"we are poor in the thea

MW00329400

JEWISH IDENTITY

JEWISH IDENTITY

Elias Friedman, O.C.D

Preface by Rev. Msgr. Eugene Kevane
Introduction by Ronda Chervin, Ph.D.

THE MIRIAM PRESS
Saint Louis, Missouri

Imprimi potest
P. Philippus Sainz de Baranda, O.C.D.
   Praepositus Generalis
   Romae, die 26 iunii 1982
Nihil obstat
Edward J. Montano, S.T.D.
   Censor Librornm
Imprimatur
† Joseph T. O'Keefe, D.D.
   Vicar-General, Archdiocese of New York
   May 26, 1987

_____

_____

The Association of Hebrew Catholics (AHC) is a non-profit corporation
registered in the states of New York, Michigan, and Missouri. The Miriam
Press is the publishing arm of the AHC. All contributions are tax-deductible in
accordance with §501(c)3 of the IRS code.

For additonal information write to:
Association of Hebrew Catholics
4120 W. Pine Blvd.
St. Louis, MO 63108
Email: ahc@hebrewcatholic.org • Web: http://hebrewcatholic.net

ISBN 0-939409-00-3 (HB)
ISBN 0-939409-01-1 (PB)

Library of Congress Catalog Card Number 87-061623
Printed and Published in the United States of America

ACKNOWLEDGMENTS

These are due in the first place to Msgr. Eugene Kevane, who has played the major role in bringing the text of *Jewish Identity* to publication. My sincere thanks go, next, to Dr. Ronda Chervin, for suggestions which have resulted in an improved presentation of the book. David Moss has shown exemplary zeal in carrying out the practicalities involved in the publication. Mrs. Margaret Fitzgerald did noble work typing and retyping the text.

My gratitude goes out to the benefactors who contributed to defraying the costs. They are too numerous to be mentioned; none will be forgotten in my prayers.

E. F.

CONTENTS

PREFACE

The uniquely frightful impact of the Holocaust bore down upon John Friedman when he was a young Jewish medical student and ardent Zionist. Casting about for understanding of the awesome reports emanating from Central Europe, heartland of the cluster of peoples once rightly called Christendom, he came upon St. Paul's Epistle to the Romans, chapters 9-11. Forcefully it came home to him that the time foreseen by St. Paul is now. "Blindness has come upon part of Israel," St. Paul writes, "until the full number of Gentiles enter in, and then all Israel will be saved...in respect to the election, they are beloved by him because of the patriarchs. God's gifts and his calls are irrevocable" (Rom. 11:25-26, 28-29).

"It is happening now," the young medical man said to himself, in a powerful insight which has ruled his thought and life ever since. This insight gives him a share in St. Paul's prophecy and makes him himself a truly prophetic figure both in Israel and in the Catholic Church today.

As a part of my teaching in the field of Catechetics, I developed a series of lectures on "The Reality of the Problem," as the *General Catechetical Directory* so honestly terms it, which teachers of the Catholic Faith face today. Earlier in the present decade, these lectures were published as *The Lord of History* (Boston: St. Paul Editions, 1980). Father Elias, the same John Friedman, now a Catholic priest of the Carmelite Monastery on Mount Carmel in Israel, happened to read this book. He wrote to me immediately. Now that a Gentile Catholic priest has written this study of the historic apostasy of the once-Christian Gentile peoples, he said, the way is clear for me to publish the book of my own lifetime of thought and study on the subject of Jewish identity. My book is predicated on the new situation in which both Christians and Jews are finding themselves. This situation results from the current fulfilment of Jesus' own prophecy on the end of "the times of the

Gentiles." "The distress in the land and the wrath against this
people will be great. The people will fall before the sword; they
will be led captive in the midst of the Gentiles. Jerusalem will
be trampled by the Gentiles, until the times of the Gentiles are
fulfilled" (Luke 21:23-24).

Does this not relate to the Great Return of the Jews to Palestine,
that immense event of this present Twentieth Century? In this
wonderful work of the God of the irrevocable election, what is the
self-understanding which results for the Jews? What is "Jewish
Identity"? What is political Zionism? What is spiritual Zionism?
How does Zionism relate to the Messiah and to all for which the
Messiah stands in the heritage of Jewish thought and life?

All these things are analyzed with great scholarship and equally
great spiritual insight in this book, *Jewish Identity.* It is important
for post-conciliar Catholic Catechetics. The Catholic Church is
beginning to recognize the new situation which Father Elias' book
studies, as the documents in the appendices bear witness. It is an
honor to respond to Father Elias' invitation to do this Preface, along
with the illuminating Introduction by the distinguished convert
from Judaism, Dr. Ronda Chervin, for a book which witnesses in
so timely a way to the God of the irrevocable election who is the
Lord of history.

> October 3, 1985, Feast of St. Therese of Lisieux
> Rev. Msgr. Eugene Kevane
> Notre Dame Pontifical Catechetical Institute
> Arlington, Virginia

INTRODUCTION

By Ronda Chervin, Ph.D.

Jewish Identity, by Father Elias Friedman, O. C. D., is a prophetic book. Written with dramatic intensity, it would have best been read without any preface or introduction were it not for one difficulty. Most readers of non-fiction are not accustomed to prophetic dramatic renditions of controversial topics. We get upset if we are not sure where an argument is leading. We want to know the end before we arrive at the middle.

For such audiences it is good to have a preface and an introduction. You will want to know who this Father Elias Friedman might be who is trying to shake you up from old peaceful stagnant concepts about Jewish Identity. You will want to know to whom this remarkable treatise is addressed. You will want to know how far he is going to go. If this description does not fit you, by all means skip my introduction and go right on to Chapter I.

Elias Friedman, O. C. D., is a Carmelite friar living at Mount Carmel in Haifa, Israel. He was born into a Jewish family in South Africa. He converted to the Catholic faith in 1943 while a doctor in the South African Medical Corps. He became a Carmelite shortly after his conversion, a priest in 1953, and the following year a member of the "Stella Maris" Monastery in Haifa, Israel.

Besides being a doctor, priest, and writer of such books as *The Redemption of Israel,* published by Sheed and Ward in 1947, he is also an internationally acclaimed poet and a historian of Carmelite origins.

The work *Jewish Identity* will certainly be of the greatest interest to Jewish converts to the Catholic faith, but it will also be of importance to Jews and Christians of all branches concerned with Jewish/Christian affairs.

The outline which follows will give the reader an idea of the

5

enormous scope and prophetic intent of *Jewish Identity.* It is a book best read several times, since the ideas are both original and inseminating.

The Argument of Jewish Identity

Jews themselves are quite unsure of what constitutes the essence of being Jewish. The celebrated case of Father Daniel Rufeisen, a Carmelite and a Jewish convert to the Roman Catholic Faith, who sought citizenship in Israel and was refused in spite of having been an anti-Nazi underground hero in World War II, brought to the fore the difficulty various Jewish groups have in defining the nature of Jewish identity.

An important review is made of definitions offered in the course of the debate in Israel. On this basis, Father Elias offers some clarifying distinctions. He suggests that the term "Jew" be used, as it was historically, to refer to those who accept the Judaic religious law. The word "Hebrew", on the other hand, refers to the *people of the election,* whether they accept the Jewish rabbinic law or not. A community is Israelite when it is in historical relation to the People of Israel prior to their dispersion from the Holy Land.

If such a distinction is accepted, it follows that so-called "Jewish converts" to Christian religions should not call themselves Jewish Christians, or Jewish Catholics, but instead Hebrew Christians, or *Hebrew Catholics,* for they are no longer under rabbinic law, but they should conceive of themselves as still part of the people of the election.

Historically, however, and even in the present, many Hebrew-Catholics are assimilated in such a way that they and their children no longer think of themselves as Hebrews.

The result of such loss of identity is not only culturally unfortunate but also constitutes a failure to respond to the irrevocable vocation of the Hebrew to be part of the people of the election. It also impedes any large-scale conversion of Jews to the Catholic religion, since assimilation, if unchecked, would eventually lead to the annihilation of the people.

A survey of the historical background leading up to and including the State of Israel presents a picture of tremendous vacillation in the attitude of the Jewish people toward the divine Election.

How shall this election factor be described? Is it a matter of heredity? Is the person born a Jew or an Israelite? Father Elias gives us an intriguing answer. No one is born a Jew. A Jew is one who accepts rabbinic law. But a person can be born an Israelite. This is an innate quality, yet not hereditary. It is personal. "It results from a transcendental relation between the person and the divine will, mediated by the community of the elect. It is because one is born into the Elect People that one is born an Israelite. The 'election factor' is irrevocable for the person so born, since the gifts of God are without repentance. It is revocable for his descendants, not by an act of will, but where the descendants have ceased to belong to a community, mediator of the 'election factor'."

Now comes one of the most controversial points in Father Elias' book, *Jewish Identity.* If there is no way of preserving the Jewish identity of the convert, due to policies of assimilation of the convert and his descendants, then it is wrong to *actively* proselytize Israelites. The term *active proselytizing* is a technical term connoting that the missionary take the initiative in trying to bring about conversion. To refrain from active proselytizing does not mean that one cannot pray for conversions, passively receive an Israelite seeking baptism into the Church, discuss religious matters with Jews, or express one's loving concern through deeds of charity. Even those who do not fully agree with this ban on active proselytizing insisted upon by Father Elias, as well as other concepts advanced in *Jewish Identity,* will still find the rest of his argument important and even essential.

Of course, the problem of Jewish identity is altered if one believes that after Christ there is no reason for Jewish people to continue to have an identity. This thesis is called revocationism. It maintains that the call of election to the Jewish people ended with the founding of a new people of God, the true Israel which is the Church of Christ. In this case, converts have no need for any outward identification of themselves as Israelites or solidarity with Jews or support of the State of Israel.

Father Elias regards revocationism as a rejection of an

irrevocable election. Instead, he will propose a Hebrew-Catholic community for converts and their descendants. With the existence of such a community, the time might end when Jews would have to regard the convert as abandoning allegiance to his people.

The theology of the Second Vatican Council refers to the Church as the People of God, but the Jewish people as still part of the plan of salvation.

The Jewish people have not lost the election, as theological anti-Semitism holds.

There is only one people of God, the followers of Christ, but others are potentially part of the people of God, the Jews most clearly so by virtue of the election which has not been revoked. "Jewry is ordained, one day, to become an effective organ for the Church. Jewry now is a part of Israel — that part which does not believe."

Anti-Semitism of Christians comes as a result of ignoring St. Paul's insistence that the Jews were still the elect, and also lack of Christian charity. Since anti-Semitic theologians thought that the Christians had replaced the Jews as the elect, it followed that it was embarrassing to have Jews still around. Violent measures were tolerated.

It is because of such revocationism (the theory that the promise was revoked) that many Christian theologians today fail to read the signs of the times in the present history of the return of the Jews to the State of Israel.

The documents of Vatican II in the teaching about the Jewish people, excerpted in the Appendix of *Jewish Identity,* mark a milestone in the refutation of revocationism and have led to the examination of anti-Semitic overtones in catechisms, prayers, and social relations.

Some claim still that Col. 3:9-11, in which St. Paul writes that there is no longer a distinction between Greek and Jew or male and female, revokes any special privileges of the Jewish people. Father Elias answers that there is no distinction regarding salvation, but that this does not imply no distinction of *roles* in the plan of salvation, just as the same passage should not be used to imply that men and women have no distinct roles.

In a bold comparison, Father Elias suggests that just as the various special rites in the Church exist for the preservation of the diverse historical communities, so should there come into being a Hebrew-Catholic community for the preservation of the Jewish community within the Catholic Church. This idea has been approved by Monsignor William A. Carew, until recently Apostolical Delegate of Jerusalem.

Father Elias argues brilliantly that it is a form of Platonism to divorce Catholicism from culture, as is done in missionary activity which assimilates to the universal Church without integration into culture.

Consulting the table of contents will give the reader an idea of the many other topics discussed in *Jewish Identity*.

Some points of particular interest include the following:

The prophecy in Luke 21:24, "Jerusalem will be trampled by the Gentiles, until the times of the Gentiles are fulfilled", can be related to the return of the Jews to Israel in our times. The end of the pagan era is signalized by the present apostasy of the originally evangelized countries from their Christian faith:

"As he walked slowly across the stage of history, the Jew took on an uncanny resemblance to Jesus: beaten, spat upon, mocked, derided, bleeding from his judicial scourging, crowned with the thorns of incomprehension, bearing his Cross on the way to Golgotha. Jewry ran the gauntlet of the nations."

"Mystically speaking, Jewry as a whole was nailed to the Cross and dies under Hitler. ...On the third day, three years after the conclusion of hostilities in 1945, Jewry rose from the dead; the State of Israel was proclaimed."

"Once faith is given, Jewry will be transformed into a powerhouse of spiritual motivation, sufficient to bring about the 'resurrection of the dead', the return to the faith of lapsed Gentility."

There is a great need in our times for a theology of history or theological prophetism to read the signs of the times. Our response to the signs of the times is not a matter of scholarship but of personal faith, submitted to ecclesiastical control. One of these signs is the increase of messianic fervor among Jews in Israel. Another is the interest of the Israeli Jew in Jesus, who is not seen as an outsider, but as a Jew from Nazareth, a native of this country, not a foreign influence as in the Diaspora.

It is against the background of the ideas given in the main text of *Jewish Identity* that we are asked to consider Father Elias' prophetic goals for a Hebrew-Catholic Association.

I. A CASE OF CONSCIENCE

On July 12, 1959, a young friar, short, round-faced, and energetic, entered the State of Israel through the busy Port of Haifa, on his way to the "Stella Maris" Monastery, principal sanctuary of the Discalced Carmelite Order, there to take up his position as a member of the community. For the next few years his presence focussed worldwide attention on the century-and-a-half-old edifice, crowning the promontory of Mount Carmel like a fortress.

The young Carmelite, known to his colleagues as Father Daniel Rufeisen, was indeed no ordinary friar, as a cursory glance at his previous career suffices to demonstrate.[1] Oswald, his original name, had been born in Poland (Zywiec, 1922), into the Orthodox Jewish family of the Rufeisens. On the fateful day the German army invaded his country, he joined the crowd of panic-stricken refugees streaming eastwards. After a series of daring adventures, during which he rendered distinguished services to the anti-Nazi underground movement, he abruptly entered the Catholic Church in 1942. His heroic conduct, especially in the rescue of hundreds of Jews from the ghetto of Mir, earned for him an award from the Russian army and an honorable place in the history of the Jewish struggle for survival in Nazi-dominated Europe.[2]

At the conclusion of hostilities in 1945, Oswald received the habit in the Discalced Carmelite Order, in which he was later ordained a priest in 1952. His name was changed to Daniel in memory of his numerous and dramatic escapes from the lions' den of the enemy.

Though he now wore the brown habit, leather girdle, and sandals of a Carmelite friar, Father Daniel nourished the passionate desire of settling in the recently-founded State of Israel. He had cultivated the sentiment ever since his early days in the Zionist Youth Movement. The unspeakable sufferings of Polish Jewry at the hands of the Nazi persecutor, of which he had borne his full share, only served to

11

strengthen the sense of solidarity with his people's tragic destiny. Having finally persuaded his religious superiors to grant him permission, he renounced his Polish citizenship and sailed off for Israel on a tourist visa allowing him a temporary sojourn of six months in the country.[3]

Immediately on arrival, Father Daniel made application for a certificate of a Jewish immigrant, which entitles the bearer to receive citizenship automatically, under the Law of Return of 1950,[4] as amended in 1952.[5] His motive was to obtain recognition of his identity as a Jew, notwithstanding his change of religion. The Minister responsible for the execution of the law[6] turned down the application on December 8, 1959. Father Daniel replied by filing an *order nisi* constraining the Minister to expose the grounds of his refusal before the Supreme Court. Because the Law of Return had prudently refrained from defining the term "Jew", the Minister defended his action by invoking a cabinet decision, instructing the relevant authorities to register any person as Jewish who, *bona fide*, had made a declaration to that effect "provided that there had been no change of *dat*", a word commonly translated as "religion".[7] Justice Cohen, dissenting from the opinion of his fellow judges, argued that the excluding clause, "providing that there had been no change of *dat*", being a cabinet decision, lacked force of law. Professor Simon later concurred.[8] To the intense disappointment of the plaintiff, the Supreme Court upheld the decision of the Minister of the Interior by a majority vote of the judges, on June 12, 1962.[9]

In his summing-up, the learned Judge President, the late Moshe Silberg, created a stir by announcing his intention to justify the Court's verdict on secular grounds, given that the Law of Return was the law of the Parliament of Israel, not of any rabbinical authority. He aroused the expectation that he was about to offer a secular definition of the term "Jew", on the basis of which the excluding clause would appear as a logical corollary. Non-Jewish opinion was confused, for secularism does not discriminate on grounds of religion.[10] *Prima facie* the excluding clause conveyed the contrary impression, that religion was the essential criterion in the determination of "Jewishness". If so, the criterion was expected to cut both ways. It was understandable that a person should cease to be called a Jew after changing his religion, but why should a Jew who had lost belief in God continue to enjoy the appreciable privileges consequent on the reception of a certificate of a Jewish immigrant? An uneasy feeling was generated that a secular argument in support of the verdict would be inevitably discriminatory, as Father Daniel's advocate had claimed in the first case.[11]

The paradox lay in the fact that Father Daniel held a view of Jewish identity even more secular than that of the Court. He had gathered the impression from his participation in the Polish Zionist Youth Movement, that Modern Zionism intended to divorce Jewish nationality from the Jewish religion, so that one could be a Jew, whether an atheist or a member of any religion at all. In bringing his case of conscience before the Supreme Court of Israel, Father Daniel was implicitly challenging the State to show reason why a Jewish convert should not be admitted to a Jewish society, ostensibly organized as a secular democracy. To his cost, he had neglected to consider several factors involved in the case: the existence of two forms of Modern Secular Zionism, moderate and extreme; the ambiguity of the word *dat;* and local jurisprudence. Father Daniel, in effect, held to an extreme form of Secular Zionism, the Court to the moderate form which maintains that Jewish nationality remained vitally attached to the Jewish religion.

Rabbinical circles were equally disturbed. They felt that a secular definition of the term "Jew" would stand in contradiction to rabbinical law. Justice Silberg, indeed, took excessive pains to make clear the status of the Jewish convert in Jewish religious tradition, quoting extensively in Aramaic from rabbinical authorities.[12] It was so much time wasted, for he had no intention of applying their criteria. Had he wished to, he could have simply declared that a Jewish apostate forfeited his rights to benefit from the Law of Return.[13]

A secular definition of the term "Jew" further risked creating a dichotomy in Israel between the religious and secularist camps by calling two nations into existence, each with its own definition of the title "Jew".

For a long time, Orthodox and secularists in Israel had been at loggerheads with one another over problems of personal status, the most common occasion being the registration of the offspring of mixed marriages. Their number had considerably increased in recent years, following the virtual annihilation of many Jewish communities during World War II. As for the children of these marriages, rabbinical law regarded the issue of a Jewish mother and a Gentile father as Jewish, whereas the issue of a Gentile mother and a Jewish father were regarded as Gentile.

The principle offends secularist logic. After all, the offspring have equal quantities of Jewish blood in both cases, if the reader will pardon us for using such crude terms to express the opposition of outlooks. Instructions for the registration of children of the second category, issued prior to the arrival of Father Daniel, had raised storms of protest in Orthodox Jewish circles.[14] Most macabre of all was the story of Aaron Steinberg, the uncircumcised and unbaptized child of a Jewish father and a Russian Orthodox mother, whose pitiful cadaver, so the press reported, had been dragged in a taxi from place to place in search of a dignified burial. An envenomed public polemic flared up, which resulted in the remains being disinterred and reburied.[15]

In the event, the verdict of the court proved to be welcome to Orthodox sentiment, for it excommunicated Father Daniel civilly from Jewish society in Israel, as effectively as the excommunication, fulminated by the rabbis of Amsterdam, had excommunicated Baruch Spinoza from the Jewish community of his time.[16] The Orthodox had been fearful lest a reassurance from the Supreme Court of Israel, that a Jewish convert remained a Jew, should set the stage for a wave of conversions to Christianity the world over; notoriously, the chief obstacle to accepting the Christian faith for a large number of Jews is the break with their people which the conversion invariably entails.

The affair of Father Daniel was by no means the first occasion for a public discussion about convert Jews in Israel,[17] though it provided the first occasion for the Supreme Court to hand down a decision in their regard, thus marking a chapter in Israeli jurisprudence.

Jacques Madaule, a French philosemite, had already remarked

that the Jewish community does not tolerate the fact that one of its members should pass over to Christianity and still pretend to belong to Judaism.

Attacking the Christian Mission, Dr. Breuer made the chilly observation that convert Jews in Israel belong to a sixth column; what the fifth column is, we leave to our readers to guess for themselves.[18] André Chouraqui, on the contrary, generously wrote that in Israel things have changed: converts reveal themselves to be excellent Israelis, devoted to their fatherland and to their people, ardently striving to create a new fraternity.[19] The editor of the "Ma'ariv", a prominent Hebrew-language daily, defended the dismissal of Rachel Ben-Giora from her post in a government school on the grounds that as one who had separated herself irrevocably from Jews and Judaism by her conversion to Protestantism, "she had no right to be instructing Jewish children".[21]

Even after the verdict against Father Daniel had been pronounced, bad feeling over matters of personal status continued to simmer between Orthodox and secularists. Two cases aroused especially heated discussion in the Israeli press, the Eitani Case (1965)[21] and the Shalit Case (1970),[22] both associated with the registration of the offspring of a Jewish father and a Gentile mother.

Rina Eitani was born of a mixed marriage of the kind described. Her Jewish father had been murdered by the Nazis. In the company of her Gentile mother and her sister, she experienced the horrors of life in the ghetto of Warsaw. In 1947 the British interned her in a camp in Cyprus with other illegal immigrants brought to Palestine by the Jewish Agency. After the establishment of the State of Israel, she became a citizen in virtue of the Law of Return. She had never considered herself a Christian, assuming innocently that personal status was always and everywhere determined through the father.[23] She acquitted herself honorably of the duty of military service in the Israeli Defense Force, lived on a Kibbutz, was married in due course to a Jew by a rabbi and reared her children as Jews. Having gained widespread popularity for her devotion to public causes, she was eventually elected municipal councillor of Upper Nazareth.

What must have been her dismay when the authorities summoned her to hand in her passport because her mother was a

Gentile, even though on the passport she was inscribed as a person of Jewish nationality. Mrs. Eitani had met all the criteria in force at the time of her arrival in the country to qualify for registration as a Jew, having declared herself, *bona fide,* to be Jewish, without ever having embraced any other religion. In addition, she had amply satisfied the criteria of subjective identification with, and objective participation in, the life of the Jewish community, the absence of which in the lives of converts in general had provided the grounds for denying access to the benefits of the Law of Return (to Father Daniel in particular). Mrs. Eitani's passport was subsequently returned to her after the judiciary had accepted the argument that the administration lacked the competence to revoke a right granted in error, after the person involved had enjoyed its exercise in good faith (estompel).[24]

Lieutenant Benjamin Shalit of the Israeli Defense Force applied to have his two children registered as of Jewish nationality, but of no religion. Himself a convinced atheist, Shalit had married a Scottish woman who shared his anti-religious sentiments and who became the mother of the two children around whom the legal drama was to be enacted. Unexpectedly, the Supreme Court, on January 23, 1970, ordered the children to be registered in conformity with the will of the parents.[25]

The fury of the Orthodox knew no bounds, for the verdict was a flagrant violation of rabbinical law.[26] They threatened to withdraw from the government coalition unless the verdict was overruled. Golda Meir, a lifelong Socialist and agnostic,[27] surrendered tamely to the ultimatum. The Law of Return was amended by the addition of the registration formula in use (1970). Henceforth Israel had a legal definition of the term "Jew". The text of the amendment ran as follows: "For the purposes of this law the term 'Jew' refers to a person born of a Jewish mother or converted to Judaism and who is not a member of another *dat ".*[28] The secularists had been routed. The Orthodox still found matter for complaint. They pressed for a further amendment: converted to Judaism *in compliance with traditional rabbinical law.* Their purpose was to exclude converts to the Conservative and Reform Synagogues, whose conversion they do not recognize. This would tighten the monopoly they enjoy as the only current of religion in the Jewish world, accredited in Israel.

The humiliation of the secularists was mitigated by a simultaneous amendment extending the benefits of the Law of Return to the non-Jewish partner of a Jewish marriage and to the couple's non-Jewish children and grandchildren. The intention was to facilitate the immigration into Israel of Russian Jews, many of whom had married non-Jews. However, the second amendment radically altered the intention of the law, which expressed Ben-Gurion's view of Zionism as the "ingathering of the exiles". Not only did Gentiles now benefit from the provisions of the Law of Return, but even a certain category of Jewish converts, as happened when the Christian spouse of a Jew turned out to be a convert as well. Evidently the legislator saw no obstacle in allowing non-Jews to participate in the life of the state, as a colorful variety of Gentile groups, Christian and Muslim Arabs, Druses, Circassians, Armenians, Copts, and others were already doing.

The particular importance of the case of Father Daniel can only be appreciated against the background of the evolution of Jewish society in Israel. The late Baruch Kurzweil added a significant subtitle, "Continuity or Revolution", to his book on modern Hebrew literature.[29] The excruciating question before him was whether modern Zionism was indeed building a state for Jews, or whether it was engendering a "new and different nation", as Leibowitz also darkly suspects.[30] The majority of Jews in Israel rightly hold that the conservation of their historical identity conditions their survival as a people. A total change of collective identity would result in the cessation of their historical existence. Two questions remain to be answered: in what does their essential identity consist and how is it to be maintained in spite of change? These are the central issues for Jewish society in Israel today.[31] They anguish Jews who have the future of their people at heart. Such issues are also a grave responsibility for Christians, one which has not always been taken seriously enough by them in the past.

The Argument from Historical Rupture

Returning to the courtroom, we find Justice Silberg initiating his summing-up. He began by announcing that it was necessary to fix the meaning of the word "Jew" in the Law of Return. He proposed to give the term a secular interpretation in contrast to its meaning in the Law of Marriages and Divorce (1953), by which law the State conferred on rabbinical courts exclusive jurisdiction over Jews in the State in these two cardinal fields of human life.

By secular interpretation the judge had in mind to draw on two fundamental principles of law: a) the aim of the legislator; b) the customary use of the term amongst Jews.

So far the line of argument sounded reasonable enough, but then Justice Silberg went on to make a compromising reflection: "And who better than us know what the content and essence of the term 'Jew' are!"[32] These were brave words indeed. Who could blame the world if it hung on the lips of the judge, in expectation that the mystery of Jewish identity was about to be revealed?

If such were the expectations of his auditors, they were doomed to disappointment. "The answer to the above question", the learned judge went on, "is, in my opinion, unequivocally clear: a Jew who has accepted Christianity cannot continue to be called a Jew." The question had been neatly sidestepped. We now knew when a Jew was *not* a Jew; we had still to learn when he *was* a Jew. To claim that the answer was "unequivocally clear" is to ask too much from the reasonable man, so often invoked by the legal profession as a norm for its evaluations. To us, the reply of Justice Silberg was clearly equivocal.

Justice Silberg then allowed himself a sudden bold generalization: "As a whole, with a very small number of exceptions, Jewish Society in Israel was agreed on one point: It is not prepared to disassociate itself from its historical past, nor to reject the heritage of its forefathers. It continues to drink from its original sources of inspiration. Forms differ, the channels differ, the conclusions differ, but the wells are not blocked, for to do without them would leave the people impoverished and bitter. Only a simpleton could believe that Zionism intends to fashion a new culture."[33]

Here was no legal argument, but a deeply-felt restatement of the ideology of Ahad-Ha'am, classical exponent of Moderate Secular Cultural Zionism. From now on it was plain sailing for the judge. "The Jewish converts, as experience teaches us, have cut themselves off completely from their people, for the simple reason that their sons and daughters marry into other peoples."[34] In consequence, guided by a healthy instinct for survival, the Jewish people were convinced that conversion was destructive of Jewish identity and closed its doors on the convert.

Justices Mani, Landau, and Berenson concurred with the line of argument developed by the Judge President, which we designate as "the argument from historical rupture". It was a weighty argument, based on irrefutable observations. Some Christian missionaries tendentiously advance the claim that a Jew who embraces Christianity is a "completed Jew". True or not, and we ourselves think that he is neither a Jew nor complete, the claim has no bearing on the argument from historical rupture, which concerns not the convert himself, but his descendants, as Justice Silberg declared with extreme precision. These are lost to their people. They cease to play any role in the moulding of its future. Sadly enough, the profound remarks of the Court fell on deaf ears, where most Christians were concerned.

Though Justice Silberg had spoken with warmth and conviction, he undermined the force of his argument by allowing the reservation: "with a very small number of exceptions".

Indubitably, the learned judge was referring to the "Young Hebrews", better known as the Canaanites and, more exactly, as the neo-Canaanites. Since the history of the movement is irrelevant here, let us begin by setting out its aims and ideals.

The neo-Canaanites are a group of Israeli Jews which aims at the foundation of a new nation in Israel, defined solely by the factors of territory and language. It renounces the pretense of continuity with the Jewish past. It does not even regard itself as issuing from Zionism. Sentimentally, its links are with the Canaanites of ancient Palestine, whence the popular epithet, Canaanites. Politically, it advocates the abolition of the Law of Return, an immigration policy open to Gentiles as well as to Jews and the legalization of mixed marriages.[35]

For Justice Silberg to have observed that the Canaanites were numerically insignificant was an evasion. What counts is that, despite a calculated program of rupture from the Jewish past, Canaanites enjoyed the benefits of the Law of Return and were registered as Jews, even against the dictates of their conscience. These facts voided the argument from historical rupture of its moral force. It entitles one to describe its use against the Jewish convert as discriminatory. Communist Jews, who, in general, are no less atheist, anti-Jewish, anti-Zionist and, like the Canaanites, intent on destroying their links with Jewish history, may also benefit from the Law of Return.

The Karaites are a sect founded in the 8th century A. D. by Persian Jews who rejected the authority of the Oral Law and of the rabbis.[36] The Orthodox prohibit marriages between Rabbinites and Karaites.[37] Nevertheless, Karaites are free to immigrate to Israel.

The Samaritans were regarded by the Fathers of the Church as Israelites but not as Jews.[38] The Samaritan religion, though based on the books of Moses, has evolved independently of Judaism. Macdonald contrasted the Samaritans of Northern Palestine with the "Judaists" of Southern Palestine,[39] from whom present-day Jews are presumed to have descended. The Chief Rabbinate of Israel prohibits marriage between Rabbinites and Samaritans,[40] and, in turn, the Samaritan high priest does not permit marriages with Jews.[41] Nonetheless, Samaritans are as free as Karaites to immigrate into Israel.

Messianic Jews profess belief in the messiahship of Jesus, while leaving the belief in his divinity optional. Some are baptized, some are not.[42] Some maintain contact with one or other of the larger Protestant churches; others keep at a distance, in defense of their Jewish identity. Messianic Jews have been known to receive immigration certificates. We know of a case of one Messianic Jew who was called up for military service in the Israel Defense Force. He declared that he had been baptized, but that he had never belonged to any Christian denomination. He was forthwith enrolled and made to undergo the three years' regulation military service.

The recent decision of the Supreme Court denying to a

Messianic Jew, Eileen Dorflinder of the USA, the benefits of the Law of Return, seems to have been motivated by the fact that not only had she been baptized but that, at a given moment, she had belonged to some Christian group. The judges decided that she had changed her *dat*, as the word is understood in Israeli law (POC 19 [1979] 127-128).

The Verdict

Whereas the secular argument of the Court used to justify the rejection of Father Daniel's claim to be a Jew was unconvincing, the verdict was entirely consonant with the legislation on personal status obtaining in the State of Israel.

As far back as 1864, the Turkish government had organized the Jewish subjects of the Ottoman Empire into a religious community or "millet", under a Chief Rabbi resident in Constantinople, the Hakam Rabbi. The Hakam Rabbi, in turn, had a representative in Palestine.

The lightning conquest of the Near East by the troops of General Allenby in 1918 broke the link between the Jews in Palestine and their patriarch in Turkey. In 1921, the Jewish inhabitants of Palestine elected their own council of rabbis, which obtained recognition from the occupying power (3-18-21). The Mandatory régime introduced minimal changes into the situation. The "millet" system continued in force in Palestine long after it had been abolished in Turkey by Kemal Ataturk.[43]

The "millet" was an ethnico-religious community with the accent on the confessional aspect.[44] Originally a method for exercising imperial power over minority groups, its convenience was recognized by the British who changed the term "millet" to "community". By 1939, the Mandatory Power had drawn up a list of ten officially recognized communities.[45] The State of Israel has since recognized, in addition, the Anglican community in Israel,[46] the Druses,[47] and the Baha'is.[48] The term *dat* is the Hebrew equivalent of "millet". It should be translated "religious community". To translate it as "religion" is ambiguous and misleading.

Until 1927, Jews in Palestine were automatically considered to belong to the local Jewish religious community. The Mandatory Power then ruled that it would recognize as members of the Jewish community only those Jews of either sex who had completed eighteen years of age and who were registered in the community.[49] Change of religious community had been regulated by an earlier ordinance.[50] The Mandatory Power clearly understood that a change of religion took place only when the person involved had been received into a new religious community and not on the basis of an internal act of faith. Religious affiliation was the sole criterion of personal status. The atheist had no status in law, since Ottoman jurisprudence had made no provision for him. The lacuna explains the anomalous position obtaining in the State of Israel, where atheist Jews are registered as Jews despite their personal convictions.

The testimony offered by Moshe Shertok illustrated very well the role of the community in determining personal status under the "millet" system. Shertok appeared before the Special Commission of the United Nations for Palestine as a representative of the Jewish Agency. He was put the question: "Whom does the Jewish Agency regard as a Jew?" He replied: "Speaking technically, in terms of the legislation in vigor in Palestine, I would say that the criterion is the Jewish religion. What is decisive is that the person should not have passed over to another religion. Even if not observant, he will be considered a Jew until he enters into another alliance with another religion, from which moment he loses his right to be regarded as a Jew. The decision depends on the religious criterion."[51]

Since Shertok confined himself to the legislation in vigor in Palestine, we must interpret the use of the word "religion" to refer to "religious community". All the same, he was guilty of gross ambiguity. No one had asked him to limit his reply to conditions in Palestine. The Jewish Agency was active throughout the Diaspora, selecting Jews for immigration to Palestine. What, the Commission could have asked, was the criterion of the Jewish Agency *before* the immigrant came to Palestine? The question of the Commission had clearly embarrassed Shertok. He chose the easy way out, for the legislation of Palestine did furnish all parties concerned with a simple, legal definition of the term "Jew".

Also, because the testimony of Moshe Shertok was adduced

by Justice Berenson against the plaintiff, Father Daniel, it is to our purpose to point out that Shertok's reply belonged to an entirely different order than the secular argument expounded by Justice Silberg. The secular argument was an ideological one: the argument from change of community was a legal one and quite the opposite of secular.

Moshe Shertok hinted at the anomalous position of the atheist Jew, who remained a member of the Jewish community, despite his personal convictions to the contrary. It is a position morally obnoxious, perhaps, but legally consistent.

The new State of Israel maintained the Mandatory legislation on personal status.[52] It was ideal from the rabbinical point of view, but no less gratifying to the religious heads of non-Jewish communities.

In both cases, religious heads enjoyed full powers in matters of marriage and divorce within their own community. Understandably, therefore, the Catholic Church in Israel has never objected to the "millet" system.

Ben-Gurion, declaring his intention to uphold the *status quo* in matters of personal status,[53] argued that its maintenance was necessary to promote the unity of the Jewish people.[54] It followed that he, a non-believing Jew, had committed himself and his party to supporting the rabbinical prohibition of marriages between Jew and Gentile from purely nationalistic motives. His stance was awkward; it invited the accusation of racialism. The "millet" system, in itself, is of course not racialist; it is fundamentally religious. There are no racialist laws on the statute book of the State of Israel.

The Mandatory ordinances concerning the Jewish community were found to be vexatious. They excluded Jewish minors from membership in the community. Many Jews neglected to register, or were unwilling to do so for reasons of conscience. The situation was corrected by the Marriage and Divorce Act of 1953, which suppressed the need for Jews to register in the community.[55] The upshot of the new law was to define a Jew as one whom the rabbis would be willing to admit into their community at the moment of marriage. The community criterion remained intact.

How surprised, therefore, we were to come upon the following passage in a book by Justice Silberg: "The authoritative criterion (of personal status in Israel) does not depend on what community the person belongs to, but on his "Jewishness", and this status cannot change even from a legal-civil point of view by a change of community".[56] In the passage quoted, Justice Silberg acknowledged the existence of an absolute quality of "Jewishness". It was his right to do so, though he was then obliged to explain to common mortals in what he thought that quality consisted. The opinion stands in contradiction to the relativization of the term "Jew", on which he had insisted in his arguments against Father Daniel. An absolute quality of "Jewishness" has to be either religious or philosophical: in either case, it is transcendental and beyond the competence of a human court of law. It enters into the area of competence of the legal profession only through the religious community to which the person concerned may belong. We leave it to readers better equipped than we are in the labyrinth of the law to reconcile the above-quoted passage with the verdict of its author against Father Daniel.

The jurisprudence in vigor in the State of Israel when Father Daniel arrived in the country justified his exclusion from the Jewish community without any need to invoke secular arguments of dubious validity. If the Court decided to make use of the secular argument, the motive has to be sought for elsewhere than in the law of the land. Father Daniel, by his affiliation to the Catholic Church, had changed his legal identity, for the purpose of Israeli law. He had become a Catholic; he had ceased to be a Jew. To grant the contrary was to admit that a person could belong to two different religious communities at one and the same time. This would be equivalent to scrapping the community legislation of the country. Whether it followed that Father Daniel should have been deprived of the right to immigrate into Israel remains an open question for the author of these pages.

Since the amendment of 1970, there is no more any need for an Israeli Court to advance secular arguments to justify the excluding clause against converts. So far as the Israeli legal profession is concerned, the tentative of Justice Silberg has become a matter of merely historical interest.

Kurt Hruby understood that beyond any charge of discrimination lies a deeper problem. "One has to safeguard Jewish identity", he wrote, "in circumstances often difficult and obscure. This is a problem which agitates Israeli opinion periodically; it is one difficult for non-Jews to grasp".[57]

The verdict against Father Daniel was precisely such a movement of defense of the national identity, unsure of its definition but convinced that the admission of Jewish converts in the Jewish community would signal the dissolution of the Jewish people. The dilemma of the Court was that of Moderate Secular Zionism. It is true that Father Daniel is no more a Jew;[58] but neither is the Secular Zionist a *Jew.* He is a secularized Israelite.

The dilemma of Moderate Secular Zionism arises from the fact that a definition of the term "Jew" requires religion as an essential element, not merely as an integral element, which is what Ahad Ha'am had proposed. Professor A. Derczansky commented pertinently that "the experience of secularization, instituted by the founders of the State of Israel, had demonstrated that their tentative has encountered the spiritual dimension of the Jewish conscience".[59]

The intention of Ahad Ha'amism to maintain the continuity of Jewish historical identity is commendable; its capacity to ensure it in practice is weak. The sentiment of continuity with the Jewish past is respectable; the substance is hollow and the application of the ideology to individual cases inevitably discriminatory.

II. HISTORY OF THE JEWISH
IDENTITY PROBLEM

The French Revolution marks the watershed between the medieval and modern periods in the history of the Jewish People. It thrust open the rusty gates of the ghetto and granted equality of political and civil rights to the public executioner and the persecuted Jew alike. The precipitate entry of Jews into Gentile society initiated a struggle for civil liberties in the countries of Europe, as the fermenting principles of the Revolution reached them one after another.[1]

Admirable as were in themselves the ideals of liberty, equality, and fraternity, beneficial as were the widening opportunities offered to Jews for advancement in all fields of social life, the underlying rationalism of the Revolution led ineluctably to the eventual destruction of the fabric on which the new freedoms were erected.

The social theory of J. J. Rousseau, which conceived society as originating in a contract between equal and autonomous individuals, was inapplicable to the Jews. They were inescapably a foreign religious community. Although equal before the law, Jews were different from others. A reaction to their entry into European society set in. Opposed to Rousseau's exaggerated individualism, Gentiles organized themselves into nation-states, each possessed by a pseudo-mystical soul, in which strangers could not participate. Modern nationalism was born. The Jew found out to his cost that constitutional equality did not guarantee social equality. A new anti-Semitism flared up out of the smouldering embers of ancient religious prejudices. The Dreyfus Affair, occurring in the very land where the principles of liberty, equality, and fraternity had been trumpeted forth with so much enthusiasm, disclosed to Theodor Herzl the frightening intensity of the new Jew-hatred. Convinced that civil emancipation had failed to solve the Jewish problem, Herzl conceived an alternative solution: a State for Jews in distress.

"If," wrote Maritain, "this emancipation was in itself a just

26

and necessary thing, and one which corresponded to a Christian aspiration, nevertheless, the hopes which the rationalist and bourgeois-optimist way of thinking, forgetful at once of the mystery of Israel and supra-individual realities, had based upon this emancipation to extinguish the Jewish problem, were soon to prove vain."[2]

The Dreyfus Affair warned of more terrible disasters ahead. Herzl, aflame with prophetic intuition which transformed the talented journalist into a political visionary, proposed that a secure shelter be provided for Jews, guaranteed by international law, which, at the same time, would put an end to the vicious circle of their wanderings. He launched his movement as an answer to Jewish suffering and humiliation, to which his own injured pride was no stranger.[3] Less than fifty years later, Hitler confirmed Herzl's worst previsions by ordering the massacre of European Jewry. Herzl had failed. True, a State for Jews did come into being, but too late to save those for whom it had been intended. An index card was filled in for each of the six million murdered Jews and deposited in the Yad Vashem Institute of Jerusalem, especially erected for the purpose; the ashes of the victims mouldered in the fields of a guilt-ridden continent.

What, in the meantime, was taking place in the inner forum of the Jewish spirit? Hruby has these excellent words à *propos:* "The problem of the identification with the surrounding milieu, now become its cultural milieu, was raised in all its brutal amplitude, when the isolation imposed for centuries on the Jewish People came to an end".[4]

The intimate contact with European culture dazzled the ghetto Jew, whose natural genius had been starved by the pitiless conditions under which he had been constrained to live. Pouring into the great centres of European life, Jews were utterly seduced by the charm of its music, the beauty of its visual arts, the grandeur of its literature. They avidly adopted European currents of thought and began to participate actively in all the intellectual and political movements of the day. Their very success in every domain added fuel to the fires of the new anti-Semitism. Since emancipation, European culture has become an indispensable part of Jewish life, but the incompatibility with the old ways of life grew in proportion to their participation in the new.

The acculturation of the modern Jew to Western civilization set off "an intellectual revolt against traditional Judaism, overwhelming in intensity and unparalleled in magnitude, the velocity and momentum of which could not be contained by any individual or group, no matter how profound and gifted".[5] Professor Y. Leibowitz has compared it to the crisis which followed the destruction of the Second Temple.[6]

A movement for the reform of traditional Judaism sprang up, which went so far as to alter the accepted view of Jewish identity. The reformers stripped Rabbinical Judaism of its national components, ceasing, for instance, to pray for the restoration of the people to their ancient homeland. Henceforth, Judaism was to be a universal religious movement open to all, on the analogy of Christianity and Islam. The object of the reformers was thus to facilitate the identification of Jews with the host-nation.[7]

Klausner's ethical monotheism became the religion of many Jews, amongst whom we can count Ben-Gurion, in the later years of his life, and Einstein.[8] Freud, Trotsky, and a host of others were radical atheists. Mixed marriages also multiplied. Conversions to Christianity were numerous,[9] so much so that Jewish writers began to complain of an epidemic.[10] But Christianity acted as a disintegrating force, uprooting from the heart of the convert all sentiment of solidarity with his people, though D'Israeli represents one of the few honorable exceptions to the rule.

In the measure that he drifted or broke away from his community of origin, the Jew suffered a loss of his Jewish identity. Raymond Aron has confessed that he did not feel himself to be a Jew anymore.[11] Chancellor Kreisky of Austria shares the sentiment. To them and to those like them applies the negative definition of Jean-Paul Sartre in all its telling irony: "The Jew is one whom other men consider to be a Jew".[12]

A manifold reaction — religious, theological, and cultural — was initiated to combat the current of assimilation and apostasy. In the United States the Conservative Synagogue, for instance, succeeded in tempering the excesses of the Reformed Synagogue. More to our purposes were the nationalist reactions. The Socialist "Bund" aimed at Jewish autonomy in the Diaspora, based on the Yiddish language. Ahad Ha'am, in contrast, proposed to found a Hebrew-speaking Cultural Centre in Palestine where Jewish identity could reconstitute itself on the basis of a secular Jewish nationalism, with the mission of arresting the assimilation of Diaspora Jews.

Ahad Ha'amism infused a secular soul into the political framework of the Zionist movement. Secularism, the common denominator between two otherwise divergent worlds of thought, rendered possible a fusion between the Political Zionism of Herzl and Ahad Ha'am's Moderate Secular Cultural Zionism. The union came to be known, pretentiously enough, as Synthetic Zionism. Justice Silberg had occasion to say that Synthetic Zionism was the prevailing ideology of the State of Israel.[13]

How Synthetic Zionism succeeded in inspiring its believers to a life of unprecedented heroism is illustrated in the spate of biographies about, and autobiographies by, the founders of the State of Israel. We recall personalities such as Ben-Gurion, Golda Meir, and Moshe Dayan, who have become household names the world over. Menahem Begin's religious faith places his Zionism in a different category, no less synthetic than that of his political opponents.

In the State of Israel, Synthetic Zionism is locked in a double confrontation: on the right, with traditional Judaism; on the left, with Extreme Secular Zionism and its small radical wing, the Canaanites. It was Father Daniel's peculiar fate to have wandered into the lines of crossfire between the three protagonists, competing for the control of Jewish history. If we understand Gershorn Scholem correctly, none of the three is destined to carry off the palm of victory.[14]

III. AHAD HA'AMISM, OR
NEW LAMPS FOR OLD

Most Jewish thinkers of the past, when seeking to provide a rationale for their religion, tried to conserve rabbinical law, in whole or in part. This was certainly not the case with Ahad Ha'am (1856-1927), the most influential exponent of Moderate Secular Cultural Zionism. After extensive studies in rabbinical literature, the young thinker lapsed into a lifelong atheism, inspired by the English empiricists Mill, Spencer and Darwin. "The ideas he popularized were by no means part of the Jewish tradition, but had their roots in the West."[1] In a state which has been translated from dream to reality, his thought has revealed its strength, but also its inherent contradictions.[2]

Traditional Jewish theology had always held fast to the belief that the specific factor in Jewish identity was the divine Election. Ahad Ha'am held no such conviction, but he recognized as a matter of fact the unity and permanence of the Jewish people throughout history. He postulated the existence of a metaphysical spirit to account for these stubborn phenomena.[3] For his part, the somber Kurzweil criticized the notion as a biological-nationalist reduction of the original belief of his ancestors in the divine Election.[4]

For Ahad Ha'am this factor, immanent in the Jewish people, guaranteed the continuity of its identity, despite change. His loyalty to a non-religious specificity of the Jewish people is what characterized his moderate form of Secular Zionism.

Let us consider a few representative disciples of the master.

A. D. Gordon (1856-1922) became the spiritual mentor of the pioneer movement in modern Zionism. He indulged in a pantheism far removed from the biblical notion of the creation. Yet he opposed the fiery Berdyczewski on the ground that it was essential to preserve the national ego. "We can accept everything from others," he taught, "we can change everything so long as we remain ourselves."[5] It is a pity that he did not explain what this national ego was, which could remain itself when all else about it had changed. St. Thomas would deny that one can change all the accidents without eventually changing the substance also.

Ben-Gurion excluded divine revelation from his scheme of things. Notwithstanding, he maintained an unshakable belief "in a fundamental difference between the Jewish People and other nations."[6] The former was unique, but wherein lay its specificity? It lay, thought Ben-Gurion, in a genius for moral enthusiasm, the cause (if you don't mind) of the historical permanence of the Jewish People.[7] Elsewhere he added that there is hidden in this people a marvelous vitamin which conserves it in existence.

Moral enthusiasm is a generic, not a specific, quality. Even some Gentiles have a genius for moral enthusiasm.

Feeling himself on unsteady ground, Ben-Gurion then discovered a vitamin with historical properties, so far unknown to medical science. If the first answer was frothy rhetoric, the second was a banal metaphor. Ben-Gurion might have been a great politician, but his intellectual training left much to be desired.

Gershom Scholem, world-famous authority on Jewish mysticism, was a deeply religious man,[8] though he never overtly professed belief in the God of Abraham. Still, he regarded it as foolish to hold that Jews are "a nation like other nations." "I share the traditional view," he is reported to have declared, "that even should we wish to be a nation like all other nations, we could not succeed. And if we did succeed, that would be the end of us."[9]

Martin Buber, whose profound spirituality impressed both Jews and Gentiles alike, once observed: "All the elements that might constitute a nation for the Jew, that might make the nation a reality, are missing: land, language, way of life. ...He does not see his substance unfold before him in his environment: it has been banished into deep loneliness and is embodied for him in only one aspect, his origin. That this substance can nevertheless become a reality for the Jew is due to the fact that his origin means more than a connection with things past: it has planted something in him that does not leave him at any hour of his life, that determines every tone, every hue in his life, all that he does and all that befalls him. ...The Jew, bound up with the world, immured in the people, dares to relate himself to God as a Jew, in the immediacy of the I and the Thou. This is Judaism's primal reality."[10]

Disloyalty to the principle of the specificity of Jewish identity is the hallmark of the extreme form of Secular Cultural Zionism. There is a great deal of oscillation between the two poles, moderate and extreme, because the inner logic of secularism is opposed to the belief in Jewish specificity. Ratosh, founder of the Canaanites, pushes his disloyalty to the utmost limits, retaining from Ahad Ha'amism only the idea of a Hebrew-speaking society in the Land of Canaan, otherwise completely divorced from links with Judaism, the Jewish people, and Zionism itself.

The New Society

Traditional Judaism offered to Jews a way of sanctification and organized them into a historical community strong enough to resist the shocks and catastrophes which threatened its survival. The second service was capital. Because we have no appropriate Geiger counter to discern which individuals carry the "election factor", the onus of identification falls entirely on the community with which the individual is affiliated. Community, identity, and identification are correlative terms.

The Traditional Jewish community had an unmistakable structure. It was governed by a multitude of religious prescriptions, at first transmitted by word of mouth, collated in the Mishnah, commented upon in the Gemara, and later codified by Maimonides (1135-1204) and Joseph Caro (1488-1575). Jewish life was deployed in the framework of a liturgical calendar punctuated by recurrent feasts and fasts to recall, for example, Passover, Shavuot, Sukkot, and Yom Hakippurim. The Jewish male was circumcised on the eighth day of his life, when he was introduced in the Alliance of Abraham. At the age of thirteen, he celebrated his Bar-Mitzvah, by which ceremony he undertook to observe the commandments of the Law. The synagogue was the center of communal life. In the absence of a central religious authority in Judaism, the Jewish community was organized on congregational lines. Marriage took place under a canopy. Divorce proceedings required the assistance of a rabbi. The status of the Jewish woman was honorable but limited. The dead were washed and buried with simplicity in the communal cemetery.

A series of human types peopled the traditional Jewish world. They provided an endless source of inspiration for a galaxy of splendid storytellers such as Mendele the Bookseller, Y. L. Perez, Sholem Aleichem, and Shai Agnon the Nobel Prize winner, to mention only a few. There were the rabbi and the rebbetzin, his wife, the ritual slaughterer of poultry and animals, the cantor, the saint, the marriage broker, the sacristan, the influential intermediary with the Gentile world, the house owner, the mendicant, the communal benefactor, the members of the village band who entertained guests on festive occasions. These types incorporated in flesh and blood the spiritual aspirations of traditional Judaism and constituted the social fabric of a thousand and more Jewish villages lying hidden on the plains of Poland and Russia. The Jewish community, so structured, became the wellspring of the Jewish identity of the individual Jew. There were also prescriptions to regulate marriage between Jew and Gentile. In a valid marriage between two Jews, the children took the personal status of the father.[11] So Jesus of Nazareth inherited the messianic title through his presumptive father, Joseph, son of David (Mt. 1:20). Intermarriage was allowed on condition that the non-Jewish partner embraced Judaism. Mixed marriages, where the partners retained each his or her own religion, were null and void. It followed that, *de facto*, the personal status of the child was invariably that of its mother. Rules governing the ritual purity of foods strengthened the régime of separation between Jew and Gentile, fertile ground for the growth of suspicion, prejudice, and hatred among the latter.

Rabbinical law allowed that a person entered the Jewish community by birth, by conversion, and, more rarely, by simple aggregation.[12] Other legalities governed the expulsion of the Jew from the community, for example in cases of apostasy. An extensive literature dealt with the status of apostate.

The traditional identity of the individual Jew was thus relative to the community of which he was a member and with which he identified himself subjectively by faith in its religious principles.[13]

A Jew was a subject of rabbinical law no less than a Catholic was a subject of canon law and a Frenchman a subject of French law.

There can be no doubt about the glacial intentions of Ahad Ha'am. He meant to make a clean sweep of the traditional Jewish community and to replace it by his Hebrew-speaking Secular Cultural Centre. Let no one be led astray by the lofty title of "Spiritual Centre", sometimes used to describe the society projected by Ahad Ha'am. The Hebrew word for the spiritual is elastic enough to admit various kinds of ambiguity. Ahad Ha'am was anything but a man with a spiritual life.

Religious Jews realized that Ahad Ha'amism posed an immense threat to the traditional identity of the Jewish community.[14]

Ahad Ha'am, for his part, indignantly denied the imputation that he intended to bring about a radical change in Jewish identity. Quite the contrary! He meant to re-establish it more securely than ever, but on fresh foundations. Let us do justice to Ahad Ha'am. He believed that Jewish identity was given in the unchangeable character of the people, only whereas in the past the national genius had produced a religious culture, he now called upon it to produce a secular culture.[15] "Seeing that national unity was falling to pieces, since religion had ceased to be a sufficient cement, the people had to be reunited by the creation of a national Cultural Centre."[16] The Centre would have an essential mission to Diaspora Jews. It would inspire them to intensify their Jewish consciousness by preserving national values and creating new ones. Ben-Gurion's vision of the ingathering of the exiles was alien to Ahad Ha'am. He meant his Centre to function like a transplanted heart, pumping fresh blood into the withering limbs of dispersed Jewry, thus annulling the tendency to assimilation and mixed marriages. He expected Jewry to conform obediently to the inevitability of progress, discard their religion, and participate instead in the new culture, emanating like a vital flood from his Centre. Critics accused Ahad Ha'am of aspiring to don the fallen mantle of Moses. Leon Simon, his admiring biographer, rejects the insinuation. However, it remains that any new way of understanding Jewish identity entails a new view of the Jewish community.

In any event, a secular Hebrew-language Cultural Centre did

come into being in the Holy Land, though its cultural influence on the Diaspora Jew had been minimal[17] and its power to check assimilation nil. Walter Laqueur dismisses it as a potential force in a mission to the Jewish people.[18] The late Eliezer Libnah commented that Zionism had set up a centre without a periphery.

In the meantime, Ahad Ha'am regarded with serenity what to others appeared to be an "abysmal opposition between the secular and the religious views of the identity of the Jewish People."[19] Confident that he was retaining the collective identity unimpaired, Ahad Ha'am blandly proceeded to employ the traditional terminology. His atheistic Cultural Centre remained a "Jewish" centre, its atheistic members "Jews", the culture itself "Judaism".

Professor Gershon Weiler is of the opinion that "the new ideas constituted a radical break in the continuity of that Jewish history which had begun with the reforms of Ezra,"[20] and went on to add that Ahad Ha'am's pretension of remaining in continuity with the Jewish past was illusion.[21] Leibowitz pertinently observed that "the use of 'Jewish' terminology, the significance of which had been deliberately perverted, did not suffice to establish historical continuity."[22] For Leibowitz, "the exploitation of religion by a secular state leads to hypocrisy, nihilism, and moral corruption."[23]

Justice Silberg adduced authorities such as Kaufmann, Mahler, and Leshinsky in defense of his verdict. We have quoted Jews of equal intellectual stature who deny that Ahad Ha'amism is equal to the task of conserving Jewish identity and ensuring its future.

The Cultural Centre and the Individual

As we had no means for detecting the "election factor" in an individual, so we have none for discerning what person possesses the Jewish national spirit. What, then, were the criteria which Ahad Ha'am adopted in selecting candidates for the Centre or excluding them from it? There could only be three, for Ahad Ha'amism was a nationalism and, like any nationalism, reposed on a historical society living in a defined territory and speaking its own language. "Zionism held that a continuing secular Jewish identity was, as a matter of social fact, only possible where Jews had achieved a territorial concentration. Moreover, to be historically valid, a nation had to be settled in its own land, the soil of its ancestors, not set up in some other place, and the people had to revive its capacity to speak its own classical language, Hebrew."[24]

These three conditions, let it be remarked, only became relevant *after* the candidate had entered the Centre. Before entry, Ahad Ha'am could ask no more of him than that he be of Jewish origin. As to the old religion, Ahad Ha'am demanded respect, not belief.

The first category of candidates qualifying for admission to the Culture Centre were persons strangely like Ahad Ha'am himself. They were men and women of Jewish origin, permeated with nostalgia for the symbols of a venerable past, but who had lost faith in the religion of Moses and were desperately in need of establishing their identity on a new basis. A crowd of eager volunteers sprang forward at the summons of the master and daringly began to implement his program. They emigrated to Palestine, learned to speak Hebrew, and laid the foundations of the Secular Cultural Centre at the price of incredible sacrifices. They were the justly admired pioneers. For them, active participation in the building of a national home meant participation in the building of a new national identity. It was an exhilarating enterprise. The pioneers revived the Hebrew language, created a system of Hebrew education, launched a Hebrew press, opened a Hebrew theatre. They and their children have held the helm of the State of Israel for three decades and have won its wars.

Identification with the Jewish past was important for Ahad Ha'am in a candidate for admission to the Cultural Centre, but not essential. At the end of his essay "Revival and Creation", in the course of which the author made the disrespectful remark that an atheist Jew was a better Jew than a religious one, Ahad Ha'am went on to treat of a "third category" of Jews. They were those "who draw a line through the past, treating it as if it had never existed, as if the nation had just now begun to exist." These people did not so much desire to revive an ancient nation as to create a new one, a foreign one.

Notwithstanding his disapproval, Ahad Ha'am was reluctant to bar them from admission to his Centre. Let them enter, he cried, but under surveillance (so we translate his meaning for the reader) in case their extreme secularism should lead to the "negation of the negation", Ahad Ha'am's quaint phrase for succumbing to the temptation of Christianity.

What transpires from the foregoing is that the residual criterion in selecting candidates for admission to the Centre would be Jewish origin and no more. The State of Israel acts precisely on this assumption when it distributes immigration certificates to anti-Zionist Communist Jews.

Theodor Herzl fell into the same line of thought. A certain Mr. de Jong, a convert Jew, applied for permission to join the newly formed Zionist movement. Herzl's answer was in the negative. He argued that the only way he and his contemporaries had of showing that they were Jews was the religion of their ancestors. This was to affirm that they were men of Jewish origin, not that they were Jews. Mr. de Jong could have replied that his ancestors also had practiced the Jewish religion.

Ahad Ha'am went so far as to invite religious Jews to collaborate with him in edifying his Secular Cultural Centre, in the spirit of the spider inviting the fly to step into its parlor. His action provoked a stinging rebuke from Kurzweil, who described it as an example of "quiet demonism".

Ahad Ha'am did not admit converts to his Centre. He literally spewed forth the suggestion, justifying himself by the same argument that Justice Silberg was to employ against Father Daniel. It seems that Ahad Ha'am protested too much. Had he not torn up traditional Judaism by the roots more radically than Christianity itself?

Ultimately then, it was not necessary to be a Jew to enter the Cultural Centre; rather one became a Jew, an Ahad Ha'amist Jew, by living in the Centre. Leibowitz made the point very clearly that it is not the Jewish people which is building a state for itself; it is the state which is moulding a people it aims at bringing into existence. So we account for a certain class of Gentile immigrant in Israel, whose presence is tolerated provided that he falls into line with the majority.

IV. AHAD HA'AM INTERROGATED

Ahad Ha'am maintained a pudic reserve about the more obvious implications of his secularism. Let us interrogate him in retrospect.

Did Ahad Ha'am intend to abandon the practice of circumcision? If not, what would be its justification in a secular centre? The question is not irrelevant. It could be addressed to all non-observing Jews who continue to practice the rite.

Did Ahad Ha'am mean to institute civil marriage and divorce? Would Ahad Ha'am have tolerated mixed marriages in his Cultural Centre? Would he have allowed equal status to the issue of mixed marriages, whether from a Jewish father and a Gentile mother, or from a Gentile father and a Jewish mother?

Did Ahad Ha'am intend granting the same status to the Reform and the Orthodox synagogues in his Cultural Centre?

Let these questions suffice. Agreed that Ahad Ha'am did not aim directly at setting up a state — he was too timid for that — but as a man deeply versed in rabbinical law, these cases and others must have crossed his mind and called for comment. Ahad Ha'am veiled his thought on such delicate matters for fear of exposing to the eyes of the Jewish world the full extent — nay, the brutality — of his break with tradition.

It is this sort of concrete question which the pressure of reality has forced into the forefront of public notice since the State of Israel has come into being. Each case hides a personal tragedy. Together, they spell out to the full the consequences of Ahad Ha'am's secularism as it impinges on the fabric of Jewish life. Each case provides an occasion for conflict between secularist and Orthodox, one exacerbated by the rapid infiltration into Israeli society of the standards of the permissive West.

Would Ahad Ha'am have finally admitted Gentiles to his Centre?

The question is particularly relevant to the case of Father Daniel.

The Court forbade Father Daniel entry into the Jewish community of Israel on the grounds that he was not a Jew for the purposes of the Law of Return; that is, for the purposes of the said law, Father Daniel was regarded as a Gentile.

The Secular Centre and the Gentile

In every age there have been Gentiles willing to enter the Jewish religious community; why should there not be Gentiles desirous of entering the Secular Centre? The rabbis prescribed conditions for admission into the Jewish religious community: circumcision for males and the ritual bath for females. Did Ahad Ha'am foresee any parallel ceremonies for admission to his Centre? Were there any conditions at all?

The problem is not an imaginary one. Far from it! The Canaanites affirm that there are twenty-eight thousand Gentile immigrants undergoing silent assimilation into Israeli society, without benefit of clergy.[1] Kurman complained that the secularists wanted conversion without any religious ceremony.[2]

After all, was it not easier for a Gentile to identify himself with a secular society than with a Jewish religious one? Were not the very principles of secularism of Gentile origin? Was there, finally, any act which the Jewish member of the Secular Centre had to perform and which a Gentile might find unacceptable in conscience?

In the State of Israel, a bewildering variety of non-Jews inevitably participate in the same cultural framework as the Jew. Arabs speak fluent Hebrew; Druses fight and die in Israel's wars; Assad Azi, a young Druse, writes Hebrew poetry. Ahad Ha'am made the study of — not the belief in — Judaism one of the signs of the good Jewish nationalist. The colorful habits of Catholic religious studying Judaism dot the campuses of Israeli universities. Recently the Vatican instructed all Catholic institutions of higher learning to make provision for studies in Judaism. Other Christian denominations do not lag behind the Catholics in this respect.

The Sentiment of Identification as a Norm

Ahad Ha'am and his disciples insisted on the importance of the sentiment of identification with the Jewish past as a hallmark of the true Jewish nationalist. Let us examine the results of thirty years of educational experience in the State of Israel under the guidance of Ahad Ha'amism.

Ben-Gurion identified himself more with the Hebrew biblical past, when the Jewish people enjoyed sovereignty, than with the two thousand years of exile when they did not. The effect was to provoke a decline in the sentiment of identification amongst Israeli youth with pre-State Diaspora Judaism. Here are some characteristic findings:

"The non-Orthodox *sabras*, or native-born Israelis, consider themselves Israelis on all accounts, while the Orthodox and most of the non-sabras of all persuasions rank as Jews."[3]

Professor Simon Herman published the results of his sociological survey. He found that:

a) the sentiment of Jewish identity is a correlative of Jewish religious observance;

b) it is threatened by a decline in religion;

c) Zionism has eroded the sentiment of Jewish identity;

d) a Jewish problem exists for Israeli youth.

Another survey by the same sociologist yielded an unexpected finding: 63% of the pupils in government schools in Israel would prefer to have been born Gentiles or in the Diaspora.[4]

Father J. Stiassny, a close observer of the Israeli scene, writes: "Many sabras openly declare themselves not to be Jews, but Israelis, indeed Canaanites."[5]

Y. Leibowitz, an Orthodox Jew, well-known in Israel for his trenchant views, records that the Zionist pioneers set up a society which was not in continuity with the Jewish past; that its link with the past had been broken; that the State of Israel was pseudo-Jewish; that a process was under way in Israel of changing the Jewish people into another people.[6]

M. Bar-on testified: "The Israeli who has been born here is not directly Jewish."[7]

Professor Emmanuel Rakman declared: "The Jewish identity of the majority of the inhabitants of Israel is on the wane."[8]

We end the list of witnesses by calling on Doron Rosenbloom, who reflected on the unprecedented difficulty experienced by the Israeli in determining the visage of the State and its identity.

The rapid de-judaization of Israeli youth formed by the cultural program of Ahad Ha'am constrained the Department of Education to introduce a course for the strengthening of Jewish consciousness amongst Israeli school children. Father Stiassny was squarely of the opinion that "the new programme has failed".[9]

Why Definitions are Dangerous

Aristotle required of a metaphysical definition that it possess a specific element coupled with generic factors.

In traditional Judaism, the divine Election played admirably the role of a specific difference, being equally present in all Israelites and absent from all Gentiles.

The generic characteristics of the Jewish people were similar in kind to those found in other peoples. They may be classified into objective and subjective. The objective components were race, language, land, history, culture; the subjective components were a sentiment of identification with the group and a willingness to participate in the moulding of its destiny.

Even in the field of generic characteristics, the Jewish people betrayed its singularity. For centuries it existed deprived of those "major criteria which contribute to assure the national cohesion in other peoples",[10] surviving in the Diaspora without a common language and a homeland. Its original Judaean chromosome pool became heavily diluted in the course of time by massive admixtures from the host nations. In Russia, for instance, an entire non-Semitic people, the Khazars of the Crimea, once embraced Judaism.

The divine election, though efficacious, was invisible. It fell to rabbinical law to conserve the community of the elect and to bear responsibility for identifying the individual Israelite.

The weakness of Ahad Ha'amism lay in the fact that the Secular Cultural Centre had no specific quality which enabled a distinction to be made between Jew and Gentile. The principles of Zionist nationalism — land, language, people — were too generic in nature to provide a criterion of distinction between them. On a purely speculative plane, there was nothing in Ahad Ha'amism to prevent a radical shift of collective identity taking place in Ahad Ha'am's projected Secular Centre.

Kurzweil grasped that the Canaanites, though numerically insignificant, were symptomatic of the intrinsic weakness of Ahad Ha'amism. The Canaanites had stripped Ahad Ha'am's doctrine of its sentimental overtones and pushed his secularism to its logical conclusion. The political triumph of the Canaanites, should the impossible occur, would entail the entire destruction of Jewish identity and the formation of a "tertium quid", the neo-Canaanite nation. The latter would be no more attached to its Jewish past than the modern Englishman is to the medieval Catholic Church which once covered his land with cathedrals and monasteries.

Moderate Secular Zionists are seized with panic at the prospect of a drift to neo-Canaanite radicalism, which their own secularism has engendered. To return in repentance to Judaism is out of the question; to take the plunge into Extreme Secularism is to sign the death warrant of Zionism. Hence the dilemma! The solution of the Moderate Secularists is to compromise with their secularist principles. They support the rabbinical establishment out of an unavowed consciousness that the latter is more capable of assuring the conservation of Jewish identity than they are. While waiting for a suitable issue from their dilemma, they punish the Canaanites by ostracism. The sharp eye of Father Stiassny did not overlook the fact that Zionists who never frequent the synagogue are the most consistent supporters of the rabbinate.[11]

Kurzweil was consequently justified in blaming Ahad Ha'amism for exposing the Jewish people to the danger of losing its historical identity. The situation, however, is not as gloomy as he pretended. In divesting Jews of the straightjacket of rabbinical law, Ahad Ha'amism had unwittingly liberated the divine component in their identity. It is this factor, not the Jewish religion, that is affirming itself with such unheard-of dynamism in Israel and in the world at large. The corresponding decline in Jewish identity concerns only the second component, the one flowing from rabbinical law. The true problem for Moderate Secular Zionism would be to discover an alternative religious community to the synagogue, as Martin Buber well understood.[12] Israelis would then cease to be secularists, which may sound paradoxical, but paradoxes have a way of providing the only reasonable solution to problems in Israel.

In the meantime, the compromise continues. Secular Zionists support the ban on mixed marriages; they exploit the "millet" system; they have been known to launch campaigns for the conversion of Christian immigrants to Judaism. [13] The same dilemma obliges them to apply the excluding clause against the entry of Jewish converts into their society.

The marriage between Moderate Secular Zionism and Orthodox Judaism creates a great deal of tension in the State of Israel. It is an uneasy union, quite unforeseen by Ahad Ha'am himself. At some time in the not-too-distant future, a divorce will take place on grounds of incompatibility.

V. WORDS! WORDS! WORDS!

There are sciences of the human word. There are arts of the human word. There is the excruciating discipline of translation, the tiresome teaching of languages, a medicine of words. Recall to mind the unhappy stammerer, the stutterer, the deaf, the dumb, the blind, and their difficulties with speaking or reading. Analphabetism is a political and social problem. Words used to communicate truth, lies, entertainment, propaganda, and advertisement are the object of an industry and a technology. The wisdom of the word tells us when to speak and when to be silent. Above all, there is the use and the abuse of words.

Father Daniel claimed to be a Jew. Was he using or abusing the term? What is its correct use? Can it be defined? André Neher thought not. Mordechai Kaplan agreed, holding that it was a miscellany. John Macdonald refused to make any scientific use of the word at all.

If there is confusion about the correct use of the word "Jew", we have only ourselves to blame. The question has been wrongly formulated. The true problem is not, in the first place, who and what is a Jew, but what is the Jewish people. One receives the impression at times that inquirers secretly prefer to stroll around the labyrinth rather than locate the exit.

A Jew can only be a member of the Jewish people, no more, no less. Not that our reply is a definition, but it puts us on the road to a solution. Neither is the term "Jewish people" self-evident. One writer lucidly observed that it had an "accidental, contingent nature".[1]

To begin with, the term "Jewish people" is not encountered in the Hebrew Bible. There we read about the Benei Yisrael, the people of Israel, or the Israelites. The people of Israel is well-defined in theology as the people of the Election, the people of the divine promises. The individual member of this people is an Israelite.

44

In the Book of Kings, it is true, the term "Israelite" is commonly limited to the Israelites of the northern kingdom of Israel, much like the word "American" has come to be applied only to citizens of the United States.

The term "Jew" is also encountered in the Old Testament, though much less frequently than "Israel". For the pre-exilic period, it connotes an inhabitant of Judah, or refers to his language. It should be translated as "Judaean", a usage adopted by modern translators of the Bible. In Gen. 25:34, we read that "when Esau was forty years old he married "Yehudit", the daughter of Beeri the Hittite". Perhaps, at that time, the term "Jew" (Yehudi) referred to the non-Israelite inhabitants of Judaea! The geographical sense persists in the New Testament where "Jew" is often used in opposition to "Galilean".

For the pre-exilic period, the religion of the people of Israel has no proper name. We call it the religion of Ancient Israel, or the religion of the Mosaic Alliance. During the Babylonian Exile the great work of committing it to writing was successfully undertaken. The result was the Five Books of Moses, or Torah. The Torah, or Written Law as it is also known, was accepted by the exiles who had returned from Babylon to rebuild the walls and temple of Jerusalem, thus becoming their canonical literature. From then on the religion of the Mosaic Alliance has a proper name, Mosaic Judaism, of which Ezra is deemed to be the founder. To the Books of Moses were progressively added those of the Prophets and the Writings to constitute, finally, the Old Testament. The Samaritans did not share in the development of the canon of Holy Scripture, confining themselves to the Torah.

Mosaic Judaism is the religion of the Mosaic Alliance, from the time it was committed to writing and accepted by the Judaeans as binding in conscience by divine authority, given the valid nature of that authority. The name is derived from Judaea, where the exiles had settled and where Mosaic Judaism was to undergo its most significant development before expiring with Jesus on the cross.

Rigorously speaking, those to whom Ezra communicated the Torah should be called "Israelitico-Judaeans", in contrast to the "Israelitico-Samarians" of northern Palestine.

A semantic evolution then occurred in the term "Judaean". To its original geographical connotation was added a religious dimension, so that the term came to signify the Judaean who observed the customs of Mosaic Judaism. A word of great utility has been coined to connote the added religious sense: "Judaite", though Macdonald uses "Judaist".

The Israelites of southern Palestine were consequently "Israelitico-Judaeans" from a geographical point of view and "Israelitico-Judaites" from a religious point of view. The Israelites of northern Palestine were "Israelitico-Samarians" from the first point of view and "Israelitico-Samaritans" from the second.

A further semantic development in the term "Judaean" arose to complicate the situation even more. The religious sense of the term "Judaean" was extended to embrace those Israelites everywhere who observed the customs peculiar to the Judaites of Judaea. Think of the analogous extension of topical names such as Asia and Africa, which initially designated no more than provinces of the present continents, which now go by those names.

Solomon Zeitlin observed, in confirmation, that the Judaean way of life became synonymous with their religion, and as such was adopted by Israelites in other parts of the world.

The Romans used the term "Jew" to designate Israelites who followed the laws of Mosaic Judaism such as circumcision, abstention from pork meat, and the strict observance of the Sabbath, customs which struck the pagan world with particular force. It was they who popularized the extended sense of the term "Jew", so much so that the use was finally adopted by Israelites themselves. The Roman preference for "Jew" is illustrated in the New Testament, when Pontius Pilate wrote out the title of the cross: "This is Jesus, King of the Jews" (Mt. 27:42). By contrast, Simeon, a Jew, blesses the newly born Messiah with the words: "Glory of your people Israel" (Lk. 2:32), and the chief priests mock Jesus, agonizing on the cross: "He is the King of Israel! Let's see him come down from that cross" (Mt. 27:42).

The Jewish preference for "Israel" is still to be observed in the Mishna, though "Jew" is used, especially when a point of rabbinical law is at stake, or when Gentiles are brought into the picture.

Josephus calls the pre-exilic Israelite a "Hebrew" and the post-exilic Israelite a "Jew". Now and again he permits himself an anachronistic use of the term. Post-Christic Judaism is particularly fond of this kind of anachronism. The Midrashim commonly call the patriarchs "Jews"; one midrash will have us believe that Jethro became a "Jew".

Philo employs "Hebrew" for the Israelites of Palestine and "Jew" for those of the Diaspora.

These examples of the varied use of the term "Jew" illustrate the absence of an international linguistic police force, empowered to prevent authors paying words a penny to make them mean what they like. They underline the insufficiency of semantics in fixing the theological meaning of words.

Pre-Christic and Post-Christic Jews

After the destruction of the temple of Jerusalem in 70 A.D., those Jews who had not accepted Christianity found themselves placed under a new religious régime which we call Rabbinism, or, bending to the pressure of historical convention, Rabbinical Judaism. The name of the new religious régime was appropriate enough, as it has been founded by the rabbis of the academy of Yavne, the most prominent of whom was the Rabbi Yohanan Ben Zakkai. It persists to the present day, being currently known as Orthodox Judaism.

The individual adherent to Rabbinism is a Rabbinite, or a Rabbinical Jew. Amongst both Jews and Gentiles the convention is to name him simply a Jew, a convention that perpetuates an ambiguity, for Rabbinism was not in formal continuity with Mosaic Judaism, which is what the unqualified use of the term "Jew" gives the unwary to understand. It was something substantially new.[2]

The Romans continued to employ "Jew", even after the destruction of the Temple. So far as they could observe, it had not brought about any significant change in the customs of the Jews: they continued to frequent the synagogue as before, to abstain from pork, to circumcise their children, and so on.

Post-Christic Jews, of course, never entertained the least suspicion that Mosaic Judaism has ceased to exist or that the new

religious régime under which they found themselves required a
different name, as did their identity.

Christians, however, should not accept the rabbinical use of
the term "Jew" at its face value, but should insist on the radical
difference between pre-Christic and post-Christic Jews. The
corollary is that Christian theology cannot formulate a definition
of the term "Jew" which covers both categories.

The Two-Factor Structure of Jewish Identity

The widespread use of the two terms, "Israelite" and "Jew",
especially in rabbinical circles, indicates a perception by rabbis of
a fundamental duality in the structure of Jewish identity, though
not all rabbinical authors express their perception clearly.

What transpires is that Jewish identity is a result of the interplay
of two factors, Election and Law. This two-factor structure of
Jewish identity is basic to our solution of Father Daniel's case of
conscience.

The term "Israelite" designates any member of the people of
Israel, object of the divine Election.

The term "Jew" designates the Israelite placed in relation to the
Law of Moses, written and interpreted.

To be an Israelite is to possess an innate quality which, if we
understand St. Paul correctly, is irrevocable at will. We say innate,
not hereditary; we say irrevocable for the person concerned, not
for his descendants.

To be a Jew is for the Israelite to be placed under the Law of
Moses, an external relation and therefore not innate and revocable
at will.

Father Daniel was born an Israelite and remained one after his
baptism. At circumcision he became a subject of the Law of Moses
and so a Jew in the conventional sense of the term. At baptism he
ceased to be under the Law of Moses and became subject to the
Law of Christ. Father Daniel was, in consequence, not entitled to
call himself a Jew; he had become an "Israelitico-Christian" or,
for short, a "Hebrew Christian".

However, by the same token, Secular Zionists who have

rejected the authority of rabbinical law are no more entitled to call themselves "Jews" than Father Daniel. They are secularized Israelites.

A one-factor theory of Jewish identity underlines the outlook of Y. Leibowitz and leads him to absurd conclusions. Leibowitz places the essence of Jewish identity in rabbinical law. Since the majority of the Jews, to talk only of the State of Israel, reject the obligation of rabbinical law, Leibowitz ruthlessly concludes that they are rapidly becoming "another" people. Does he mean to insinuate that they are on the way to becoming Gentiles? The word "another" in Hebrew is a synonym for apostate, so perhaps he suspected the worst. Arguing from the same premises, Leibowitz affirms that relations between Israeli and Diaspora Jews are fictitious. They have become two different peoples. In this way, Leibowitz has achieved the rare distinction of infuriating both Secular Zionists and Orthodox Jews, for which latter a Jew remains a Jew, though he may sin.

Leibowitz is right enough in believing that the de-judaization of the Israeli Jew is an irreversible process; he is right in pointing to a certain rift which has appeared of late between Israeli and Diaspora Jewry. He is wrong about his fundamental conception of Jewish identity. Its essence does not reside in rabbinical law; it resides in the divine Election. The Israeli can cease to be a Jew; he cannot cease to be an Israelite. The perpetuity of the essential identity of the people is guaranteed by a divine promise. Leibowitz is causing himself unnecessary bitterness of spirit in believing otherwise and is to be blamed for creating an atmosphere of pessimism concerning the future of the nation.

VI. JESUS AND JEWISH IDENTITY:
FROM MOSAIC JUDAISM TO THE CHURCH

The advent of Jesus Christ, the Son of God, changed human history; it inevitably changed Jewish identity. The bearing on the case of conscience of Father Daniel is immediate. Here was a Jew who had become a Christian; was he still a Jew? The final answer lies in the impact of Jesus on Jewish identity.

The passage from Judaism to Christianity rouses the passions of Jew and Gentile alike. The Jew accuses the Christian missionary of attempting to destroy the physical integrity of the people, though not, of course, by physical means. Father Hruby seems to accept the assessment, for he says: "If Israel refuses to identify itself with the new Israel, which the Church pretends to be, it is because such an identification would lead, *ipso facto*, to the end of the Jewish people."[1] We find the forecast alarmist — at any rate avoidable — but the ground has to be cleared of the multiple ambiguities in the terms employed before light appears.

Christians are surprised to learn that belief in a Jewish Messiah should appear to imperil the existence of the Jewish people. They are bewildered and hurt at the resentment their well-intentioned missionary overtures encounter among Jews. When the so-called "Anti-Mission Law" was passed in the Knesset, the parliament of Israel, the reaction of Christians was one of heated indignation. We concede that they had a case to air; what we do not justify was the absence of any effort of comprehension among Christians of the Jewish point of view. Standing on their side of the fence, Jews have always observed with feelings of outrage the alienation of the convert from his people and the assimilation of his descendants into the Gentile community. What is more, the very thought of adding the religious pluralism of the Christian world to that obtaining already in the Jewish world is enough to fill the Jew with horror. Is it to be wondered at that religious and secularist Jews combine forces to resist the Christian missionary, who proclaims salvation for the individual and prepares the earthly extermination of the people?

Jesus of Nazareth had no such intention. Had he not come to save the Jews? (cf. Mt. 1:21) He himself was a Jew, born in Bethlehem of a Jewish mother, Mary, and circumcised on the eighth day of his life. He was of the tribe of Judah (cf. Heb. 7:14), a scion of the royal house of David (cf. 2 Tim. 2:8; Rm. 2:26). Jesus directed his public ministry to the lost sheep of Israel, whom he loved and for whom he was to die before dying for others (Jn. 11:51-52).

When the Samaritan woman rounded on him pertly, saying: "You are a Jew. How can you ask me, a Samaritan and a woman, for a drink?" (Jn. 4:9), he does not reject the attribution. By announcing to the confused woman that "salvation comes from the Jews" (cf. Jn. 4: 22), he implicitly acknowledges that he was a Jew. The author of the Apocalypse bestowed on the Risen Christ the epithet "Lion of the tribe of Judah" (cf. Rv. 5:5).

St. Peter teaches that Jesus had come to grant Israel "repentance and forgiveness of sins" (cf. Acts 5:31); not a destructive aim, surely.

Some are of the opinion that "there is no shred of evidence that Jesus, at any point, repudiated his obligation to the Law, to which both his birth and circumcision committed him".[2] The statement is true, as far as it goes. Jesus had no plan to change Mosaic Judaism *during his lifetime.* The passage "not an iota will pass from the Law, till all has been accomplished," may be an interpolation from judaising elements in the Primitive Church, as some exegetes are inclined to think; they certainly express the attitude of Jesus to the Law, prior to Calvary. Modern revolutionaries are different. They are men in a hurry; they strive to introduce radical changes in the established order before their death. Not so Jesus! Two swords were enough for his purposes. The Church which he aimed to set up was to be the work, not of Jesus himself, but of his Spirit; to procure this gift for mankind, Jesus knew he had first to die and rise again from the dead.

It was a principle of Mosaic Judaism that a Judaite was bound to the observance of the law as long as he lived; death liberated him from his obligation (cf. Rm. 7:1-2; 1 Cor. 7:39). Jesus remained faithful to the Law until his death. On the third day he rose from the dead, free to institute his Church. He was no more a Judaite; he was an Israelite of a Judaean ancestry, "of David's line" (cf. Rv. 22:16), and of Judaite origin.

The same principle holds good for the convert. In baptism he dies with Christ and is absolved from the obligation to observe the Law of Moses. After baptism he rises to a new life, an Israelite but no more a Jew, subject to the Law of Christ only. "It was through the law that I died to the law, to live for God" (Gal. 2:19-20). One commentator finds the passage obscure. A reference to rabbinical teaching will make its meaning clear. In setting up his Church, Jesus did no violence to Mosaic Judaism, contrary to what many Christians imagine. Jesus and Mosaic Judaism died together on the cross; they rose together on the third day, transfigured.

We are now in a better position to judge how erroneous are certain positions summarized by Eugene Fisher. Some scholars, for instance, hold that post-Christic Judaism and Christianity are both "in full and valid covenant with God", and that "Christianity is an alternate form of the Sinai covenant, which remains in force"; or again, "that the Christian covenant thus perfects and fulfills, not Sinai, but the covenant with Noah". One asks oneself in astonishment (if what these positions pretend are true) why any Jew should ever have become a Christian, beginning with St. Peter and St. Paul.

Whereas some appear to hold that Jesus left Mosaic Judaism intact, Larcher goes to the opposite extreme: "He (Jesus) foresaw and posed successively the acts which were to lead to a rupture with Judaism".[3] To give Larcher his due, his thesis vacillates between continuity and a break in the passage from Mosaic Judaism to the Church. Elsewhere, he modifies his previous stances: "Jesus, in virtue of the same divine authority, could have declared the Torah abrogated, incomplete and imperfect word of God, eclipsed by the perfect and definitive Word. He did not do so." Again, he concedes that the Torah "continues to indicate the will and intention of God".

Larcher, expressing a broad current of opinion amongst Christian theologians, maintains that Jesus put aside all that was material, temporal, and nationalist in Mosaic Judaism. What, then, is the residual value of the Old Testament for the Christian? The Old Testament, Larcher replies, retains no more than a "pedagogic value" for the new Israel. In consequence, Larcher regards as illegitimate any attempt to apply the prophecies of the Old Testament for the purpose of explaining the return of Jews to the Holy Land. How should a Christian explain it? "The answer to those questions," he writes, "escapes us entirely, for the designs of God are impenetrable in advance." We incline our head piously at the thought, but, in fact, have not the designs of God advanced? Is not the re-establishment of the Jews in the Holy Land a reality? Larcher finds facts embarrassing. His rejection of Zionism is short and harsh. The most he is prepared to admit, and that grudgingly, is that maybe the Jewish people constitute a special case. We see no sign that Zionists are going to fold up their tents and steal away, in order to facilitate matters for Larcher.

Rijk was more candid. He confessed that theologians are, ultimately, uncertain about the residual value of the Old Testament for Christians.

Adolf Darlap was positively humble. On the status of the Old Testament in Christianity, he admitted "that it is not so easy to define what remains and what has been suppresssed."[4]

Perhaps Darlap's question should not be raised at all. The passage from Mosaic Judaism to the Church was the work of the Holy Spirit and its results are transmitted to us by tradition. The theologian registers them retrospectively. Seventh Day Adventists appear to enter where angels fear to tread when they conclude that the sanctification of Saturday is preceptive for Christians.

In the meantime, the Church tenaciously held to the belief that books of the Old Testament had been composed under the inspiration of the Holy Spirit, no less than those of the New Testament. Catholic theology taught that the Old Testament was a legitimate source for demonstration of theological propositions, on a par with tradition and the teaching authority of the Church. Ecumenical councils quoted the Old Testament as if its quotations were demonstrative, not merely illustrative.

The truth is that the redemptive death of Jesus introduced a dual ferment of continuities and discontinuities into every order of Mosaic Judaism. Jesus compared the action of the kingdom of God to yeast fermenting a paste. Newman used the image of a caterpillar which undergoes metamorphosis in its silky cocoon, to issue therefrom a butterfly.

Newman, in fact, succeeded where others failed. He laid down the principle which explained the transition from Mosaic Judaism to the Church.

"Let us recollect," he began, "why the prescriptions of the Law are abrogated and we shall understand in what sense. They were abolished because they were types and because Christ their antitype is come. True then as far as they are types they are abolished, but not as far as they are religious services and principles and elements of religious worship. That is, we must distinguish between the precept itself and the particular fulfilment of it under the Jewish law, the Jewish rite."[5]

Continuing in the same line, Newman went on: "Not only do forms and ordinances remain under the Gospel as equally as before, but as it is plain from the very chapter on which I am commenting, what was in use before is not so much superseded by the Gospel ordinances, as changed into them. What took place under the Law is a pattern, what was commanded is a rule under the Gospel. The substance remains, the use, the meaning, the circumstances, the benefit is changed, grace is added, life is infused, the body is of Christ, but it is in great measure that same body which was in being before he came. The Gospel has not put aside, it has incorporated into itself the revelation which went before it."

Newman summed up his thought on the passage from Mosaic Judaism to the Church in a lapidary sentence: "The Jewish Church and the Christian are really one."[6] David Flusser, surprisingly enough, comes to a similar conclusion, to be interpreted, naturally, in terms of his own premises.[7]

Let us apply Newman's illuminating distinctions in some detail.

Doctrine

The rigorous monotheism of the Old Testament prophets was unhesitatingly accepted by the Gospel. On one occasion, Jesus recited the opening sentence of the "Shema": Hear O Israel, the Lord our God, the Lord is one God. To this monotheism was added the doctrine of the Trinity. The Christian accepts that monotheism is a dogma or revealed truth of the Old Testament and, if revealed, then preceptive.

The eschatology of Mosaic Judaism was taken over almost in its entirety by the Church. The Apocrypha and the pseudepigrapha of the Old Testament dealt in a vivid and imaginative way with last things, the end of history, the ultimate destiny of souls. To these beliefs and others the Church added that on the last day it would be Jesus the Lord, come in glory, who would judge the living and the dead.

Morals

Christianity retained the Ten Commandments, only "illustrated, tempered, and spiritualized," as Newman would have said. Cicognani and others have argued that the Ten Commandments reappear in Christianity because they represent the natural law. The remark does not cover the precept of Sabbath observance. The Jewish Sabbath became the Lord's Day in Christianity on the authority of tradition. The Lord laid down no precept concerning it. It was sufficient for Christians to consecrate one day a week to God, what day being of secondary importance. Not even the Jewish component of Sabbatical repose was retained, for in the first centuries of the Christian era the Church lacked the political power to impose one day of rest a week on Christians. If courts, banks, and businesses close down on Sundays, we are beholden for it to Constantine the Great. It may come as a surprise to Christians to be reminded that the Sabbatical repose they practice on Sundays is not of divine but of ecclesiastical law.[8]

Newman wrote in confirmation: "And so again the Ten Commandments belong to the Law, yet we read them still in the Communion Service as binding upon ourselves, yet not in the mere letter; the Gospel has turned the letter into spirit."

Marriage

Monogamy and the indissolubility of Christian marriage are preceptive for Christians. Jesus defended these principles by invoking Gn. 2:24. Cicognani inferred from this that Christian marriage is indissoluble only because Jesus confirmed the teaching of Genesis. Did he not force an interpretation on the text from *a priori* motives? To us, the more natural reading is that Jesus invoked Genesis because it contained a teaching preceptive for the People of God in both phases of its existence.

Scripture

The Church retained the Sacred Scripture of Mosaic Judaism in the most spontaneous manner imaginable. Where Christianity differed from Judaism was in its interpretation of the messianic prophecies and the provisional status it accorded to the institutions of the Mosaic Law (cf. Mt. 23:1-3).

Ritual

The sacrifice of the Cross rendered obsolete the bloody offerings of the old order (cf. Heb. 9:11-14). The principle of the sacrifice was not abolished, but the kind of sacrifice offered. Simultaneously, the ministerial priesthood of Aaron was replaced by the priesthood of Jesus. Protestants err who assert that Jesus ever intended abolishing a sacrificing priesthood.

Newman expounds the matter with his customary energy and clarity: "Persons sometimes urge that there is no code of duty in the New Testament, no ceremonial, no rules for Church policy. Certainly not! They are unnecessary; they are already given in the Old. Why should the Old Testament be retained in the Christian Church but to be used? There we are to look for our forms, our rites, our policy, only illustrated, spiritualized by the Gospel. The precepts remain, the observance of them is changed."[9] How far are we not from Larcher!

In the light of Newman's teaching, we stand dismayed when Hruby affirms: "Israel is entitled, legitimately, in the order which is theirs, to expect that in time the Temple will be restored."[10] Christians, in the order which is theirs, may think otherwise. At all events, one Israeli religious leader has expressed his disappointment at the marginal degree of enthusiasm the project of restoring the

Temple arouses in the Israeli public. In the first place, the Temple would have to be built on the site now occupied by world-renowned Muslim sanctuaries, an unthinkable violation of the status quo governing holy places in Jerusalem. What is more, bloody sacrifices being offered in public would hardly be an agreeable sight.

Christianity inherited from the old dispensation its ministerial priesthood and the distinction between the priesthood and the laity, one which lives on in the consciousness of Jews to the present day, though the Jewish priest or "Cohen" has not exercised his functions for nigh on two thousand years. Lastly, the Christian Church abided by the rule of Mosaic Judaism, which reserved the priesthood to males, in opposition to the pagan world, where the priestess was an accepted institution.

Ecclesiastical Authority

After recounting the parable of the homicidal vine-dressers, Jesus added the ominous words: "For this reason, I tell you, the Kingdom of God will be taken away from you and given to a nation that will yield a rich harvest. When the chief priests and the Pharisees heard these parables, they realized he was speaking about them" (Mt. 21:43-45).

If we delete the phrase "and the Pharisees" as a gloss, which some exegetes recommend, the passage suits our purpose even better. Jesus is using the passive voice to avoid pronouncing the name of God, in accordance with the custom of his time. What he meant to say was, therefore, that God was about to withdraw whatever kind of divine authority had been bestowed on the priesthood of Mosaic Judaism in order to transfer it to others. Protestants argue from this passage that Jesus intended to transfer authority to Peter, in the latter's merely individual capacity. They err. The authority in question was not the authority of the chief priest of that time but of his office, which had existed for centuries before.

The priesthood of the Old Law had been established as preceptive for the People of God in whatever phase of its existence. The discontinuity introduced by the Gospel ferment lay in the transfer of the same authority from the House of Aaron to Peter, the Apostles, and their legitimate successors. Since none of these came from the Jewish priesthood, Jesus effectively opened the priesthood to any man qualified for the office.

The transfer of priestly authority, announced prophetically by Jesus, is one of the principle axes in the transition from Mosaic Judaism to the Church. The corollary is that the Church is in formal continuity with Mosaic Judaism, which is the burden of Newman's magnificent essay on the subject. The transfer of authority establishes on an unassailable foundation the essential identity between the two great phases of the public revelation of God to mankind. Mosaic Judaism was the People of God under the Law of Moses; the Church was the same people under the Law of Christ.

The second corollary is that when the transfer of divine authority had come into effect, it left Jewish religious leaders destitute of divine authority. Indeed, the obsolescence of the temple system in the generation that followed the resurrection of Jesus was rapid, ending in its physical destruction in 70 A.D, when Providence confirmed the dispositions taken by God. The temple burned, and with it the genealogical records required to demonstrate the validity of the Jewish priesthood. Today a Jew bearing the name "Cohen" can only adduce family tradition in support of his claim to be of priestly descent. What court of law would deem that sufficient evidence after an interval of two thousand years?

Even more so than the Jewish priesthood was Rabbinism, which succeeded Mosaic Judaism as the religion of the people, deprived of divine authority. True, the people which now came under the control of the rabbis were still authentic Israelites. Their history would unfold under the régime of the election; despite the exile, they would retain a link with the land of Israel. But these were attributes of the people, not of their new religious régime. They held for secularized Israelites no less than for religious ones, for the material object of the election is the people, not its religious beliefs or opinions.

We gladly concede that Rabbinism possesses values, many of which have been gravely neglected by the Christian clergy, and which the latter can recuperate in friendly discussion with Jews. However, all religions have their respective values, though one and one only is valid, the religion of Jesus Christ.

The Legal Prescriptions

The sacrifices of the Old Law were replaced by a new one, more efficacious than the blood of goats and bull calves (cf. Heb. 9:12), the old priesthood by a new one, the old legal and ritual prescriptions by a new legislation and a new ritual. The Law, it is said, was abrogated. Notwithstanding, the idea of abrogation can only be analogical, when applied to the supernatural order. Christianity abrogated the prescriptions of the Old Law, to replace them with others. The kingdom of God was to be taken away from the chief priests; it had therefore existed in Mosaic Judaism. In the Church the kingdom entered a new phase, without loss of its essential identity and structures.

Cicognani recognized the similarity between the institutions of Mosaic Judaism and the Church, without being able to account for it. Was it therefore accidental? Larcher found Mosaic Judaism unrecognizable in the Church. For Newman, the similarity is essential. Are there not in both a chief priest, assisted by secondary priests and counseled by legal experts? Are there not found in both priests ordained to offer sacrifices on consecrated altars? Both have a priesthood distinguished from a laity also called to holiness of life. Both have a Holy Scripture, a large part of which is shared. The histories of both are illustrated by prophets, monks, saints, martyrs, and confessors.

Post-Christic Rabbinism, in contrast, has no chief priest, no Sanhedrin, no sacrificing priesthood, no altars, no monastic institutions. Yes, Rabbinites can be saved in the synagogue, like Muslims in Islam and Buddhists in Buddhism. Their salvation depends on the good disposition of individuals, encouraged by the occasions which their religion may offer them to pose saving acts of faith. Their salvation does not demonstrate the validity of Rabbinism.

For Eugene Fisher to pretend that the Jewish covenant-unbiblical expression remains valid after Christ, that Rabbinism is sufficient for salvation on its own terms, that it does not need to be perfected by Christianity and other sophisms of the like, is to deny that Jesus Christ died to save all men, the Jews first. We welcome Fr. Fisher's appeal for a revision of the theology of post-Christic Judaism and the Jewish people; we agree that the revision involves a change of heart for Christians, not only a change in theological perspectives. But must Fisher revise Christian truth in the process? His book is titled *Faith Without Prejudice*; it is certainly not a book about "Faith Without Bias".

Cardinal Newman speaks the mind of the Church when he denies forcibly that any essential change of identity took place in the transition from Mosaic Judaism to the Church. He asks rhetorically: "What likeness is there between a church spread over the whole earth and a church pent up in one corner of it, between a national church and a Catholic? I answer, surely the mere extent of a church and its fortunes generally are but an accident of its being; externals cannot destroy identity if it exists, which is something inward."[11]

"But further," he continues, "it may be objected that the change was internal, not external; not only did the Church change from local to Catholic, but it became a Church of the Gentiles instead of a Church of the Jews."[12]

"I consider," he answers in reply, "that the word *remnant*, so constantly used in scripture, is a token of the identity of the Church in the mind of her Divine Creator, before and after the coming of Christ. Express and precise as are the sacred writers in declaring that the Gentiles shall be rejected, still, instead of stating the solemn appointment of God in a simple contrast between the two dispensations, they are accustomed to speak of the Remnant of Israel inheriting the Gentiles."[13]

Father Benoit is of the same opinion: that this universal expansion of the new elected people is not, in any way, brought about by the expulsion of the Jews, but by the addition of the pagans. The latter were not substituted for the former, as one says sometimes, they were associated to them.

The Gentiles were branches of the wild olive tree, grafted against their natural inclination into the cultivated olive tree (cf. Rm. 11:19), not by any metaphysical necessity, but by the decree of a merciful God and, conditionally, on their remaining faithful to their calling (cf. Rm. 11:20-21).

The Church of Christ was, therefore, not in contradiction to Mosaic Judaism. It did not oppose Mosaic Judaism; it was opposed to the survival of Mosaic Judaism. Mosaic Judaism did not disappear like a child who is reported missing to the police. It grew up. The adult does not abrogate the child. The child is assumed into the adult. They are the same person in different stages of its existence.

Christianity and the Social Régime of Mosaic Judaism

Jesus did not neglect to provide his people with new institutions to take the place of the old. He chose the Twelve and instructed them in the mysteries of the kingdom. He guided their first steps in the field of the apostolate. At Emmaus, the Risen Christ continues his teaching office (cf. Lk. 24:13-35). After Pentecost, the Twelve appear as a well-organized group: Peter at the head, John and James his intimate confidantes. The group was able to make serious decisions, to replace Judas the traitor by Matthias, and to admit the Gentiles.

Jesus left behind him an organized Church, the members of which were all Israelites, a Church of the Hebrews. Christ, its mystical head, was himself an Israelite, Mary and the Apostles were Israelites. Since the Church existed before the admission of the Gentiles, it is in essence Israelite. Gentiles only belong to the integrality of the Church, given that Christianity cannot be rightly conceived without the mission to the Gentiles.

The Church of the Hebrews was not a new sect of Judaism, not a kind of Reformed Synagogue. It represented the definitive form of the kingdom of God on earth, eschatologically oriented.[14]

Mosaic Judaism had been a *dat*. The word is of Persian origin, signifying "decree" or "royal decree". It was extended to describe the religion of Moses, which appeared to Jew and Gentile alike as representing a system of divine decrees. The sense of *dat* is excellently brought out in the Book of Esther. Haman complains to his king about the Jews: "Their laws (dateihem) are different from those of all the nations and they ignore the royal edicts (datei hamelech)" (cf. Est. 3:8). The Latin word "religio" has a wider and a narrower sense. The wider sense corresponds to the ordinary sense of the word religion. The narrower sense is confined to ecclesiastical circles: it signifies a religious order under its rule and constitutions. It is to this second and narrower sense of the word "religio" that the Hebrew "dat" approximates.

The Risen Christ had abolished the Jewish *dat*, though all his immediate disciples did not appreciate the extent of the change which he had effectuated in Mosaic Judaism. Many continued to circumcise their children, pray in the temple, frequent the synagogue, and call themselves Jews. Nor was there, at first, a proper name for the new religion. Jews such as St. James and the members of the community of Jerusalem held that the Law of Moses was still necessary for salvation. They were Judaeo-Christians.

On certain occasions St. Paul, too, called himself a Jew (cf. Acts 22:3). In a famous confrontation between them, St. Paul upbraids St. Peter, saying: "...you who are a Jew are living according to Gentile ways" (Gal. 2:14). Was St. Paul justified in calling St. Peter a Jew?

On the face of it, he was not! St. Paul had a very clear notion whom he thought was a Jew, and whom he thought was not a Jew. A Jew, for St. Paul, was one who trusted in the Law (cf. Rm. 2:17), who knew God's will through the Law, and who was a subject of the Law (cf. Rm. 3:19). The Gentiles, on the other hand, were those "who do not have the Law" (Rm. 2:12).

What St. Paul had in mind, and what he should have said, perhaps, was that he and St. Peter were of Jewish origin, for they had now "died to the Law" (Rm. 7:4).

At such an inchoative stage in the history of Christianity, it would be unfair to expect from St. Paul a more rigorous and consistent terminology. Ultimately, St. Paul directed his mission to the Gentiles. The Jewish adherents to the new way were few in number. St. Paul did not positively enjoin on them to abandon the customs of their ancestors, but he had undermined their *raison d'être*. If the Law was not necessary for the salvation of the Gentiles, neither was it necessary for the salvation of the Jews. St. Paul himself was prepared at times to practice the Law. He circumcised Timothy, he fulfilled his vows in the temple; but these were done in pursuit of his missionary policy of being all things to all men. The fact remains that St. Paul was still entitled to pose such acts, for the converts had not yet been expelled from the synagogue. They were obliged to leave the synagogue only after the destruction of the temple.

The right to pose acts of the Jewish religion entitles a person to be called a Jew. The principle holds to this very day in rabbinical law. For instance, a convert man may give his Jewish wife a bill of divorce, valid in the eyes of a rabbinical court. In the same measure, the convert is a Jew in the act for Rabbinical Judaism and not only in potency, as Kurman would have it.

But St. Paul no more considered that the Law of Moses bound his conscience. He was not a Judaeo-Christian in the strict sense of the term. What is more, his teaching on the caducity of the Law of Moses plunged the Judaeo-Christians into a profound dilemma. St. Paul declared the wall of separation between Jew and Gentile to have been overthrown by Jesus Christ. The special consequence was that the régime of social separation between Jew and Gentile was suppressed. A Christian of Jewish origin was now free to marry a Christian of Gentile origin. As the Judaeo-Christians saw it, and the rabbis with them, the way now lay wide open for the dissolution of the Jewish people in a flood of Gentile proselytes to the new religion.

The Judaeo-Christians recoiled from the prospect. Unable to find a solution to their dilemma consonant with the spirit of Christian fraternity, they entrenched themselves behind the régime of social separation between Jew and Gentile, so characteristic of Mosaic Judaism. Their bishops turned down the invitation to attend the Council of Nicaea, thus branding Judaeo-Christianity as heretical in the eyes of the Catholic world. The hostility of Gentile Christians from without and sectarianism from within brought about the disappearance of the various currents which together made up the Church of the Circumcised.

Testa and Bagatti have pioneered studies in the remarkable world of the Judaeo-Christians. They have traced the manifold influence of their culture on the development of Christianity. Our purpose requires from us to insist on the fact of their disappearance from the stage of history.

Daniélou maintained that even if all Israel had embraced Christianity, the continuity of Israel would not have been threatened. How could he know? The history of Judaeo-Christianity belies his facile optimism. It was an experiment which failed, in which Christianity did not succeed in conserving a community of Israelite Christians. The lesson for us is that not every community of Israelite Christians bears with it a guarantee of survival. How much more successful have not the rabbis been!

In the personal experience of the author of these pages, to guarantee the continuity of Jewry's history, in the hypothesis of an entry *en masse* of Jews into the faith, steps would have to be taken and obstacles overcome which Daniélou either ignored or preferred not to mention.

The problem of terminology vexes converts to this day, as we see in the case of Father Daniel. Many designate themselves Jews, relying on the example of St. Paul. But circumstances have changed since the first days of the Church, making it inexact for converts to apply to themselves the term "Jew". If they insist on so doing, they invite the question as to what they mean by the word.

Protestant circles favor "Hebrew-Christian". So did David Goldstein. The trouble is that the word "Hebrew" has come to have a double nuance. It could signify an Israelite, abstraction being made as to whether Israelites are the Elect People or not; or it could signify an Israelite in the mouth of the one who actively denies that post-Christic Jewry, in particular, is still the object of the Election. The latter is the use adopted by the Canaanites. The courts of the State of Israel have declared that "Hebrew" and "Jew" are synonymous in the eyes of the law.

During World War II, Christians of Jewish origin were classified as "Christians of Jewish descent". The Nazis, who employed a racial criterion in the determination of Jewish identity, were known to round up Jewish converts and send them to the camps of extermination, where they met with the same fate as their fellow Jews.

The expression "Jewish-Christian" is often carelessly bandied about. It appears to us incorrect and thoroughly ambiguous.

Gentile courts of law are willing to accept the declaration of any person that he is a Jew, but facts of that kind have no theological value.

An Israelite who today accedes to the Christian faith is not a Judaeo-Christian. Not only did Judaeo-Christians frequent the synagogue until their expulsion from it around the year 80 of the Christian era, they believed that the Law of Moses was still valid. Today, Jewish converts may not attend synagogue services habitually. Such behavior would be considered inconsistent with their Christian confession of faith by both Jews and Gentiles alike.

Messianic Jews number about three thousand in the State of Israel. They have been the object of study by Pastor Kavarme of the Norwegian Church, Haifa. Some accept the divinity of Christ and have been baptized. Others, like the Ebionites of old, reject the doctrine. The different currents agree in believing Jesus to be the Messiah. They resemble the early Judaeo-Christians in their resolve to retain their historical identity. This attitude expresses itself in their rejection of the title "Christian", which they confine to Gentile Christians, classical persecutors of the Jewish people. Another tendency is to adopt a régime of social separation from recognized Christian denominations.

According to Pastor Kavarme, the Messianic Jews in Israel are already divided amongst themselves on doctrinal issues. If a house divided against itself must fall, then their future is not assured. Nor can their fragile organization offer the Jewish people what it is obscurely seeking: a firm guarantee against the dissolution of their historical identity, in the event of its embracing the Christian faith.

VII. FROM MOSAIC JUDAISM
TO RABBINISM

From the ascension of Jesus to the destruction of the second temple in 70 AD, the institutions of the Old Dispensation continued to function: daily sacrifices were offered, the prescribed pilgrimages to Jerusalem took place, feast days were celebrated with pomp and splendor, customs were maintained. Inwardly, what had been a divinely approved order was now a hollow façade, doomed to inevitable destruction (cf. Mt. 24:1-3; Lk. 23:28-31).

During the siege of the city by the Roman army, Yohanan Ben Zakkai, a prominent rabbi, foreseeing the ultimate fate of Jerusalem and its priesthood, begged the permission of Vespasian to quit the besieged town and join the sages of Yavne. The future Roman emperor, obviously well informed of the peaceful dispositions of the venerable old man, granted his request. At Yavne, Yohanan Ben Zakkai devoted himself to creating an alternative center of supreme legislative authority for the Jewish people, capable of replacing the old Sanhedrin. After an eventful history, punctuated by several displacements of its seat, the new Sanhedrin was finally dissolved at the time of suppression of the Palestinian Jewish Patriarchate in 425 AD. Post-Christic Rabbinism, founded by Yohanan Ben Zakkai and his colleagues at Yavne, continued to flourish. Today it is even enjoying a certain prosperity in Israel, with the help of state subsidies. Oswald Rufeisen was born under its régime.

The suppression of the temple priesthood left Rabbinism with a problematic authority. Symptomatic was the struggle that opposed Yohanan Ben Zakkai himself to his colleagues at Yavne. Towards the end of the second century, Judah the Patriarch, conscious of some inner weakness in the substitute rabbinical Sanhedrin, transferred authority to the Mishna. The Mishna was no other than the Oral Law, of Pharisaic inspiration, dominated by the school of Hillel and committed to writing by a team of rabbis under the editorial direction of Judah himself. The rapid adoption of the

Mishna by Diaspora Jews proves that there existed a deeply-felt need for a central authority. But a written authority only served to underline the absence of a living one. A written law requires interpretation and adaptation to circumstances. The result was that the authority passed from the Mishna into the hands of its authorized interpreters, the rabbis. In theory, each rabbi had an equal authority to interpret the law. Naturally, some rabbis were more learned than others. The tendency was for people to turn to those rabbis in each generation who had achieved the highest reputation for their knowledge of the law. These renowned rabbis sometimes entered into association with one another to form an unelected body of legal experts known as the Great Ones of the Torah. In turn, the authority of the rabbi was limited by the community of believers. The rabbi never issued a decision which he thought would not be acceptable to the community. Herbert Wouk concluded, reasonably enough, that ultimate authority in post-Christic Judaism lies with the community of the faithful. What community, we ask? In point of fact, no rabbi has effective authority over all communities in the Jewish world.

Rabbis were permitted to adapt the law, provided that their adaptations did not amount to new legislation. It was a fine point to know just when a rabbinical decision was in fact an adaptation or when it had transgressed and became a new law. Theoretically, rabbis claimed a kind of infallibility, since the sum total of their decisions throughout the ages was esteemed never to have passed the boundary set by their limited authority as interpreters of the law. The difficulty here is that Rabbinical Judaism has no defined dogma, so that the exact line between the changeable and the unchangeable has never been drawn. Moore has no doubt that rabbis took liberties with the Law of Moses when the needs of the hour required it. The flaw in rabbinical authority provided a handle for the reformers of the nineteenth century, who argued that since rabbis had made new laws in the past they, the reformers, were entitled to make new laws for the present. The reformers erred in their appreciation of post-Christic Rabbinism. What characterized it was not real fidelity to the Written and the Oral Law but the will to remain as faithful as possible to the Written and the Oral Law. In other words, the criterion was subjective, not objective. It followed that reformed Judaism, where that criterion was not found, could not be in moral continuity with Rabbinism. It was another religion.

Professor Leibowitz has put forward a pressing plea for the updating of traditional rabbinical law in the State of Israel. He takes the example of postmortems required by doctors and opposed by rabbinical circles. Draft furnaces in Israeli steel factories must be kept burning on Saturdays, in violation of the precept of Sabbatical repose. Leibowitz, an Orthodox Jew, calls on the rabbinate to introduce new legislation. By this one word, he has driven himself into opposition to rabbinical tradition, which has never admitted that rabbis possess legislative power.

Rabbi Maimon (1875-1962) advocated reassembling the Sanhedrin to overcome the difficulties of the hour. His proposal was dropped. Henrietta Szold was amongst its most spirited opponents and the reasons are not far to seek. Who would be the candidates for election? Who would be the electors? How would they sanction any new legislation? How would they avoid becoming tools in the hands of politicians? New legislation would almost certainly create schism amongst rabbis, for their conservative elements are opposed to change. Let Catholics recall the analogous case of Monsignor Lefèbvre in the wake of Vatican II.

The one positive result of Rabbi Maimon's campaign was to stress the fact that Rabbinism had never been anything more than a stop-gap religion, what A. M. Naftal calls a "temporary substitute for the Temple,"[1] the truncated remains of Mosaic Judaism, neither divine in origin nor inspired in its historical development.

Ben-Gurion and Golda Meir often represented to the rabbinate the need for a reform of rabbinical law. Equally consistently, the rabbinate has refused to espouse the idea, a refusal which Herbert Wouk saw as a "fatal intransigence". The rabbinate is undoubtedly aware of the reasonableness of the arguments in favor of reform. The Mishna was compiled during the Exile and reflects its conditions, especially the absence of political sovereignty. Weiler maintains that the Mishna cannot furnish legislation for a state. He is not alone in his opinion. What prevents the rabbinate from acceding to the demand for reform is the lack of legislative power.

The consciousness of the limits of their authority pays tribute to Jesus, who deprived rabbis of it in the first place. Indeed, rabbis cannot even dispense from the Law. The rabbi is not a bishop; an assembly of rabbis is not a synod. The synagogue has no organ comparable to an Ecumenical Council, as Leo Baeck recognized.

The Oral Law is for Rabbinism what dogma is for the Catholic Church. A synagogue remains orthodox for as long as it remains faithful to the traditional codifications of the Oral Law, Rabbinism being an orthopraxy rather than an orthodoxy. The very moment a synagogue legislates for a change in the Oral Law it becomes a reformed synagogue.

Although a visibly profound change of religious régime had occurred when the temple was destroyed, post-Christic Judaism consistently denied that any alteration in the status of Mosaic Judaism had been decreed. Exile and dispersion were explained, not as due to a sin against the Alliance, but as the consequence of the evil conduct of man against man, to gratuitous enmity between Jews. This interpretation alluded to the bloodthirsty fighting between fanatical factions at the siege of Jerusalem, the murder of the moderates, the incredible burning down of grain stores, all of which behavior weakened resistance in the face of the enemy.

For Rabbinism, the cessation of the sacrifices was a mere historical contingency, a suspension of the régime, not its suppression. In time the temple would be rebuilt, the priesthood reassembled, and sacrifices once more offered on Mount Zion. We ourselves have encountered a young Jewish maiden who, putting on a brave face, declared her readiness to conduct a flock of sheep to Jerusalem should the temple be restored. In 1967, when Jerusalem was recaptured by the Israeli army, a group of determined rabbis began to prepare their seminarians in the intricacies of the law concerning bloody sacrifices, just in case...! Secularist Zionists, for their part, are rather appalled at the thought of bloody sacrifices being offered in public on the threshold of the year 2000 AD.

Breuer expressed the basic assumption of Rabbinism when he wrote that the Mosaic Law remains valid by divine law, because it has never been abrogated by any authoritative body. Rabbinism regards itself as the legitimate *dat* of the Elect People, the Chosen

People, the People of God, without qualification. A Christian, Fisher notwithstanding, cannot accept this self-evaluation of the rabbis.

Jewish Identity and Rabbinism

Rabbinical Judaism grasped well enough, in practice, the "two-factor" structure of Jewish identity. It perceived that Jewish identity derived from both Election and Law, from doctrine and community.

For Jewish doctrine, Judaism was the religion of the Jewish people, the individual Jew a member of the Jewish religion.

Rabbinical law, on the other hand, proposed two formulas. The first would have been acceptable to St. Paul: a Jew is the subject of rabbinical law. Such is the view of the nomocrats, to mention only Moses Mendelsohn (1729-1786), J. D. Soloveichic (1903-), Leibowitz, and Herman Wouk.

We encountered the second formula in the case of Father Daniel; a Jew is a person born of a Jewish mother, or who becomes a Jew by conversion. Note that the excluding clause is not part of tradition but is in keeping with its spirit.

The second formula is no definition of Jewish identity, if only because it is forbidden to allow the term to be defined to enter the definition. One could simply ask: when is a Jewish mother Jewish?

What is more, it creates the false impression that Jewish identity depends in some way on biology, that race is a constituent of "Jewishness".

Another disadvantage of the formula is that it implies that "Jewishness" is innate; nay, hereditary. So one writer came to the preposterous conclusion that millions of Spaniards are Jewish because they are descendants of the Marranos.

Since a Gentile becomes a Jew by conversion, it is obvious that "Jewishness" is neither innate nor hereditary.

The second formula is far from exhausting rabbinical law on the question of personal status. It is no more than a derivative formula. The primary principle of Jewish personal status was already announced by Philo: "Sons and daughters belong to the house of the male parent".[2]

The Talmudical Encyclopaedia enlarge on Philo's statement.

We read: "A Jew who consorts with a Jewess and begets a child by her is legally its father, even if the woman is forbidden to him; but if a Jew has intercourse with a Canaanitish slave woman, even if she is permitted to him, for instance, if he is a Hebrew slave; or if he consorts with a heathen woman, the issue does not rank as his".

In practice, in a valid union between a Jew and Jewess, the offspring take the personal status of the father; in an invalid union, between a Jew and a Gentile, the status of the offspring follows that of the mother. As a matter of fact, therefore, the personal status of the offspring is always that of the mother.

Is a Person Born Jewish?

It is commonly said that a person is born Jewish. St. Paul echoes the prevailing usage: "We are Jews by birth, not sinners of Gentile origin" (Gal. 2:15).

The expression is acceptable enough, provided that one does not fall into the error of believing it to mean that Jewishness is an innate quality, like the color of the eyes. Quite the contrary: "To be born a Jew" is synonymous with "being born under the Law".

Not every Israelite is "born under the Law". The description may apply to a child born into a Jewish religious family, where it has a real prospect of acquiring the Jewish religion. An Israelite male child born into a Jewish religious milieu is circumcised on the eighth day of his life. At the age of thirteen, the young boy celebrates his bar-mitzvah, when, ideally, he acknowledges the obligation in conscience to observe rabbinical law. In the measure that he really observes the prescriptions of the law, he becomes a more and more perfect Jew. Should he neglect his religious duties, he becomes a non-practicing Jew. Should he deny the obligation in conscience to observe rabbinical law, he ceases to be a Jew and may be pronounced an apostate.

How different is the case of an Israelite child not born into a Jewish religious milieu and who has no real chance of acquiring the Jewish religion! Of him it cannot be said that he was born a Jew. In the State of Israel he might be automatically registered as a Jew, but registration would only make him a nominal Jew. It happens that even in atheistic kibbutzim male children are circumcised at birth, though without any religious ceremony, in order to conform, it being feared that at school or in the army the uncircumcised person might be subject to discrimination of one kind or another. All Israelites in Israel are obliged by the law to marry and divorce through the rabbinate. These acts are equally powerless to confer on them the content of "Jewishness" so long as the persons concerned do not accept rabbinical practice as binding their consciences by divine authority.

As we see it, "Israelite" is a word which carries with it the opposite significance. A person is born an Israelite in the sense of possessing at birth an innate quality which we call the "election factor". The quality is not hereditary. It is personal. It results from a transcendental relation between the person and the divine will, mediated by the community of the elect. It is because one is born into the elect people that one is born an Israelite. The "election factor" is irrevocable for the person so born, because the gifts of God are without repentance. It is revocable for his descendants, not by an act of will but where the descendants have ceased to belong to a community, mediator of the "election factor".

A "Hebrew" is a person considered a member of the Jewish people or of the people of Israel, making abstraction of the question whether the people has or has not a transcendental dimension to its identity.

A person born a Hebrew is automatically an Israelite. St. Paul exclaims: "…being of the stock of Israel and the tribe of Benjamin, a Hebrew of Hebrew origins" (Phil. 3:5); and again he exclaims: "Are they Hebrews? So am I! Are they Israelites? So am I!" (2 Cor. 11:22).

Not so Yonatan Ratosh, founder of the Canaanites! An avowed atheist, he applied to be registered as a "Hebrew" rather than as a "Jew", in order to deny the religious character of the Jewish people.

The Community, Source of Jewish Identity

The rabbinical formula, "a Jew is one born of a Jewish mother or converted to the Jewish religion", is a roundabout way of stating that a person may be aggregated to the Jewish community by birth or by conversion. Talmudic law allows for a third channel of aggregation, quiet assimilation. In the absence of any evidence to the contrary, a person is to be believed when he declares he is a Jew. Returning Marranos accepted to observe the commandments of rabbinical law, but the determining factor in their readmission was their willingness to become part of the Jewish community.

The plain sense of the foregoing is that the rabbis regard the Jewish community as the source of the Jewish identity of its members. The identification of the individual Jew would then consist in demonstrating that he had become a member of the community in one of the ways indicated. Since many persons in the State of Israel are survivors of communities annihilated by the Nazis, the authorities had to go by their personal declaration in the absence of objective control. The way was thus open for many a Gentile to slip into the community. Their presence is suspected, but overlooked, so long as they show willingness to assimilate to Israeli society. Willingness to assimilate, in turn, is a disposition hard to evaluate where the majority are not observant Jews. To compensate, heavy emphasis is placed on a negative criterion: the Gentile undergoing quiet assimilation is expected scrupulously to avoid contact with the non-Jewish clergy.

The power of the community to mediate the "election factor" derives from the Election itself. The people of Israel are the material object of the Election, thus each of its constituent communities is capable of mediating the "election factor".

Alleged Inseparability of Jews and Judaism

The rabbis claim that the Jewish people is inseparable from Judaism. They are playing a powerful card, appealing to the sentiment of nationalism to rally the support of the people for orthodoxy. In the State of Israel the claim sounds less convincing, given that the majority of Israelis have already separated themselves from their ancestral religion. Leibowitz, an Orthodox Jew himself, declares as much, not without personal anguish, to the horror and indignation of his fellow Orthodox.

We concede that the terms *Jew* and *Judaism, Jew* and *the Jewish people* are inseparable; not so the realities. Newman observed that the people had lived under several religious régimes in the course of its eventful history. It had to pass from the ancient religion of the Mosaic Alliance to that of Mosaic Judaism, its fundamental continuity being retained. Later it passed from Mosaic Judaism to Rabbinical Judaism. In modern times, many Jews have passed from Rabbinical Judaism to the Reform Synagogue. Ahad Ha'amists pass from Rabbinical Judaism to the Cultural Centre.

The true inseparables are not Jews and Judaism but the people and their Election. Do what they may, the people cannot shake off the all-pervading influence of the God of Israel. During the Second World War, Orthodox Jews, Zionists, and converts were subject to the same atrocious tortures, driven into the same gas chambers, there to suffer the same death by slow suffocation. The Zionist State, to the dismay of Zionists, has existed under the constant menace of physical destruction, a menace at times almost palpable.

The Israeli Jew is confused about his identity because spontaneously he adopts a "one-factor" theory of Jewish identity. He argues, much like Leibowitz, that if he admits that he is not a Jew he is confessing himself to have become a Gentile. Against this conclusion, his self-understanding rebels. He is, therefore, reluctant to discontinue the practice of calling himself a Jew, though the name sits awkwardly on his lips. The theory of Ahad Ha'am still influences him, according to which Jewish identity is an inseparable attribute of the people. Ahad Ha'am was, of course, wrong. It is not "Jewishness" that is an inseparable attribute of the people, but the "election factor".

Another motive which hinders the Secular Zionist from admitting the almost evident truth, to wit, that he is no more a Jew, is the fear of burning his boats with the Diaspora, where traditional views of Jewish identity are still prevalent.

In the meantime, as the "Jewish" identity of the Secular Zionist wanes, his "Israelite" identity waxes, not through the practice of the Jewish religion but through a day-to-day commitment to participation in the people's historical destiny.

No one had a more profound insight into the nature of the crisis of identity besetting the modern Jew than Hayyim Nahman Bialik (1873-1934). Bialik received a talmudical education but revolted when the literature of the "Enlightenment" movement fell into his eager young hands. He rejected the Talmud as a living code of life though, unlike others, he retained a vivid faith in the essential doctrines of Judaism. He adopted the program of Ahad Ha'am for the creation of a Hebrew Cultural Centre in Palestine, but from far loftier motives. He was, in the last resort, a Spiritual and not a Cultural Zionist, in the pure tradition of the medieval poet, Yehudah Halevi, who had linked the return of Jews to the Holy Land with a renewal of their religious vocation.

Bialik was acutely aware of the disastrous consequences of the rejection of rabbinical law for the Jewish community. It meant the suppression of circumcision, of the bar-mitzvah ceremony, of marriage under a canopy, of the liturgical calendar, of the dietary prohibitions, of any criterion for distinguishing between Jew and Gentile—in short, the utter collapse of the historical community into which he, Bialik, had been born. He was not beguiled by the unstable synthesis of a secularist culture within a religious framework, which characterized the Secular Zionist compromise. Only a new religious synthesis could, in his eyes, restore equilibrium.

Bialik did not feel himself empowered from on high to found a new religious order. He terminates his essay, "Halakha Veagadah", with a cry of anguish: "We bend our necks. Where is the iron yoke? Why does the strong hand and the outstretched arm not lend themselves to us?"

What Bialik was invoking was nothing less than a divine intervention. His failure to discover a new law was part of the heritage he left to future generations, a heritage of questions without answers. It marked the line where his prophetic vocation ended.

André Chouraqui is no less alive to the role of rabbinical law in conserving the historical community of post-Christic Jewry. He made the point in his response to Daniélou: "In this exile it was no longer faith that saved, but the Law alone that permitted the sociological existence of those who survived exile". Lamentably enough, Daniélou did not understand what Chouraqui was trying to communicate to him. Chouraqui was endeavoring to explain that to call upon the Jewish people to convert to Christianity, without at the same time providing them with a cognate community framework, was to vow their historical identity to destruction. Chouraqui, in laying so much emphasis on the extrinsic utility of rabbinical law in conserving Jewish identity, unwittingly opened up a possibility which Professor Bergman had foreseen. "It is not enough," wrote Bergman, as if in answer to Chouraqui, "to see in the religion of Israel a means for the assurance of our existence, for, if religion had no other function than that, it is possible to imagine its substitution by another means which would fulfill the same function."

Secular Zionism does, in fact, do no more than echo the position of Chouraqui. It freely recognized the value he assigns to rabbinical law in the preservation of post-Christic Jewry, but pretends that the civil law of the State of Israel has taken over that function, rendering the role of rabbinical law superfluous.

Over thirty years of experience demonstrate that a secular law and a secular community are inadequate to the task of furnishing the Israeli "Jew" with an unambiguous identity. The search for a solution must continue.

When Is a Community a Jewish Community?

The stress we have laid on the community as mediator of the collective identity of the Jew obliges us to examine the credentials of a certain number of historical groups commonly held to be "Jewish".[3]

The Samaritan community has dwindled to a pitiful handful, four hundred or so persons. The Samaritans represent the ten tribes of northern Israel. They are Israelites, "Israelitico-Samaritans" if you like. They have never been Jews and their religion has never been influenced by Judaism.

The Karaites date from the second half of the eighth century. The community was founded by a Persian Jew, who revolted against the authority of the Oral Law while remaining faithful to the Bible. Karaites thus ceased to be Rabbinites, indeed clashed with them at times. The Israelite identity of the community is not in question, but the Karaites are not Jews in the sense determined by historical convention.

The Reform Synagogue was launched in Germany during the last century. It regards obedience to the Oral Law as optional, not obligatory, thus ceasing to be Rabbinite. The Reform Synagogue is pseudo-Jewish; its rabbis function as pastors, rather than as authorized interpreters of the Oral Law, their traditional function.

Are Reformed Jews Israelites? The question is a disturbing one, perhaps, but has to be raised.

The "Pittsburgh Platform" (1885) declared that the Reform community was a religious community, with no national attributes. It made clear that the Reform intended to create a universal brotherhood on the lines of Christianity, Islam, or the Baha'is. The "Pittsburgh Platform," by its implicit denial of any distinction between Jew and Gentile, that is to say by its denial of the "election factor", abandoned the traditional notion of Jewish identity, imperiling the Israelite character of the community. The Reformers gradually became aware of the danger to their Israelite identity, a danger which they had created for themselves. The "Columbus Platform" of 1937 showed a renewed recognition of the existence of a collective soul, of which the community was the body. A pro-Zionist orientation was given to the movement and a parade of Jewish symbols recommended.

The Conservative Synagogue was set up in the United States in reaction to the excesses of the Reform, which it eventually succeeded in curbing. It retained the principle of fidelity to the Oral Law, so remaining within the ambit of traditional Rabbinical Judaism. Its legal innovations have been timid. The Conservative Synagogue is a community of neo-Rabbinical Jews.

The religious current instituted by Samuel Raphael Hirsch (1808-1888) is a form of neo-Orthodoxy. Rabbinical law was rigorously observed, but the need for liturgical adaptations was recognized, as well as the need for cultural promotion of the rabbi.

The Doenmeh sect was a community of crypto-Jews who practiced Islam in public and Judaism in secret. They appeared at first to have retained their traditional Jewish identity, though they deviated seriously from the Orthodox moral code. Their absorption into the Muslim community of Turkey now seems complete.

The Marranos were crypto-Jews who practiced Catholicism in public and Judaism in secret. The majority ended up being absorbed into the Spanish Church. A handful, especially on the island of Majorca, still keep up Jewish customs, even tending to intermarry. These habits are insufficient to regard them as Israelites. They are Spanish Catholics with judaizing tendencies.

The Black Jews of Dimona in Israel are self-chosen Jews. Their group has no historical roots in Jewish history.

The Falashas of Ethiopia are a dwindling community whose religion is based on the Greek version of the Old Testament translated into Ge'ez. The Talmud never reached the Falashas. Their religious heads are known as priests, not as rabbis. Their origins are obscure, but they appear to be descendants of proselytes. By this insertion into the Jewish people they qualify at least as Israelites. The attitude of the Rabbinate of Israel toward the Falashas has been vacillating. The Jewish Agency favors their immigration into Israel; a significant movement of immigration of Falashas has taken place recently.

The Benei Israel is a community of Indian Jews, also descendants of proselytes. There can be no reasonable doubt that they are Israelites but, like the Falashas, they lack a rabbinical tradition. On arrival in Israel, they were dismayed to find that their Jewish credentials were not recognized by the Rabbinate. In spite of initial difficulties, many appear now to have been successfully integrated into Israeli society.

To sum up, a community is Jewish in the sense of the term fixed by historical convention when it is ruled by rabbinical law; it is Israelite when it is in historical relation with the People of Israel prior to their dispersion from the Holy Land.

The Identity of Post-Christic Jewry

We recall several principles already employed in the preceding pages in the Christian assessment of Rabbinism.

- Divine authority in matters of religion was transferred by God from Mosaic Judaism to the Church.
- Jewish identity results from the interplay of two factors,

Election and Law, or doctrine and community.

- The term "Jewish people" is contracted from "Israelitico-Jewish" people.

- The providential status of Rabbinism should be distinguished from that of the people, which the rabbis guide.

Jesus had never denied a measure of divine authority to the Mosaic priesthood; "Go off and present yourself to the priest," he ordered the leper whom he had cured, "and offer for your cure what Moses prescribed" (Mk. 1:44).

"The Scribes and the Pharisees have succeeded Moses" (Mt. 23:2), though the extent of their authority as against the priests seems to have been an object of controversy amongst them and is not easy for us to fix. In any case, Jesus predicted that it would be taken away from them and bestowed on others. Rabbinism is thus devoid of divine authority. The Jewish People, in contrast, is retained under the Election.

Jacques Maritain, who married a Jewess and is counted amongst the great philosemites of modern times by a host of his countrymen such as Leon Bloy, Peguy, Claudel, could write: "The Mystical Body of Israel is an unfaithful and repudiated Church—and that is why Moses had figuratively given forth the bill of divorce—repudiated as a Church, not as a people, and ever awaited by the bridegroom, who has never ceased to love her".[4]

The invalidation by Christianity of Rabbinism is our answer to the nomocrats, who exalt rabbinical law to the point of turning it into an incarnate logos, a rationalistic logos, not a divine logos. From the beginning of his public ministry, Jesus took a stand against the teaching of the rabbis (cf. Mt. 15:1-9), complaining that their tradition broke away from the commandments of God and that it made God's word null and void (cf. Mt. 15:6). He warned his disciples against the yeast of the Pharisees (cf. Mt. 16:6). Rabbinical theology tended towards a semi-Pelagianism. The observance of the Law gave the Jew a right to salvation. Man could, by the exercise of his will, overcome his evil inclination. As a result, the role of the Messiah became problematical for the rabbis, less and less essential to rabbinical thought. The series of pseudo-Messiahs that sprang up in the course of Jewish history were brought into existence by the pressure of historical circumstances rather than from any inner development of rabbinical theology. Rabbinism discounted the value of prophetic interventions, relying more and more on the power of naked human reason. For the Jewish theologian, Frank Rosenzweig, the post-Christic Jewish people was itself the Messiah, the suffering Servant of Yahve, vicariously atoning for the sins of the Gentiles through the very suffering the latter inflict on the former.

Since the massacre of the six million Jews of Europe, the thesis of Rosenzweig takes on a new dimension. It earns our deep respect if not our entire agreement. In effect, the Servant of Yahve had done no wrong (cf. Is. 53:9); he was innocent. The exile of the Jewish People is a sign of sin, however one may choose to define the sin. Rosenzweig's victim, therefore, is not innocent, or not purely innocent.

André Chouraqui had a rare perception of the altered status of Rabbinism before God. He had this to say: "Let us go back to the epoch of Jesus. The Jewish world was not yet a nomocracy, but a theocracy. God reigned; he was present in the Temple; his priests were the intermediaries with the people. The Law in this economy was of secondary importance. What was primary was the living God present in the Temple, the priest and the sacrifices that purified for faults committed against the Law. When the Temple disappeared, the spiritual structure of the Jewish world was overthrown. I should like you, first of all, and every other Christian, to be aware of this revolution, which transformed the very essence of Israel's spiritual life. With the Temple destroyed, Israel knew the pangs of supreme tragedy, that of the exile from God himself."[5]

The Christian is perhaps more aware of the catastrophe from which Rabbinism emerged than Chouraqui may imagine. Anyway, Chouraqui would surely agree that if what he says is true and God is in exile from the post-Christic Jewish People, the latter is automatically disqualified from playing a positive role in the economy of salvation. Consequently, we reject the affirmation of Gregory Baum, according to which "Judaism continues to exercise a positive role in God's plan of salvation".[6] What role did devolve on it we hope to consider later.

If post-Christic Judaism were in any way valid, as Fisher pretends, the Jewish convert would be obliged to practice it even after his entry into the Church, which no one would be prepared to concede.

The invalidation of Rabbinical Judaism should not be received as an offense. After all, Judaism invalidates Christianity.

No one today intends to denigrate the exceptional value of Rabbinical Judaism. It believes in the one true God, creator of heaven and earth, of all things visible and invisible, who created the universe by the power of His word, without the help of the angels. It believes in the revelation of God to mankind, the inspiration of Holy Scripture, the spiritual nature of man, the election of Israel, the Four Last Things, a Messiah to come. It offers the Jew occasions of making saving acts of faith, hope, and charity, and encourages him to observe the Ten Commandments. Jews may be saved in it, as Muslims in Islam, depending on their subjective dispositions. "With all Jews in whom grace dwells, as with all souls of good faith, the work of the Cross is present, but veiled and unperceived and involuntarily experienced. Despite himself and in an obscuring mist, the pious Jew, the Jew of the spirit, carries the gentle Cross and thus betrays Judaism without realizing what he does."[7]

Not only did Calvary invalidate post-Christic Judaism, it invalidated all existing religions insofar as they might have possessed any valid content, leaving one sole valid religion for all mankind, the religion of Christ. The same is true for any religion that has come into being since Calvary, or that human ingenuity may invent for the future.

VIII. THE THEOLOGICAL IDENTITY OF
THE POST-CHRISTIC JEWISH PEOPLE

Christianity passes an irrevocable act of invalidity on Rabbinical Judaism. Does the act extend to the people? Many Christians have thought so, many continue to think so, misled by the tendency to block Jews and Judaism together. The outcome is a widespread sentiment that God revoked the Election of the Jews and that they henceforth possess no transcendental dimension.

In reply, we ask what, in general, is an election. The word signifies a choice and an elevation to an office. The notion is functional; in isolated grandeur, it is meaningless.

The Election of Abraham should be distinguished from the election of grace. The first is collective, the second personal. The first applies exclusively to Israel, the second to Gentiles also. The first is a call to collective sanctity, the second accords sanctity to the individual.

The material object of the Election has been defined by Hruby with admirable precision: "The divine election is directed to the people as such, insofar as it is a collectivity." The words in italics are in the original.[1] We add: to the people, not to their religious beliefs or opinions.

In the Epistle to the Romans, St. Paul puts himself a question: "Has God rejected his people? Of course not! I myself as an Israelite, descended from Abraham, of the tribe of Benjamin. No, God has not rejected his people whom he foreknew." (Rm. 11:1-2)

What is St. Paul's logic? He is asserting that because *he* has remained chosen, the *people* has remained chosen. What, then, is the link between individual and collectivity? The answer is that a person is an Israelite only by virtue of his belonging to the collectivity, direct object of the Election. Therefore, if St. Paul remained chosen, his people remained chosen, notwithstanding the divergence of views between them on the subject of Jesus.

The Election of Abraham extends to Israelites in all generation

Both Trotsky and St. Paul were equally Israelites, the former materially speaking, the latter spiritually as well.

The effect of the Election was to create a people whose name is Israel.[2] The Election furnishes this people with the specific element in its identity. It is the transcendental source of its unity, gathering into one an extraordinary multiplicity of historical groupings. By its nature it distinguishes Israel from the Gentiles, who are not the direct object of the Election.

From the Election flows a special providence which will govern the history of Israel until the end of time. Inversely, inspection of the history of Israel can reveal the existence of a special providence and provide a motive of credibility in the Election of Abraham. Such was the spiritual itinerary followed by Yehudah Halevi in medieval times and Isaac Breuer in modern times.

The final aim of the Election is the vocation of Israel to bear collective witness to the Messiah. It will be compelled to do so in every phase of its history, positively or negatively, in ways varying with "its stand toward salvation", to use the apt phrase of Cardinal Journet.

The possession of a meaningful historical function makes of Israel a sign among the nations. Its entire history becomes intelligible in the light of the logos. The sign will be positive, negative, or ambivalent, depending on how faithful Israel is to its vocation.

Yehudah Halevi (1075-1141) is the great Jewish theologian of the Election. He recognized that the Exile expressed the negative status of post-Christic Jewry. He failed to explain sufficiently why the sign had become negative.

The intelligibility of Israel's history makes possible a systematic interpretation of its constituent phases and, beyond this, an interpretation of human history as a whole.

The variation in the quality of the sign obliges us to distinguish between a variable and an invariable element in the special relation between Israel and God established by the Election. The invariable element is the sheer, naked existence of the relation; the variable element is the functional content of the relation at any given phase of salvation history.

Journet observed *à propos*: "Not only Israel's spiritual destinies — that goes without saying — but even its temporal destinies, with their share of the banal and the commonplace, will be forever dependent on the most staggering supernatural mystery it is given to us to know. This solidarity cannot be broken or shaken off. But the way in which Israel is made aware, though always divine, varies from age to age with Israel's stand towards salvation."[3] The full identity of Israel is no static etiquette; it takes body and consistency from the role it plays, at any time, in the plan of salvation.

There are several corollaries to the Election. The first is that it is irrevocable. For this we have the word of St. Paul. It guarantees Israel's survival. Israel is perennial and indestructible, qualities which Hilaire Belloc recognized to have been demonstrated in the history of post-Christic Jewry. The irrevocability of the Election regards the Jewish convert as well and determines his special status in the Church. With St. Paul, each convert could say proudly "I myself am an Israelite" (Rm. 11:1). So was the Risen Christ, so were Mary and the Apostles, so is the Mystical Body of Christ. Converts who try to dissimulate their Israelite identity sin against the Election. In no better case is the clergy when it ignores the special status of the convert.

The irrevocability of the Election authorizes one to reject the policy of the active proselytizing of Israelites in circumstances which expose their specific identity and that of their descendants to deterioration and loss. For, being a violation of the divine order, it has never succeeded on any but a very limited scale. Naturally, Hitler's policy of genocide, designed to destroy the bearers of the Election, was a sin of immeasurable proportions, the full consequences of which have yet to dawn on the Christian world.

The vocation of God echoes in the mind of the Israelite, creating in it a collective consciousness, a collective identity, what Bonsirven called "a singular soul". It expresses itself in a sentiment of cohesiveness, characteristic of Jews, combined with a sense of mutual responsibility on the group level, if not always on the individual level.

Martin Buber gave solemn expression to the self-understanding of the Jew: "We know," he wrote, "that there, within that reality, we are not rejected by God, that in this discipline or punishment, God's hand holds us and does not let us go, holds us within this fire and does not let us fall."[4]

The vocation of Israel opens a way to God which does not exist for the Gentile. It furnishes Buber with the argument that a mediator between Jewry and God was unnecessary, seeing that a road to a direct dialogue with God was open to the Jew at all times. Then came the Holocaust and the terrible silence of God, when it became apparent that the dialogue with God was more difficult than Buber had imagined.

It is paradoxical that precisely at a time when a sensitive Christian such as Marcel Dubois is reflecting on the theological importance of Jewish self-understanding, Leibowitz, an Orthodox Jew, dismisses it as mere subjectivity.

The Election called Israel to a primacy of spiritual responsibility; it became a privileged instrument in the designs of God. Let us not permit our imagination to play us tricks. The privileges of Israel, enumerated by St. Paul, have nothing in common with the abuse of their position by the aristocrats of the *Ancien Régime* in France. Amongst the privileges listed in the Epistle to the Romans are: the adoption of sons, the glory and the covenants, the Law and the promises (d. Rm. 9:1-8). There is, in addition, a permanent link with the Holy Land (d. Gn. 15:18-19). What rights to the land that link bestows on Jewry today is at the heart of the Judeao-Arab conflict. Undoubtedly, the advent of Jesus introduced both continuities and discontinuities on this point, as it did in all the orders of Mosaic Judaism.

In itself, the Election of Abraham is a transcendental act of God. Its presence and its activity can be gauged only in the measure that they are reflected in the life and history of the people. A community of the elect becomes a corollary of the Election. Then, if the "election factor" has to produce its fruits, a law for the community becomes another corollary. The Law of Moses fulfilled precisely this function; it grouped Israelites into a sort of Mystical Body, to borrow the phrase from Maritain, the physical boundaries of which it rendered visible.

Mosaic Judaism, Rabbinism, the Conservative and Reform

Synagogues, each in its turn gave expression to the consciousness that Jews have of the necessity of belonging to a cognate community, if the historical identity of the group is to be preserved.

The Election, we have said, imposed on Israel a vocation. In the pre-Christic era, it consisted in preparing for the revelation of the Messiah. Prophets and saints wrote and edited a sacred scripture, developing doctrine and defending it against corrosive factors working for its destruction.

It was an error widely accepted in Christian circles to believe that in preparing to receive its Messiah Israel exhausted its vocation, the argument being that once the Christ came, Israel was left without any *raison d'être* at all.

Vatican Council II took pains to correct this impression. It taught that "the principal [not the only] purpose to which the plan of the Old Covenant was directed was to prepare for the coming both of Christ, the universal Redeemer, and of the messianic kingdom". The words in brackets are by the late Professor C. A. Rijk.[5] Paragraph fourteen of the same Constitution on Divine Revelation defines the secondary purpose: to make the plan of salvation known to the Gentiles with greater clarity. The secondary purpose is illustrated by the salvific activity of the Risen Christ, Israel *par excellence*, in his Mystical Body the Church, and by the enduring influence of Mary and the Apostles in procuring the extension of the kingdom. No one may separate the historical Jesus from the prolongation of his life in his Mystical Body. It is this secondary responsibility which waits to be discharged by Jewry on its accession to the faith.

Why did God choose Israel? There is no serious answer to the question. We note, however, the practical dynamism of the Jew, his adaptability, resourcefulness, tenacity, and idealism: qualities of the perfect missionary. We note also how suitable is the Holy Land to be launching site for a world mission, corridor, as it is, linking three continents.

Is Post-Christic Jewry the People of God?

For Rabbinical Judaism, there has never been any doubt: Jewry is the People of God without qualification. The Christian cannot agree. Vatican Council II described the People of God as being composed of believers in Jesus Christ and identified it with the Church. There may have been Christians who were tempted to imagine that the Council meant to exclude the Jews entirely from the title. Others began to toy with the idea that there were two Peoples of God, equal and parallel.

Not so! The same Council Constitution defined in unambiguous terms the correct relation existing between the two collectivities. There is one, and only one, People of God. Others are potentially part of the People of God. This is true in the first place of Jews, by virtue of the Election, for the gifts and calling of God are without repentance. Jewry is ordained, one day, to become an effective organ of the Church.

The teaching of the Council touching on the theological identity of post-Christic Jewry merits every praise. Until the Council, the theology of Jewry prevalent in the Christian world was a distinctly negative one: in *Lumen Gentium*, the Council initiated a positive theology of the Jewish people. The change, packed in a few short sentences, is little short of revolutionary. We hail it as inspired by the Holy Spirit.

Is Jewry the Chosen People?

Again, Rabbinical Judaism has no hesitation in equating post-Christic Jewry with the Chosen People. Again, the Christian must beg to differ. The rabbinical formula is imprecise rather than incorrect. The Jewish People is a part of the Chosen People, a part of the Elect People, a part of Israel. Even prior to the Dispersion, Jewry represented no more than two of the twelve tribes of Israel. The advent of Jesus Christ provoked another division in the people, between those who believed in him and those who were incredulous. "Do not suppose," Jesus warned his disciples, "that my mission on earth is to spread peace. My mission is to spread, not peace, but division. I have come to set a man at odds with his father, a daughter with her mother, a daughter-in-law with her mother-in-law; in short, to make a man's enemies those of his own household" (Mt. 10: 34-36).

St. Paul sums up succinctly the theological identity of post-Christic Jewry in the Christian perspective: "Blindness has come upon part of Israel" (Rm. 11:25). Jewry is a section of Israel; the corresponding section became the Church. For the Christian world, Jewry is that section of Israel which did not believe.

IX. HAS THE ELECTION BEEN REVOKED?

The sentiment is widespread among Christians, theologians, and laymen alike, that God punished post-Christic Jewry for not believing in Jesus Christ by withdrawing from them the privilege of the Election.

The thesis is directed not at Rabbinical Judaism but at the Jewish People. It defines the theological anti-Semitism of Christianity. It is the fundamental premise of a pseudo-theology of Jewry, which has wrought incalculable harm. It is the remote cause of modern racial anti-Semitism.

Father Benoit, for example, permits himself to write: "The Church cannot agree that the Jewish people is still the Chosen People, for it is henceforth conscious of possessing that election".[1] And why should we ignore the testimony of Jewish self-consciousness that it has not been dispossessed of its election? Father Benoit answers: "The Christian Church cannot recognize it to be a Church equally valid in the designs of God." In contradiction, however, Father Benoit concedes that Jewry retains a theological mission of a kind "which it has momentarily lost and for which it is searching in an obscure and painfully fumbling way." He even appeals to Jewry to realize that by reconciling itself with the Church, it stands to gain "a fulfillment of its veritable and eternal vocation."

We agree with Frizzel, who finds these words enigmatic.[2] Since Father Benoit admits that Jewry has an eternal vocation, how could it ever have been lost? Again, if it has a vocation, it has to be chosen or elected in one sense or another. Is not its election the source of its vocation?

Father Benoit's manifest error, however, has been to pass the act of invalidation of the Jewish religion over to the Jewish People. It brings him into conflict with the teaching of Vatican Council II, which has taught Christians that the Jewish People is retained under the régime of the Election.

Father George is no less embarrassed and embarrassing. He begins by boldly affirming that "Israel is a people like the others, without any religious specification".[3] Elsewhere, he observes harshly: "From henceforth, this people is no more for Luke than a people like all others, a profane people, because it has renounced its mission. It has lost the title of People of God." Father George concedes that St. Luke does not write anywhere about a rejection of Israel. Indeed, he reveals to us that St. Luke even announces their future conversion (cf. Lk. 13:35).

We ask, in surprise, if St. Luke never wrote a line about the rejection of the Jews, how could Father George in the first place have attributed to him the view that Jewry had become a "profane people"? We ask: if Jewry is the object of inspired prophecy in the New Testament, how is it that it is "a people like the others", a people "without any religious specification"?

We protest. It is no reply to the urgent needs of the hour to pronounce solemnly on what post-Christic Jewry is not; one needs to know what Jewry is.

The author of a series of unsigned articles in the *Civilta Cattolica* reveals to us how deep is the sentiment of the revocation of the Election in the clergy. He blandly emits the following opinion: "The conversion of Israel would be the definitive solution (to the Jewish problem), but on condition that the Jews turned Christians, lose their Jewish nationality, as occurs in individual conversions, at least in the second or third generation."[4] He goes on to express his chagrin, as it already seemed to him doubtful whether Jewry would agree to abandon its historical identity in the event of an accession *en masse* to the faith.

How strange is the blindness not to grasp that it is precisely the policy of assimilating Jewish converts which raises the major obstacle in the way of Jewish accession to the faith? P. Figueras makes it clear that the real "scandal of the Cross" for Jews was the danger, inherent in conversion, of the disappearance of Israel among the nations.[5]

Bishop Scandar declared at Vatican II that the Jews were no more children of Abraham. Bishop Colombo left them in possession of natural rights only, insisting that otherwise they had no further *raison d'être.*

Madame D. Judant, the Council teaching notwithstanding, continued to hold that God had rejected forever the incredulous majority of the Jews. The Archbishop of Paris naturally refused to grant her book the *imprimatur.*

The revocationist tradition is rooted in the mentality of the Fathers of the Church. At the same time, Schoeps and Travers Herford were wrong to believe that it represented the authoritative teaching of the Catholic Church. Bonsirven granted freely the right of Jewry to nourish a belief in its Election, with the reservations which Christian theology imposes. Pius IX accepted the postulatum in favor of Jewry drawn up by the Lémann brothers, in which the Jews are described as "most dear to God because of the Fathers", a phrase from St. Paul, to be used again by the Fathers of Vatican Council II. The warmth of feeling for Jews exhibited by the signatories of the postulatum, five hundred Catholic bishops, is most touching to read about.

The revocationist current prevailed in the Church for so long because there had been no official teaching on the theological status of post-Christic Jewry. Vatican Council II has remedied the deficiency, at least in part. Cardinal Bea had every reason to see in the declaration of the Council concerning the Jewish People a milestone in the relations between the two groups. If Jewish critics of the "the Jewish document" had appreciated at the time what a blow the Council had dealt to theological anti-Semitism, they would have given it a more cordial welcome.

The answer of the Council Fathers to the question whether the Election had been revoked or not was unambiguous. "Nevertheless," we read, "according to the Apostle, the Jews still remain most dear to God, because of the Fathers, for he does not repent of the gifts he makes, nor of the calls he issues." (Vatican II, *Nostra Aetate,* No. 4)

The Constitution, *Lumen Gentium,* paragraph 16, completed the official teaching enunciated in *Nostra Aetate,* paragraph 4. It refrained from equating Jewry with the Elect People, but declared it to be *secundum electionem,* a precious formula, which we translate "held under the régime of the Election".

In the wake of the Council, the Commission of the French

Episcopate for Relations with Judaism issued an important document reiterating the teaching of the Council: "Contrary to the view supported by an antiquated exegesis and open to criticism, one may not deduce from the New Testament that the Jewish People has been deprived of its election."[6]

The declarations of the Council laid the foundations for a revision of the received theology of post-Christic Jewry and Judaism. It has engendered a new interest in Rabbinism and provoked numerous initiatives for improving social relations between Jews and Gentiles. Books of catechism have been examined and purified from anti-Semitic overtones. Liturgical prayers and Church decoration have also received attention. Much, of course, remains to be done, but where Catholics are concerned the process is irreversible. To date, we know of no parallel declarations on the part of the Orthodox Christian churches, with their long history of anti-Semitism.

The teaching of Vatican Council II concerning Jewry dealt a mortal blow to the theory of substitution of the Jews by the Gentiles. With the mass apostasy taking place amongst the Gentiles, the theory is less ventilated now than previously. It had sprung up in patristic times, in the heat of an anti-Jewish polemic, when historical appearances lent credit to its plausibility.

Already, St. Paul had had occasion to remonstrate with his Gentile neophytes for imagining themselves to be superior to the Jews. He reminded them that if they were superior it was entirely due to their faith. In any case, they did not support the root, but rather the root supported them (cf. Rm. 11:18-19). His remarks would seem sufficient to have prevented the theory of substitution from ever having appeared, but Gentiles have been strangely heedless about St. Paul's admonitions regarding their behavior towards the Jews.

The revocation thesis became the rationale of a negative theology of post-Christic Jewry. It placed the soul of the Gentile on the knife-edge of an obsessive insistence on Jewish incredulity with the ever-present danger of falling over into an emotionally charged anti-Semitism. Many yielded and, in falling, violated the golden precept of Christian charity. Jews were able to charge that Gentile Christians did not really love them. The revocation thesis discredited Rabbinism as unworthy of serious study. It led to a subtle depreciation of the Old Testament, to a persistence of Marcionite traits in Christian theology. It is at the origin of much of the odious legislation against Jews introduced by Christian kings and rulers.

The revocators supported their thesis by appealing to the destruction of the Temple, to the exile and the dispersion of the Jews. The survival of Jewry and the vitality of Rabbinism became irritating problems for the theologian. Since the Jew had no further *raison d'être*, why had not divine providence shown more consistency in ensuring his disappearance?

Psychologically, the revocators did their best to make sure that the Jews did disappear. They turned them into a ghost-people, a non-people, as unsubstantial as it was subjectively possible to make them out to be. Any affirmation of identity by the Jew was felt to be a monstrous contradiction, an insupportable absurdity. The resentment of the Jew at the disdainful conduct of the Gentile can be imagined. Vri Zvi Greenberg, the Hebrew poet, gave voice to the pent-up wrath of the Jew of his generation at Gentile arrogance. Much in Zionism can be explained as a Jewish reaction to the humiliating sneers of the Gentile.

Having reduced the Jew to the lay state, so to speak, the revocators found alternative explanations for the historical facts. The continued existence of the Jewish People was attributed to a blind instinct for survival; their refusal to believe, to a meaningless obstinacy; their sufferings vain, if not deserved; anti-Semitism, a popular reaction to their inassimilability; Jewish inassimilability, an exasperating exhibition of racial pride; the return of the Jews to Palestine, a freak historical phenomenon, doomed to failure.

The foregoing mentality projected itself into books of catechism and sermons as "the teaching of contempt". Here Jules Isaac scored his greatest triumph. He presented a suitable memorandum to John XXIII and found the good pope only too willing to take the matter up. The result is to be found in the declarations of Vatican Council II on the theological status of post-Christic Jewry. Jews in Israel are known to have wept at the death of John XXIII.[7]

The revocators chose to ignore St. Paul's warning to the Gentiles that a similar fate would befall them if, like the Jews, they sinned by incredulity. Today we see that millions have. Dried-up branches which no longer bear fruit are being torn out of the olive tree and cast away. They exhibit signs of decadence, more evident than what anti-Semitic propaganda had attributed to Jews. In them are fulfilled the words of Jesus: "The last state of that man becomes worse than the first" (Mt. 12:45).

The most serious consequence of the revocationist mentality was to make impossible a reading of the signs of the times. There remained a profound reluctance to accord a providential significance to the modern history of post-Christic Jewry. There was a general failure of theological apperception, an inability to integrate the modern Jewish scene into Christian theology.

The theory of revocation influenced the pastoral handling of the convert of Jewish origin. Since the Jew was seen as deprived of theological status, even more so the convert. Clerical policy towards the convert was to admit him into the Church under the same conditions as the non-Jewish convert. It was a régime of frank assimilation. That the Jewish convert was the bearer of an ancient civilization counted for nothing. The policy was carried out with an unruffled conscience. The effect of the policy was to break the historical identity of the Jewish convert on the wheel of a pseudo-theology, essentially destructive in nature. The results lie around us for all to see. Whereas Jews exhibit a marvelous spirit of cohesion, Jewish converts are incapable of common action. They are intimidated by the pressure to conform. The clergy, in general, is suspicious of any attempt on the part of the convert to assert his historical identity. It regards the traditional policy of assimilating the convert as inevitable, and justified if not positively desirable, as we see in priests tainted with anti-Semitism. The convert is expected to submit docilely to the process of absorption, under pain of rousing the Gentile Christian to exasperation. Nothing less than an instruction from the official Church could alter the situation.

The impression made on the Jew by the régime of assimilation was disastrous. It outraged him in the deepest fibres of his self-understanding. Secularists and religious Jews closed ranks in defense against the menace of the Christian Mission. The insensibility of the Christian missionary to his bungling was as deep as his ignorance of the profound currents that were sweeping across the length and breadth of the Jewish world.

In the wake of the Council, the Catholics have tended to abandon active proselytizing of Jews, though pockets of resistance remain. These circles are unconvinced. They appeal to the command of the Risen Christ to go out and baptize all peoples. Motivated by a laudable desire to spread the faith, these zealous missionaries are nonetheless, in my view, fanatical in their resort to the naked principle of proselytizing without consulting circumstances. Where Jews are concerned, the most important circumstance is the existence of the "election factor". Not to take it into consideration is to act irresponsibly towards Jewish destiny. Kurt Hruby tried valiantly to counteract the imprudent zeal of the proselytizers. Writing with the force of personal conviction, he had this to say: "The man touched by the message of the Church is not isolated from his context, a sort of monad, but first of all a member of a human community." He concluded his address with an appeal: "Nothing less than a profound modification of a theological order could change this point of view. What is necessary is an interpretation of the plan of God, less exclusive, which to all appearances continues to reserve a place for Israel according to the principles proper to the plan."[8] The revision called for by Hruby takes on a note of urgency, if the best interests of the Church are to be served in the post-conciliar period.

X. OBJECTIONS AND REFUTATIONS

The revocationist mentality is so deep-rooted in Christian milieux that we feel obliged to refute some of the more common ways in which it is encountered.

1. The purpose of the Election was to give Christ to the world; when that purpose was fulfilled, the Election fell away from the Jewish People. We reply, denying that the purpose of the Election was limited to giving the historical Jesus to the world; we agree that the purpose of the Election was to give the world both Jesus and his prolongation in the Church.

The objection gratuitously assimilates Election and Law. It is the Law that has come to an end in Christ (cf. Rom. 10:4), not the Election.

2. The Church inherits the promises of Mosaic Judaism, leaving post-Christic Jewry dispossessed of its privileges. We reply: The Church is Israel, under the New Law, as Mosaic Judaism was Israel under the Old Law. Israel has extended its titles to the Gentiles by way of a communication, not by way of a transfer of privileges. It is in this light that we should understand the following texts:

1 Pet. 2:10 "Once you were no people, but now you are God's people."

1 Pet. 2:9 "You, however, are a chosen race, a royal priesthood, a holy nation, a people He claims for his own."

Col. 3:12 "You are God's chosen ones."

Post-Christic Jewry is a section of Israel and, as such, shares its privileges.

3. Christianity is a universal religion, incompatible with the granting of privileges to any one people. We reply: God has granted privileges to the People of Israel; the granting of further privileges is neither possible to man nor required of him. The objection leans on several biblical texts:

Gal. 3:27-28 "All of you who have been baptized into Christ

have clothed yourselves with Him. There does not exist among you Jew or Greek, slave or freeman, male or female. All are one in Christ Jesus."

We reply, denying that St. Paul intends to teach that there are no differences at all between Jew and Greek, slave and free, male and female. We agree that he teaches that there are no differences between them in the conditions of personal salvation, hence the words "in that image", "in Christ Jesus".

Clearly, however, St. Paul does not extend his egalitarianism to all the planes of human discourse. In Gal. 3:28, St. Paul teaches that there are no distinctions between male and female, yet in 1 Cor. 11:3, he affirms that man is the head of the woman. In 1 Tim. 2:14, he furnishes a theological argument in favor of women's subordination to man. He instructs women to cover their heads in the assembly as a sign of subordinate status (cf. 1 Cor. 11:10). St. Paul opposed fighting the abolition of slavery at that time, teaching that everyone should remain in the place allotted to him by providence.

The Catholic Church came under pressure to ordain women priests from the Catholic Movement for the Liberation of Women, which based its claims precisely on the passage from Gal. 3:28 cited above. Immediately, the Sacred Congregation for the Doctrine of the Faith issued a declaration explaining that Gal. 3:28 required a nuanced exegesis: "This passage is in no way related to the ministry; it affirms only the universal vocation and the divine filiation, which is the same for all."[1]

Does not the reply hold where Jew and Greek are concerned? Their universal vocation is the same; their role in the plan of salvation different.

The spiritual equality of souls is not in contradiction to a diversity of functions in the Mystical Body (cf. 1 Cor. 12:12-30). The spirit is one, the vocations many. It does not exclude a hierarchy among vocations. The Church has always regarded the religious state as superior to the lay state. But to whom more is given, more is demanded. St. Paul himself indicates how grave is the responsibility attached to the Election: "Yes, affliction and anguish will come upon every man who has done evil, the Jew first, then the Greek. But there will be glory, honor, and peace for everyone who has done good, likewise the Jew first, then the Greek. With God there is no favoritism" (Rm. 2:9-11). "It is the power of God leading everyone who believes in it to salvation, the Jew first, then the Greek" (Rm. 1:16). "The word of God has to be declared to you first of all; but since you reject it and thus convict yourselves as unworthy of everlasting life, we now turn to the Gentiles" (Acts 13:46).

The existence of a primacy of honor accorded by the Bible to Israel is hard for some Gentiles to accept. We ourselves have heard a highly placed ecclesiastic expostulate: "The Church cannot accord special privileges to one people in preference to another". Quite right: it is unnecessary; they have been accorded by God already. The sufferings of Jews across the ages, and in particular during World War II, vividly illustrate the exigencies that accompany the privileges of the Election. It is a terrible thing to fall into the hands of the living God. According to Jewish legend, God first offered the Torah to the Gentiles before he offered it to Israel. The Gentiles declined to accept it.

Spiritual egalitarianism does not imply uniformity. To this principle the oriental rites of the Church bear witness. What we call rites are really historical communities who cherish their own liturgical traditions with the encouragement of the official Church. Unlike Jewry, their distinctive identity is not a matter of revelation but arises from historical contingencies only.

The objection which opposes a universalist Church to a particularist Jewry issues from a platonising concept of universality which exalts the abstract in order to depreciate the concrete. This view of Christianity is not Christian but pagan. C. A. Rijk confessed his dilemma: "The question then is how we reconcile the universalism of the Church's mission with the recognition of Jewish identity and its particular place in the salvation plan of the Lord? Today we are only at the beginning of a serious approach to this problem, so I cannot give a definite answer." These words of Rijk should be a warning to Catholics not to be over-bold or over-confident in approaching the problems of the apostolate to the Jews.

We see to what a sterile end a platonising conception of universality led a specialist like Rijk.

For another author, the very universality of the Church demands "the setting up of communities of Christians composed of converts and for whom Hebrew would be the liturgical language".[2] The idea has met with the approval of the Apostolical Delegate of Jerusalem, Archbishop William A. Carew, who, in reply to the author of these pages, wrote: "I personally believe we should enable Jews to accept Christ and the Church without assimilation, just as Syrian, Armenian and other Orthodox when returning to Catholicism."

Has not the Catholic religion been strongest where it has been identified with a national culture? Take the examples of Ireland and Poland! In the absence of insertion into the local culture, Christianity runs the risk of remaining a marginal phenomenon, which seems to be its fate in Japan. The Election of Israel is an example given by God to us to be imitated.

The ideal world of Plato was detached from the mundane world. In Christianity it enters the mundane world. The Logos became man and dwelt amongst us, becoming a man of a particular race, place, religion, language, even dialect.

Professor Martin Versfeld wisely observed that "the Old Testament with its actuality is unintelligible from a Platonic point of view."[3] The same is true of the New Testament. Daniélou gave us a fine example of the platonising mind at work when he said: "The Christian is absolutely not linked to any particular race, any human type or any country." We unhesitatingly assert the opposite and believe we come closer to the truth: "The Christian is absolutely always linked to a particular race, a particular human type and a particular country." Daniélou's platonising mentality was symptomatic of the extent to which he himself had been influenced by Greece. Understood in that way, universalism can be a double-edged sword. If Catholics use it against Jews, Protestants use it against Catholics. In the name of the platonising mentality, Protestants find rosaries and statues, for instance, repugnant. They offend the ethereal interpretation of the Gospel which, in one degree or another, is the hallmark of Protestantism.

Kurt Hruby strenuously combated the platonising mentality: "It is, in effect, impossible," he said, "to separate the individual from his ethnic, sociological, and cultural context"; and again, "the notion of ethnic and cultural community is rarely touched upon ...but modern theological currents react to this abstract presentation, too often cut out of the heart of spiritual realities".

Newman asked pertinently how the platonising view of Christianity explained the fact that the pope had to be bishop of Rome. Is that not a case, we inquire of Daniélou, where Christianity is irrevocably attached to a particular country, to a particular city and to a particular form of human culture?

Newman went on to argue pointedly: "If St. Peter, who is the very witness and foundation of unity, has placed himself at Rome forever, instead of wandering from kingdom and kingdom and from city to city, if he thus has given local, nay, almost national attributes to the Holy See, we may be sure that there is nothing judaical or otherwise secular or carnal if we throw ourselves directly and with a special warmth of attachment upon the country or the place in which we personally find ourselves, drink in its particular spirit and glory in the characteristic tokens of a Divine Presence which have been bestowed upon it."[4]

As we see, there is much pertinence in Hruby's appeal to strip our mind of the concretions of time in order, thus purified, to rethink the mission of the Church amongst men.

XI. THE MORAL DIMENSION OF POST-CHRISTIC JEWISH IDENTITY

Thus far, we have reached two principal conclusions bearing on the identity of post-Christic Jewry: 1. That Rabbinism, as a religion, is invalid; 2. that Rabbinites are retained under the régime of the Election. There is more, however, to the problem. Jesus not only died, he was judically put to death. Since he was the Son of God, who was responsible? Who was guilty? What was the nature of the sin? What were its consequences?

The moral dimension of post-Christic Jewish identity is forced upon our attention, for the task is not an agreeable one. No one likes to be the object of a moral judgement. No one finds it pleasant to listen to outsiders sitting in judgement on the group to which he belongs. In the present case, there is the maddening difficulty of framing a suitable form of words to describe the intervention of an infinite God in finite historical events.

The consolation of the author is that others sit in judgement on Christianity. Judaism regards the belief in the Blessed Trinity as a form of polytheism. It is incredulous about the Immaculate Conception of Mary and the Virgin Birth of Jesus. Protestants have been known to denounce the papacy in terms of burning indignation, employing every verbal extremity to excoriate the cult of the Madonna and the bestowing of papal indulgences.

We feel no need to apologize or to be hypersensitive. Our intention is not to give offense but to analyze the effects on post-Christic Jewish identity of the death of Jesus.

The Believing Minority

Already in the Old Testament a moral schism appears in the people. Of the twelve tribes, ten are lost; only two remain. Of the Jews exiled in Babylon, a pious remnant returns to rebuild Jerusalem. The revolt of the Maccabees pits a nationalist party against the Hellenizers.

In the drama of Calvary, a minority of Judaites had been set aside to believe. Their importance far outstrips their numerical inferiority. The disappearance of the category might have been inevitable, but it disturbed the equilibrium of theological thinking about the intimate nature of the Church. Florival agrees that "this equilibrium could be reestablished by recognizing the specific privileged role of a revived Church of Jerusalem".[1] Florival's opinion may upset Gentile Christians. It appears to challenge the monopoly which they have enjoyed in the Church for so long. The elder brother in the parable of the Prodigal Son manifests a similar lack of sympathy when his errant brother returns home.

In the Old Dispensation, the believing minority had magnificent tasks to carry out: the rebuilding of the Temple, the writing and compilation of the Old Testament, the defense of the faith against Hellenism. Their saints and prophets are venerated by Christians everywhere.

In the New Dispensation, the believing minority had even more splendid tasks placed upon them. They founded the Church, both the Church of the Hebrews and the Church of the Gentiles. They wrote an inspired literature, assembled in the New Testament.

They extended the Old Testament line of saints, martyrs, prophets and confessors, the greatest in the Christian world.

By fidelity to the purposes of the Election, the believing minority of the New Law became a positive sign of the times. Its members were crowned with an immense glory and elevated by God to the spiritual government of humanity. It constituted Israel *par excellence*, the cultivated olive tree, ready to receive the ingrafting of the Gentiles. The merits of the believing minority helped to procure the survival of the unbelieving majority, which shared in some way the sacred character of the tree. One day the latter will link hands with the former in a common confession of faith, so that both sections of Israel will be saved.

The Unbelieving Majority

Vatican Council II treated with delicate charity and theological accuracy the moral aspects of the rejection of Jesus by the majority of his contemporaries.

To appreciate the salutary intervention of the Fathers of the Council, we should keep in mind certain essential distinctions, well known to books of Catholic moral theology but strangely overlooked by Catholics in dealing with the moral dimensions of Calvary.

Responsibility should not be confused with culpability. Responsibility is a quality of human actions, both good and bad. It arises because human conduct stamps the human character for good or evil, so granting to others the right to question the agent about his actions. If he has done well, he merits praise; if he has done evil, he merits blame and punishment.

Culpability, on the other hand, is confined to bad conduct. It is present when the agent merits blame or punishment for the evil he has perpetrated. Only the agent and his willing collaborators can be held personally responsible for an action. If the action is bad, they become automatically culpable.

Culpability, however, can be incurred by a person, without reference to any specific action, as when he assents to a sinful proposition. For instance, a person who supports the legitimacy of therapeutic abortion is guilty of the sin of abortion, though he may never have had a hand in procuring one. Naturally, he is responsible for his opinion, but not for any particular operation that may have been performed.

We call capital responsibility the responsibility proper to heads of groups: the decisions of a general involve the lives of his soldiers, those of parents the lives of their children, those of statesmen the lives of citizens. The unjust decision of a chief may render his subjects collectively guilty if they consent, even passively, to follow him in any given matter.

Culpability is diminished by ignorance, or whatever factor diminishes the freedom of choice. It may occur, then, that whereas the action is in itself evil, culpability may not always be imputable, or at least not entirely so. For instance, a child brought up in a criminal milieu may commit a crime, but since his conscience has been poorly formed, the moral guilt cannot be fully imputed to him. What degree of subjective culpability should be imputed to him is best left to the judgement of Almighty God.

The Sin of the Unbelieving Majority

In the passion and death of Jesus, Jews and Gentiles were implicated. On both sides there were a number of responsible agents; on both sides there were guilty persons. To pretend to fairness, we should consider each group separately.

The chief priests at the time of the trial of Jesus were responsible for the maintenance of religious order in Israel in the same sense that Pontius Pilate was responsible for the maintenance of order in the political sphere. The chief priests were representative of the Jewish People and, beyond the Jewish People, of humanity as a whole, if we are to believe Flick and Alszeghy.[2] Confronting the Son of God as he stood before them in the person of Jesus of Nazareth, the chief priests, as the religious leaders of the people, were in duty bound to identify correctly the accused and to examine impartially his messianic claims. This they omitted to do. Instead, they delivered him over to Pilate. In failing thus to carry out their duty as the circumstances imposed it on them, the chief priests became guilty of a grave miscarriage of justice. This holds true whether the chief priests convoked the full Sanhedrin or, what seems more likely, a "kangaroo court", hastily assembled for the purpose. In the latter hypothesis, their guilt would be aggravated. In the later steps of the trial, the chief priests exercised undue pressure on the judge, Pilate, to pronounce sentence of death on the prisoner.

The responsibility of the chief priests was capital: it set the tone for the people, which the latter followed, for the most part passively. Naturally, they were unaware that Jesus was the Son of God. To oppose God as God is proper to Satan.

All the same, Maritain considers that the chief priests were conscious of doing wrong. He writes: "One day Israel stumbled and was caught in a trap, it stumbled against God—and in what an encounter, never to be repeated! Israel did not know what it was doing, but its leaders knew that they were making their choice against God. In one of those acts of free will that involve the destiny of a whole community, the priests of Israel, the bad watchers of the vineyard, the slayers of the prophets, with excellent reasons of political prudence, chose the world, and to that choice their whole people was henceforth bound, until it changes of its own accord."[3]

The Fathers of the Council taught that the chief priests had their part of personal responsibility and guilt for the death of Jesus, but that these "may not be imputed indiscriminately to all Jews of that time, much less to Jews of our time" (*Nostra Aetate*, paragraph 4).

Eugene Fisher is of the opinion that the chief priests were not truly the religious leaders of the day.

Jules Isaac drew up a list of objections aiming to minimize, if not to nullify, the responsibility and culpability of the Temple authorities in the trial and death of Jesus. Like Fisher, he argued that the evil character of the heads of the Sanhedrin, a point admitted by the Talmud itself, disqualified them from the right to be considered the true representatives of the people. We reply that responsibility inheres in the office; the use or abuse of the office determines whether the holder is worthy of praise or blame. It does not invalidate responsibility.

Jules Isaac went on: "Throughout Christendom, for the last eighteen centuries, one teaches currently that the Jewish people, fully responsible for the crucifixion, committed the inexpiable crime of deicide."[4] What echoes in these lines is the hateful cry, "Christ-Killers", which anti-Semitic mobs hurled at the Jews. On this score Jules Isaac achieved an historic triumph. The Council corrected a dangerously loose terminology, limiting responsibility to "the Jewish authorities together with their followers", who at the time pressed for the death of Jesus (cf. Jn. 19:1-7), and exempting all others.

The Council Fathers formulated their declaration, bearing in mind the strict notion of responsibility used in Catholic moral theology, which avoids the deplorable ambiguity of identifying responsibility and culpability.

The charge of culpability is pressed against the Jews in Palestine and in the Diaspora, against those who heard and saw Jesus and against those who had not. Their cases are not markedly different.

The majority of Jews in the Palestine of the time had no hand in the conspiracy against Jesus. They were not in any way directly responsible for his death. We infer from the intense activity of the Lord in the brief period of his public ministry that he offered most of them the possibility of hearing him and being eyewitness to his miracles. Nevertheless, they did not believe.

They became culpable, not directly of his death, but of the sin of incredulity. Those who did believe made a personal option; the others did not, in obedience to their religious superiors. Since to follow the lead given by one's chief is a duty of subordinates, we may see their behavior as a mitigating circumstance.

St. Peter says to them: "Yet I know, my brothers, that you acted out of ignorance, just as your leaders did" (Acts 3:17). Where the leaders were concerned, the ignorance was affected: they were not concerned to discover the truth, out of antipathy for the person of Jesus.

As for the majority, they were collectively culpable of incredulity, but who would hasten to throw the first stone? Who would impute culpability to them? It is for God to pronounce how far they are to be regarded as subjectively culpable, not for man.

Beyond the immediate actors and spectators of the drama of Calvary stands sinful humanity. Millions have never believed in Jesus, either because they have not heard of him, or because social structures make belief morally impossible. Are we accustomed to blame them for it? Yet, objectively speaking, it remains that whoever does not recognize Jesus to be the Son of God is culpable of incredulity.

True, the incredulity of Palestinian Jews made the passion and death of Jesus morally necessary, but from that no one is entitled to charge them with direct personal responsibility for Calvary.

St. Thomas deals with the moral standing of all the parties concerned in the death of Jesus.[5] From his treatise, Bishop Meyer drew the conclusion that no Jew, contemporary of Jesus, was formally and subjectively guilty of deicide.

Unlike St. Thomas, the Council had no intention of preparing a treatise on the subject. Following the massacre of the six million Jews by the Nazis, the Fathers of the Council saw themselves under a grave obligation to respond to the appeal of Jules Isaac and undermine one of the supports of Christian anti-Semitism.

The meaning of Calvary far transcends the visible scene described in the pages of the Gospel. We are present at a cosmic drama which touches us all. The Eternal Father, out of his love for man, willed to offer up his only-begotten Son in expiation for the sin of mankind. Mankind as a whole is guilty of deicide.

The Exegetical Crux

The New Testament furnishes texts which have been exploited by the anti-Semites. We present some examples:

I Thess. 2:15: "The Jews who killed the Lord Jesus."

Acts 3:15: "You put to death the Author of life."

Acts 2:23-24: "You even made use of pagans to crucify and kill him. God freed him from death's bitter pangs, however, and raised him up again."

How are we to reconcile texts like these with the declarations of the Council? How are we to explain them to impressionable young children receiving their catechism lessons?

In answer, let us consult the Old Testament. David sent Uriah, the Hittite, to his death, inspired by an adulterous lust for the latter's beautiful wife, Bathsheba. Nathan, the prophet, fearlessly upbraids the royal sinner: "You have cut down Uriah the Hittite with the sword" (2 Sam. 12:9). David, in fact, had done nothing of the kind. In the same episode, Nathan enlarges on his words: "(You) killed him with the sword of the Ammonites" (2 Sam. 12:9). Nathan's first formula was shorthand prophetic rhetoric; his second formula corrected the liberties of the first.

In the passage we cited from SS. Peter and Paul, we encounter the same prophetic rhetoric, also on the occasion of the death of an innocent man. The Jews to whom our saints addressed themselves had not killed Jesus. At most, they had assented to the initiative taken by their leaders.

A nuanced exegesis of the above-quoted passages and others of a similar tenor is an important duty of the post-conciliar catechist.

The Sin of the Romans

Pontius Pilate, the Roman governor of Judea, was responsible for the maintenance of law and order in the providence. He became guilty of a grave miscarriage of justice when, out of motives of the basest self-interest, he ordered Jesus, whom he had declared publicly to be innocent, to be delivered up to death.

Pontius Pilate and the Roman soldiery who carried out the sentence of crucifixion represented the Gentiles in the drama of Calvary. "God," writes St. Paul, "has imprisoned all in disobedience that he might have mercy on all" (Rm. 11:32).

Had not Jesus himself prophesied: "There the Son of Man will be handed over to the chief priests and scribes, who will condemn him to death. They will turn him over to the Gentiles, to be made sport of and flogged and crucified" (Mt. 20:17-19). In this passage we find a crystal-clear *résumé* of the dual role of the chief priests and their collaborators on the one hand, and Pilate and his agents on the other.

The hierarchy of responsibility is defined by Jesus in equally clear terms in another passage. Standing before Pilate, Jesus says: "He who handed me over to you is guilty of the greater sin" (Jn. 19:11). He was alluding to the chief priest, Kaiapha, and perhaps to Judas Iscariot as well. In light of his words, we criticize as tendentious a sentence by P. Lapide: "Four centuries ago, the teaching authority of the Catholic Church, the Council of Trent, stated that Pontius Pilate was ultimately responsible for Jesus' death sentence." Agreed, Pilate was ultimately responsible for the sentence of death, not for Jesus' death, as such. Pilate was interested in Jesus only as a possible political agitator (cf. Lk. 23:13). The chief priests condemn Jesus for blasphemy (cf. Mt. 26:65; Mk. 14:61-64). Jesus, therefore, judged Kaiapha to be more guilty than Pilate.

The Sin of the Diaspora

The moral status of Diaspora Jews has also been one of collective guilt for the sin of incredulity.

Let the judgement not appear to be too harsh for the delicate-minded reader. Already, the Fourth Book of Ezra attributed the exile of post-Christic Jewry to collective sin. Rabbinical literature has never surmised any differently. The Christian and the Jew only part ways over the nature of the sin. Again we repeat, post-Christic Jewry is not responsible for the crucifixion of Jesus; it is guilty of not believing in him.

J. Isaac wrote defensively: "One has no right to affirm that the Jewish People as a whole, rejected Jesus. It is infinitely more probable that the Jewish People as a whole did not even know about him."

The objection is beside the point. Diaspora Jewry did not reject Jesus; it rejected Christianity.

Jesus himself had prophesied: "This good news of the kingdom will be proclaimed throughout the world as a witness to all the nations. Only after that will the end come" (Mt. 24:14). By "end", the fall of Jerusalem is meant.

St. Paul, as if anticipating the objection of Jules Isaac, asks: "I ask you, have they not heard? Certainly they have, for their voice has sounded over the whole earth, and their words to the limits of the world. I put the question again, did Israel really not understand?" (Rm. 10:18-19)

In each successive generation, Diaspora Jewry was to repeat its act of collective unbelief, so maintaining a negative attitude toward God's plan of salvation. St. Paul counseled his Gentile proselytes to bow their heads in fear and trembling before the sacred mystery, lest a similar fate overtake them (cf. Rm. 11:20-21). It has. The warning went unheeded. If the truth be told, St. Paul had done more than give a warning; he had prophesied.

Though a poor consolation to Jews in their grief, it may help them to put their case into perspective to learn their collective culpability is no isolated phenomenon. From the point of view of the Catholic faith, the entire Orthodox Christian world is collectively culpable of the sin of schism, however unpopular it may be in these ecumenical times to recall the fact. Likewise, the Protestant world is collectively culpable of the sin of heresy. It has now become, in addition, collectively culpable for the apostasy of the Gentiles. Jesus had warned: "A kingdom torn by strife is headed for its downfall. A town or household split into factions cannot last" (Mt. 12:25; Mk. 3:23-25). When Luther divided the kingdom, did he reflect on these words of Jesus? The kingdom lies in ruins about us; we pick our way between the debris as best we can. Even the Jewish Kabbalists at the time saw in the advent of Luther a sign of the breakup of the Church and the approach of the end of days.[6]

Post-Protestant culture, especially in its philosophical and intellectual aspects, is collectively culpable for the massacre of the six million Jews. Jewish scholars, inquiring into the causes of Nazism, have begun to realize that Nazism was no freak phenomenon in European history, but an almost logical outcome of German idealism, notably Hegelianism.

Of course, we are aware that Orthodox Christians and Protestants, in turn, accuse Catholics of sinning against Christian truth.

Let us confess together that there is a sin of the world from which Jesus came to redeem us.

The incredulity of the Jews brought riches to the Gentiles (cf. Rm. 11:12). These latter were progressively incorporated into the kingdom of God, baptized and elevated by the Spirit, and given the mission of the Jews to bear collective witness to Jesus Christ. A Christendom arose, stretching from Ireland to Russia. The roll call of its saints, doctors, martyrs, confessors, and virgins is glorious. The Gentiles had become a positive sign of the times. How different was to be the destiny of the Jews we shall now consider.

XII. THE HISTORICAL CONSEQUENCES
OF THE SIN OF UNBELIEF

Unbelief had both spiritual and historical consequences for the Jewish People. At the death of Jesus, the veil of the sanctuary split from top to bottom (cf. Mt. 27:51), symbolizing the departure of the divine presence. The rabbinical view is that the divine presence went into exile when the Temple was destroyed a generation later. To imagine the impossible, should the Temple be rebuilt, are rabbis certain that the divine presence would automatically return to occupy it?

The blindness of post-Christic Jewry to the infinite treasures of grace earned for mankind by the mediation of Jesus was and remains a terrible consequence of unbelief, one which has jeopardized the salvation of many. What is more, forty years after Calvary a chain of disasters overtook Jewry, the result of which was to fix its status in the iron framework of an exile which was to last for nigh on two thousand years. The chain of disasters to which we refer are the following:

-The failure of the Jewish revolt against the Romans.
-The destruction of the Temple.
-The destruction of Jerusalem.
-The suppression of Mosaic Judaism.
-The exile, known to rabbinical literature as the "Roman" or "Edomite" exile. The rabbis date it from the crushing of the Bar Kokhba revolt by Hadrean in 135 AD.
-The long story of suffering and humiliation, culminating in the brutal extermination of six million European Jews, by which the Nazis initiated their plan for the total destruction of Jewry.

These calamities constitute a prophetic series set out in the relevant chapters of Leviticus and Deuteronomy. Rabbinical literature has not failed to see them in this light, being powerfully struck by the parallel between the destruction of the First and the

Second Temples.

Jesus prophesied the series as a whole and in detail. Whether to his words the Primitive Church added or subtracted here and there is little to our purpose. The search for the *ipsissima verba* of Jesus is an exercise of limited importance. What we read in the New Testament are not precisely the words of Jesus; they are the words of the Spirit of Jesus and its intentions are clear: to link the events in question to the plan of salvation.

The National Prophecies of Jesus

Bossuet sets out at length the national prophecies of Jesus in his celebrated "Discourse on Universal History", one of the classical treatises on the Christian theology of history. His considerations retain their value, though the tone of the author in dealing with Jewish destiny will not please the post-conciliar reader.

The Series As A Whole

Mt. 23:35-36: "Until retribution overtakes you for all the blood of the just ones shed on earth, from the blood of holy Abel to the blood of Zechariah son of Barachiah, whom you murdered between the temple building and the altar. All this, I assure you, will be the fate of the present generation."

In Detail

Lk. 21:20: *The siege of Jerusalem:* "When you see Jerusalem encircled by soldiers."

Lk. 21:20: *The destruction of Jerusalem:* "Know that its devastation is near." "Jerusalem will be trampled by the Gentiles" (Lk. 21:24).

Mt. 24:2: *The destruction of the Temple:* "Do you see all of these buildings? I assure you, no one stone will be left on another—it will all be torn down."

Mt. 23:38: *The departure of the divine presence:* "You will find your temple deserted."

Lk. 21:24: *The defeat of Jewish arms:* "The people will fall before the sword."

Lk. 21:24: *Exile:* "They will be led captive in the midst of the Gentiles."

It has been objected that the dispersion of the Jews had begun well before 70 AD. Our answer is that what is at stake is not the physical fact of dispersion but its theological significance.

Newman freely admitted the existence of a wide dispersion of Jews prior to Jesus, and even accorded it a positive value, as the preparation for the diffusion of the Gospel. He unhesitatingly regarded the dispersion of post-Christic Jewry as the accomplishment of prophecy. Writing about "the well-known chapter of Deuteronomy which so strikingly anticipates the nature of their punishment", he observes: "That passage translated into Greek as many as three hundred and fifty years before the siege of Jerusalem by Titus has on it the marks of a wonderful prophecy."1

Chouraqui pretended that there is no normal people that does not have its dispersion, going on to compare the dispersion of the Jews to that of the French, the Spanish, the Italians, the Irish, and the Germans. Pure sophistry! Chouraqui knew well enough that the dispersion of the Jews was a matter of revelation. It was one of the consequences of the breaking of the Alliance, of the infidelity of Jewry to its vocation. The dispersion of others is no more than analogical.

Lk. 21:24: The prolonged occupation of the Holy Land by Gentiles: "Jerusalem will be trampled by the Gentiles, until the times of the Gentiles are fulfilled."

Since Jerusalem was the capital city and often a synonym for the Holy Land, Jesus effectively predicted the government of the Holy Land by Gentiles, during a providential age. In the same period the national sovereignty of the Jews would be suspended.

History has vindicated this prophecy of Jesus in the most irrefutable way. Here there can be no prophecy after the event.

Mt. 21:43, 45: The transfer of ecclesiastical authority: "The kingdom of God will be taken away from you and given to a nation that will yield a rich harvest. When the chief priests and the Pharisees heard these parables, they realized he was speaking about them."

Lk. 13:28-29: Transfer of the mission to the Gentiles: "There will be wailing and grinding of teeth when you see Abraham, Isaac, Jacob, and all the prophets safe in the kingdom of God, and you yourselves rejected. People will come from the east and the west, from the north and the south, and will take their place at the feast in the kingdom of God."

Mk. 13:30: The beginning of the tribulations: "I assure you this generation will not pass away, until all these things take place." "Jesus turned to them and said: "Daughters of Jerusalem, do not weep for me. Weep for yourselves and for your children. The days are coming when they will say: 'Happy are the sterile, the wombs that never bore, and the breast that never nursed'" (Lk. 23:28-29).

Lk. 21:24: The end of the tribulations: "Jerusalem will be trampled by the Gentiles, until the times of the Gentiles are fulfilled."

One commentator of the Bible agrees that "the age of the pagans" is the period in which pagans will have taken the place of the Jews, according to Paul (cf. Rm. 11:11-32); this period will end with the conversion of all Israel.[2]

Our first observation is that, however obscure may be the phrase, "until the age of the pagans is completely over", there will, without a doubt, be such a period. Supposing then that "the age of the pagans is completely over", what, we ask, will happen to Jerusalem? The answer is plain: it will fall back once again into the hands of the Jews. It follows, therefore, that Jesus is implicitly predicting in Lk. 21, 24 the return of the Jews to the Holy Land after a long exile.

But in 1967, Jerusalem did fall back into the hands of the Jews; so we must conclude that "the age of the pagans" is completely over.

In Lk. 21: 24, Jesus is coordinating the return of the Jews to the Holy Land with the end of a spiritual epoch in the religious history of the Gentiles. During this epoch, the Gentiles will have taken over the mission of the Jews. The insinuation is that the Gentiles would then lose their mission, or that it would be taken away from them to be restored to the Jews, once again in possession of Jerusalem. We affirm that time to be now.

Hobbes (1588-1679) wound up his classic on political philosophy, *Leviathan*, with a cynical passage. He foresaw that the work of Henry VIII and Queen Elizabeth in breaking with Rome might have untoward effects and warned: "An assembly of spirits worse than he (the spirit of Rome) may enter and inhabit this clean-swept house and make the end thereof worse than the beginning." They did.

John Donne, in his great poem, *The Anatomy of the World*, summed up his forebodings of disaster for Christendom: "It's all in pieces, all coherence gone."

In his introduction to Feuerbach's, *The Essence of Christianity*, Karl Barth made the observation: "It is for us Protestant theologians, a matter of special concern, that Feuerbach, for his own purposes, could readily make use of Luther." These purposes were entirely atheistic. Barth then goes on to trace the progressive decline of Christian faith in Protestant theology, through Gottfried, Wegscheider, de Wette, and others, until he arrives at the blatant atheism of Feuerbach.

Oswald Spengler was conscious that "something has come to end".

Karl Jaspers had the sentiment of a break with all previous history: "In the Occident," he stresses, "the process has a radical character found in no other place."

Harold Laski triumphantly announced that the nations of Christendom "have ceased to be Christian in anything but name."

William James saw Christianity as entirely displaced from the thoughts of a large part of his generation.

William McDougall was of the opinion that not only the evidence for revelation no longer suffices, but the world at large, especially our Western civilization, is unmistakably drifting away from these beliefs.

The contributor to the article on Protestantism in the British Encyclopaedia recognizes that while "huge majorities of the population, as in Scandinavia and England, are baptized members of established Protestant churches, only a small percentage of these are attendants at worship services or responsive to the disciplines of the church". He describes the religious situation in these countries as one of "massive apostasy".

On the Catholic side, Giuseppe de Rosa, reviewing the book of

Professor Savine S. Acquaviva entitled, *L 'ecclisi del sacro nella civiltá industriale*, reflects: "We are certainly moving toward the end of Christendom, but not toward the end of Christianity."[3] Delumeau is of the same opinion.[4] We concur. The evidence is overwhelming. The apostacy of the Gentiles is a fact. Is it a sign? If so, a sign of what? The best exegesis of Lk. 21:24 is to be found in the contemporary scene. Why is the clergy reluctant to accept it? Perhaps it feels that the perspective opened is too pessimistic. Perhaps it imagines that we are affirming a numerically total apostasy, which would be a mistake. The truth lies deeper. Visible phenomena, historical or otherwise, furnish no more than motives for credibility; they cannot oblige a person to believe. To accept a sign one must believe. The clergy knows the facts; it will not believe the sign.

Lk. 21: 22: *The national prophecies of Jesus, based on the Old Testament:* "These indeed will be days of retribution, when all that is written must be fulfilled."

Commenting on the passage, one exegete refers us to Dn. 9:27 only; but Jesus foresees that all Scripture will be fulfilled in the expected tribulations. And so, indeed, it is.

The Old Testament belongs, essentially, to the genre of religious historiosophy: it is, in the first place, a religious interpretation of history—past, present, and future. The explanation it offers draws on the experience of Israel in Canaan and was formulated in terms of a redemptive cycle by the great pre-exilic and exilic prophets. The redemptive cycle reflects the salvific will of God towards man. It is at the heart of divine providence. It is the mystery hidden from the beginning of the world and finally revealed in Christ Jesus.

The constituent elements of the cycle are three in number: an alliance, sin against the alliance with its concomitant consequences, and the restoration of the alliance by a merciful act of divine indulgence.

Molding images taken from the common culture of ancient Mesopotamia, the redemptive cycle was projected retrospectively in the story of Original Sin, which incidentally has no correspondent in Mesopotamian mythology.[5] The sacred author could have had no historiographical information about the origins of mankind, none at all. The truth of the story is purely historiosophical, the redemptive cycle being true for mankind from the beginning. The story presents God and man in a state of alliance, a word used by Ben Sirah to describe their relation (cf. Sir. 17:22). Whether the relation was actual or virtual, as Flick and Alszeghy propose, is for the dogmatic theologian to pronounce. At all events, it was an alliance, like the relation between God and Israel was an alliance. God addresses his revealed word to the first parents, representative of humanity at that moment, as he addresses his word to the prophets of Israel. His revealed word comports a prohibition; the Law of Moses abounds in prohibitions. The woman disobeys the revealed word of God, preferring to listen to words from another quarter. She induces her husband to sin. Why was Eve made to sin first? The theme is one of the threads which runs through the fabric of the Old Testament. Did not the wives of Solomon turn his mind from the truth, causing him to lose possession of the God-given wisdom for which he had prayed? Was not Delilah responsible for blinding of Samson, symbol of the loss of his God-given charismatic strength? Adam and Eve are exiled from the Garden of Eden, as Israel would be exiled from the Holy Land. Recall that the Garden is a holy place where God dwells, a miniature Holy Land. The consequences of sin for Adam and Eve—expulsion, suffering and humiliation—are those listed in Lv. 26 and Dt. 28 for the breaking of the Sinaitic alliance by Israel.[3b]

The exemplarity of the story of Original Sin for the history of Israel was recognized by Nahmanides (1194-1270) in his commentary on the Torah. He saw the story reflected in Lv. 26 and Dt. 28.

In a similar vein, the Kabbala attributes the following view to Rabbi Simeon Ben Yohai: "The precepts of the Torah, which the Holy One has given to Israel, are all laid down in the first chapter of Genesis in summary."[6]

The story of the Universal Deluge was probably based on the tradition of local inundation of remarkable proportions. The tradition served to illustrate the continued violation of the Adamic Alliance and the punishment that overtakes the descendants of the first couple; Noah represents the notion of redemption. The tradition is given a universal moral framework of striking proportions.

At all events, the redemptive cycle is prophetic retrospectively and prospectively. It extends to the history of post-Christic Jewry, to that of the Church and, what is more, to the inner life of each individual.

Newman had no difficulty in accepting Dt. 28 as prophetical for the history of post-Christic Jewry. "In some way they did sin," he wrote. "Whatever their sin be, is corroborated by the well-known chapter in the Book of Deuteronomy, which so strikingly anticipates the nature of their punishment"; and again, "No one can surely read the twenty-eighth chapter of Deuteronomy and then survey the actual state of the Jew at this time and since Our Lord came without being sure that their present state is indeed a fulfilment of the prophecy."[7]

The redemptive cycle can only be used by being applied. The sacred authors made of its application a system and a method.

We have dealt briefly with the application for the redemptive cycle to the origins of humanity. The tradition of a universal deluge, known to many peoples, was seized upon and used to illustrate how the Adamic Alliance was violated by sinful humanity and the consequent punishment meted out to it by the Almighty. The family of Noah is the exception, according to the principle that only a remnant is saved.

A ruined ziggurat served as the nucleus for the story of the Tower of Babel. The historical basis, flimsy enough, is worked up to illustrate how man sins by presumption and is dispersed in punishment.

In the story of Exodus from Egypt, the accent is placed on suffering, redemption, and the conclusion of alliance, the alliance of Sinai.

The Book of Judges offers an excellent illustration of the method followed by the sacred authors. The redemptive cycle is forced repeatedly on material from an obscure period of Israelite history, making an unfavorable impression on the modern reader, who feels that the sacred authors are governed by an *esprit de systeme*. His scandal is unjustified. The intention of the sacred authors was not to offer a scientific account of the age of the Judges, but to teach the theology of the redemptive cycle. The very concept of scientia history was unknown to him, being a recent product of European culture. At the same time, the sacred authors had no intention of falsifying. They reported traditions in the form available to them. What in any biblical passage belongs to historiosophy and what to historiography is for the exegete to determine.

The redemptive cycle was very successfully applied to the period of the Babylonian Exile, where it provided a magnificent and convincing interpretation of events. Nehemiah was overwhelmed by the force of the prophetic teaching. In the citadel of Susa, he prayed to Yahve: "Confessing the sins which we of Israel have committed against you, I and my father's house included. Grievously have we offended you, not keeping the commandments, the statutes, and the ordinances which you committed to your servant Moses. But remember, I pray, the promise which you gave through Moses, your servant, when you said: 'Should you prove faithless, I will scatter you among the nations; but should you return to me and carefully keep my commandments, even though your outcasts have been driven to the farthest corner of the world, I will gather them from there, and bring them back to the place which I have chosen as the dwelling place for my name.'" (Ne. 1:6-9)

The prayer of Nehemiah is steeped in the theology of the redemptive cycle and its concomitant spirituality. In the same way, Baruch was a disciple of the prophetical school of historical interpretation (cf. Ba. 1:20).

The redemptive cycle also looked forward to the Messiah and the messianic kingdom when the alliance, broken at the beginning with humanity as a whole, would be renewed. These prophecies are accomplished in the person of Jesus. At the beginning, man had refused to listen to the revealed Word of God, how the Word itself was made flesh and dwelt amongst us. By his passion and death, Jesus reconciled mankind to God (cf. Rm. 3:25), establishing the New Alliance with those who believed in him. There would be Jews who did not believe. To them he applied the predictions of Lv. 26 and Dt. 28 about the consequences for Israel of the breaking of the alliance.

Newman had an extraordinarily clear grasp of the principle of the application of prophecy. He explains: "This, I say, is what many persons are slow to understand. They think that the Old Testament must be supposed to be our rule directly and literally, or not at all; and since we cannot put ourselves under it absolutely and without explanation, they conclude that in no sense is it binding on us... surely there is such a thing as the application of Scripture; this is not a very difficult or strange idea. Surely we cannot make any practical use even of St. Paul's Epistles, without application. They are written to Ephesians or Colossians; we apply them to the case of the Englishmen. They speak of customs and fortunes which do not belong to us; we cannot take them literally; we must adapt them to our own case; we must apply them to ourselves."[8]

The application of the redemptive cycle to the history of post-Christic Jewry obliges us to nuance biblical terminology. Jesus spoke of "a time of vengeance" and "days of punishment". In Mt. 11:21, he curses Corazain and Capharnaum. As a Judaite under the Law of Moses, Jesus had the right to use the terminology of the Old Testament, as rabbis do to this day. The Christian's case is different. He is a disciple of the Risen Christ. It is forbidden to him to take vengeance or to curse. To curse is to wish someone harm; to wish someone harm is to offend against Christian charity.

Maritain counsels us: "Such words as 'penalty' or 'punishment', which we are obliged to use when we seek to elucidate human matters from the viewpoint of the divine conduct of history, must be deprived of any anthropomorphic connotation, and they become pitiably inadequate if we fail to do so. In any case there is no more absurd abuse than to believe it to be the affair of poor creatures to foster their pride and injustice by applying to their neighbors, as if they were the police force of God, 'penalties' and 'punishments', which concern only the Creator in his intimate dealings of love with those who have been called by Him."[9]

Flannery asks: "Must we really understand Israel's dispersion as a punitive intervention of God? It would seem that the more demonstrable divine intervention is not to have Israel remain scattered over the face of the earth, but to preserve her in the face of the many dangers that threaten her with extinction."[10]

The Fathers of the Council showed a fine sensibility in *Nostra Aetate* to the problem of terminology by decreeing that "Jews should not be represented as rejected by God or accursed, as if this followed from Holy Scripture".

Nations have no after-life; they undergo their purgatory, their hell, their paradise, on earth. What we call punishment is, for the most part, what they bring on themselves in consequence of sin, given the intervention of a saving providence.

We should not imagine that God imposed a blanket punishment of two thousand years' exile on the Jewish people for their incredulity. The tribulations that overtook them a generation after the Ascension were provoked by the fatal decision of Jewish leadership to take up arms against the Romans. Jesus opposed the militarists, just as Jeremiah had opposed those of his own time. "Give to Caesar what is Caesar's, but give to God what is God's" (Mt. 22:21). Jesus ardently desired to enlist the entire Jewish people in his project for the evangelization of the Roman Empire and, beyond that, of the world. He counseled the disciples to flee when the time came and not to fight (cf. Mt. 24:15-21). As a matter of fact, the Judeao-Christians did not participate in the war against the Romans, but fled to Pella beyond the Jordan.

The unbelieving majority opted for a program of military salvation. They failed miserably. The Temple burned, Jerusalem was destroyed, independence was lost, the exile initiated. We are, therefore, compelled to reject the pretension of Chouraqui that "the Jews could not take any other attitude but to be against the Roman Empire". The disciples of Jesus did! What is more, during the centuries of persecution, the Christians never revolted against their Roman persecutors.

In each successive age, the Jews repeated their collective act of incredulity, with resultant strains in their relation with the world. "The disorders affecting the relation of man with the transcendent and those affecting his relation with the world and other men condition each other reciprocally."[11]

The tendency of the new "pro-Judaeis" literature is to lay the blame for Jewish suffering almost exclusively on Christians. Yet when Zionists returned to the Holy Land, they found themselves embroiled with the Muslims in a conflict no less interminable.

At all events, it our duty to avoid the excesses of language of which Bossuet is guilty in treating of the destiny of post-Christic Jewry. The Jews remain most beloved by God, on account of the Fathers.

Mt. 23:37-38: *Jesus interprets post-Christic Jewish history in the light of his own person:* "O Jerusalem, Jerusalem, murderess of prophets and stoner of those who were sent to you! How often have I yearned to gather your children, as a mother bird gathers her young under her wings, but you refused me. Recall the saying, 'You will find your temple deserted.'"

In these tender words, impregnated with a profound, personal pathos, Jesus draws all Jewish history unto himself, as unto the luminous focus of its ultimate intelligibility. He is, self-confessedly, the final explanation of Jewish destiny, the occasion, not the cause, of its tragedy, the stumbling block it encountered and over which it fell. Only the divinity of Jesus suffices to account for the extent and the depth of Jewish suffering and to endow it with a positive value. The Jews fell into the hand of the living God. Is not Jesus reported to have said: "The man who falls on that stone will be smashed to pieces. It will make dust of anyone on whom it falls." (Lk. 20:18) Whatever way you choose to put it, whether God punishes men or men punish themselves, the harsh facts remain what they are.

The Role of Post-Christic Rabbinical Judaism

God activates all our movements, not all our intentions. He supported Rabbinism because he wishes men to believe, even when they do not possess the whole truth. But he sustained Rabbinism for the special reason that it provided post-Christic Jewry with a community framework, indispensable for the conservation of the "election factor". By the same token, it seems that God has never permitted the Christian mission to the Jews to succeed on a large scale, despite the great saints who tried to promote it. Zionists recognize the role of the Synagogue in preserving the physical integrity of the Jewish people throughout the Exile. Moses Hess, though not a practicing Jew, enthusiastically supported Rabbinical Judaism on the grounds that it was still playing a vital role in the life of the people which, nonetheless, would cease to be needed one day, after the State had been set up. He foresaw the advent of a suitable alternative but was unable to specify its nature.

Many are the values of Rabbinism. We signal out for special praise the solid witness it has always borne to the "election factor" in Jewish identity. It has been strong in defense of the community principle, so ignored by the clergy. Its notion of the vocation of Jewry has been uniformly lofty. The author of these pages acknowledges the beauty of the Jewish family—that of Edith Stein comes to mind—when it is faithful to the collective call to sanctity.

Role of the Post-Christic Jewish People

Exile has been the lot of Jewry for nigh on two thousand years. It was a condition in which the people lacked national independence, lived at the mercy of the good graces of the Gentile, often to be humiliated and put to death. The exile was a negative sign of the times, a visible symptom of the broken alliance, which was its root cause. "I have said," commented Cardinal Newman, "they were in God's favor under a covenant—perhaps they did not fulfill the conditions of it. This indeed seems to be their own account of the matter, though it is not clear to them what their breach of engagement was." "This grand drama," he continued, "so impressed with the characters of a supernatural agency, concerns us here only in its bearing upon the evidence of Christianity."[12] How true. However, to put it as the anti-Semites did, that Jewry suffered because it had crucified Jesus, was vindictive, cruel, and false.

"The passion of Israel," observed Maritain, "is not like that of the Church, a passion of co-redemption, completing what is lacking in the suffering of the Saviour. This passion is not suffered for the eternal salvation of souls, but for the stimulation and emancipation of temporal life. It is the passion of a scapegoat enmeshed in the earthly destiny of the world and in the ways of the world mixed with sin, a scapegoat against which the impure sufferings of the world strike back, when the world seeks vengeance for the misfortunes of its history upon what activated that history."[13]

Like Jesus, Jewry was a victim; unlike Jesus, it was not pure and innocent. All the same, insofar as it was innocent of the monstrous calumnies of the anti-Semites, object of satanic hatred, of unjust prejudices and violent jealousy, Jewish suffering acquired a quasi-redemptive value, which all innocent suffering merits.

The ultimate value of Jewish suffering should be sought for elsewhere than in the present. It lies in the future. The Exile may be compared to a coal mine, its dusty galleries dark and dangerous within, but once coal is extracted it is capable of furnishing light, heat, and power to mankind.

During the Exile, Jewry stored up immense quantities of spiritual energy, waiting to be released when the Exile should come to an end.

As he walked slowly across the stage of history, the Jew took on an uncanny resemblance to Jesus: beaten, spat upon, mocked, derided, bleeding from his judicial scourging, crowned with the thorns of incomprehension, bearing his cross on the way to Golgotha. Jewry ran the gauntlet of the nations.

"The Jewish Diaspora within Christian Europe," summed up Maritain, "is one long *Via Dolorosa.*"

Mystically speaking, Jewry as a whole was nailed to the cross and died under Hitler. "We all died in Auschwitz," cried out that great soul A. J. Heschel, in the name of all the Jews of his time. On the third day, three years after the conclusion of hostilities in 1945, Jewry rose from the dead; the State of Israel was proclaimed.

The parallel between the destiny of Jesus and the destiny of the Jewish people has struck Jews also. Marc Chagall has painted Jesus hanging from the cross, draped in the ritual shawl of the Orthodox. Some Jews explain the Holocaust in the light of the sacrifice of Isaac, a distant image of Jesus. Already early rabbinical literature had attributed a redemptive value to the sacrifice of Isaac, more correctly called then the binding of Isaac.

In the absence of the key, the Holocaust remains impenetrable for the modern Jew. The State of Israel sets aside one day in the year on which to recall the awful catastrophe. Public figures are given the opportunity to address the nation and to express its sentiments. We have watched Golda Meir on television on one such occasion, confessing she had no explanation to offer for the tragedy. Neither have religious leaders any consolation to extend. One affirmed that the State was the answer to the Holocaust, which was not exactly to give a religious reply.

Sidri Israeli wrote with bitterness: "The Holocaust is simply unintelligible. Whether it be art, religion, or ideology, there is no symbolic universe that could attempt to assimilate the Holocaust without the risk of being shaken to the foundations." Sidra Israeli was wrong for the first limb of the sentence, but not for the second. The Holocaust can be integrated into the framework of a Christian interpretation of Jewish history, but only by shattering the Gentile phase of the plan of salvation.

Jesus prophesied: "The Son of Man is going to be delivered into the hands of men who will put him to death, and he will be raised up on the third day" (Mt. 17:22-23). In these words Jesus prophesied his own death, the fate of his Mystical Body in the course of Church history, and the fate of post-Christic Jewry. Jews, too, would be handed over to the Gentiles to be put to death by them, only to rise on the third day. Not even the feeling of being abandoned by God would be absent from the parallel.

The purpose of this similarity of destiny is obvious. The people of the Messiah had to be molded into the image of their Messiah, in order to learn who the true Messiah was. At the time of Jesus, Jewry had not associated the Messiah with the suffering Servant of Yahve, about whom we read in the fifty-third chapter of Isaiah. They were taught to do so by being made to recapitulate the great phases in the life of the divine Saviour: humiliation, suffering, death, resurrection.

Rabbinism is anti-Christian; the Jewish people has ever lived in imitation of Christ. What is more, in Jewish martyrdom Jesus himself is martyred. This corresponds well with the intuition of the Jewish sages that God shares his people's suffering. The accession of Jewry to the faith, far from being a break in Jewish history, will be its consummation; it will bring the Jew to the full consciousness of the sense of his own identity and existence. Once faith is given, Jewry will be transformed into a powerhouse of spiritual motivation, sufficient to bring about the "resurrection of the dead", the return to the faith of lapsed Gentility. Jews have suffered and continue to .fer in view of the role that they are destined to play in the salvation history of mankind.

The Holocaust and the Gentiles

On one occasion Jesus prophesied to his disciples: "You will be hated by all on account of me" (Mt. 10:22). Persecution is a note of the true Church; on another plane it is a note of Jewish identity.

Anti-Semitism is the hatred of the Jew by reason of his origin. Its causes are multiple; the passion it arouses is amongst the ugliest that disfigure the human soul.

There are factors of secondary importance: the dislike of the unlike, to make the use of Zangwill's phrase, economic rivalry, ignorance, religious prejudice. The rabbinical régime of separation aroused suspicions. These attitudes and sentiments turn into anti-Semitism only when the soul yields to hatred and sins against Christian charity in the process. The main effect of anti-Semitism has been to drive a wedge between the Jews and Jesus, whose cause the anti-Semites have so badly served.

The presence of the Jew became a measure of the Gentile's capacity for charity. In his own way, the Jew revealed the secrets of the Gentile's heart and brought judgement upon him.

In the age of apostasy, the charity of the Gentile grew cold and his capacity for hatred increased. This anyway is the master intuition of Jacob Talmon in his book, *The Age of Violence*, to formulate the thesis in Christian terms. Civil emancipation notwithstanding, the condition of European Jewry unexpectedly deteriorated until it disappeared in a whirlpool of infernal passion. An apathetic humanity watched as a spiritual ice age spread over Europe.

As Pope Paul VI reflected, "These perhaps are the days foretold by Christ: 'Evils will be multiplied and the charity of many will grow cold.'"[14] What characterized Eichman is what characterizes Satan: not hot passion, but an ice-cold indifference to humane considerations. Let no one be misled by Pope Paul's way of speaking. What he meant to affirm was: "These *are* the days foretold by Christ."

It was God's turn to act. John XXIII threw open a thousand

closed windows in the Christian soul, as if preparing to receive the ingrafting of the Jews; the Jews, as if in preparation for their ingrafting, set up a State and captured Jerusalem. The eschatological importance of the latter may have escaped the attention of Christians; it did not escape that of Jews. Hayyim Hazaz, one of the most distinguished of modern Hebrew novelists, was prompted to write on that occasion: "And now, as in the last days of the ancient world, we are perhaps invited to save Europe from shipwreck." Hazaz had had a glimpse of the shape of things to come. Ten years have passed since then and the vision has faded. The ship of State has run into stormy waters and is itself in need of a new pilot. Nevertheless, Hazaz was right in divining that some extraordinary change had occurred in the plan of salvation.

Modern Zionism has persistently reflected events in the Gentile world. The Russian pogroms of 1881 provoked the establishment of the "Lovers of Zion" movement. The Dreyfus affair was the immediate cause of Political Zionism. The First World War occasioned the Balfour Declaration, by which the British government came out in favor of a national home for Jews in Palestine. The Second World War provided the background for the rise of the State of Israel, a fact about which Nahum Goldberg had no doubt at all.

What we add is that the relation between Jew and Gentile is more than historical; it is also theological. "There is no answer to Auschwitz," cried out Heschel despairingly, in the name of all Jews. Yes, there is an answer to Auschwitz, God's answer, the ingrafting of the Jews and the glory of the "resurrection of the dead" to follow.

The Cultural Contribution of Post-Christic Jewry

During the entire period of the Exile, post-Christic Jewry displayed its inexhaustible energy and high endowments by rendering innumerable services to human culture. They have been evaluated by scholars like Cecil Roth. They underscore the absence of any corresponding contribution to the salvation of mankind. The Secular Zionist, in his turn, should understand that the more he promotes the secularist program at home the less apt he becomes to promote a spiritual mission abroad. The Gentile world knows enough about science and technology, lesbianism, the joys of suicide, and other paragraphs in the secularist program for a brave new world. Israel may have raised expectations; it has not satisfied them.

Mt. 24:12: The future: "Love of most will grow cold."

Mt. 23:39: "You will not see me from this time on until you declare, 'Blessed is He who comes in the name of the Lord.'"

Rm. 11:25-26: "Brothers, I do not want you to be ignorant of this mystery lest you be conceited; blindness has come upon part of Israel until the full number of Gentiles enter in, and then all Israel will be saved."

In the foregoing passage from the Epistle to the Romans, St. Paul reveals the final destiny of post-Christic Jewry: it will accede to the Christian faith.

When will the accession occur?

Some Christians are quick to reply: "We ignore it entirely!" They have, we gather, answers neither for the Jewish present nor for the Jewish future.

We admit the question is equivocal. No one is demanding to be shown the timetable of divine providence. What Jesus asks of us is to read the signs of the times. He demanded it of the Jews of his own time, of the crowds that listened to him as well as of the learned. The signs then must have been transparent enough for all to see and these to be blamed by Jesus for not understanding. The problem of the signs of the times is not one of chronology, but of interpretation.

St. Paul announces that the accession of Jewry to the faith will take place after "the full number of Gentiles enter in" (Rm. 11:25). He is alluding to the peoples of the Roman Empire, it being evident that he was not alluding to the existence of the Chinese, the Japanese, and other far-off peoples.

In the Epistle to the Romans, Chapter 11, St. Paul offers us another clue: "Since their rejection meant the reconciliation of the world, do you know what their admission will mean? Nothing less than a resurrection from the dead."

St. Paul is enlarging on what he had written in Rm. 11:12: "But if their transgression and their diminishing have meant riches for the Gentile world, how much more their full number!"

We conclude, therefore, that the expression "resurrection from the dead" refers in the first place to the Gentiles. St. Paul is saying, perhaps in a veiled manner, that the Gentiles will one day abandon the faith he has offered them and die spiritually. The admission of the Jews would signal their resurrection.

Elsewhere, St. Paul predicts even more clearly that his auditors must expect a great apostasy: "Since the mass apostasy has not yet occurred, nor the man of lawlessness been revealed—that son of perdition and adversary who exalts himself above every so-called god proposed for worship, he who seats himself in God's temple and even declares himself to be God." (2 Thess. 2:3-4) In passing we recall that A. N. Whitehead described Hegel's philosophical attitude as that of a god. Is the personality cult, affected by modern dictators, anything else but an implicit claim on their part to have superseded the divinity?

In 1 Tim. 4:1, St. Paul goes on to reveal: "The Spirit distinctly says that in later times some will turn away from the faith." In 2 Tim. 3:1-5, he adds another revelation: "Do not forget this: there will be terrible times in the last days. Men will be lovers of self and of money, proud, arrogant, abusive, disobedient to their parents, ungrateful, profane, inhuman, implacable, slanderous, licentious, brutal, hating the good. They will be treacherous, reckless, pompous, lovers of pleasure rather than of God as they make a pretense of religion but negate its power."

In Rm. 11:19-23, St. Paul adumbrates the coincidence in time of the admission of the Jews and the apostasy of the Gentiles. In addressing himself to his Gentile neophytes, in an attempt to soften their arrogant attitude toward Jews, he develops his famous image of the olive tree and the branches: "You will say, 'Branches were cut off that I might be grafted in.' Well and good. They were cut off because of unbelief and you are there because of faith. Do not be haughty on that account, but fearful. If God did not spare the natural branches, he will certainly not spare you. Consider the kindness and the severity of God—severity toward those who fell, kindness toward you, provided you remain in his kindness; if you do not, you too will be cut off. And if the Jews do not remain in their unbelief they will be grafted back on, for God is able to do this."

From the whole tenor of the passage it can be inferred that the ingrafting of the Jews and the retrenchment of the Gentiles are presented as parts of a simultaneous process.

St. Jerome supports our exegesis: "Their sins occasioned the salvation of the Gentiles and again the incredulity of the Gentiles will occasion the conversion of Israel. You will find both in the Apostle (St. Paul)." (*Comm. to the Song of Songs*, Homily I)

St. John Chrysostom agrees: "Seeing the Gentiles abusing little by little their grace, God will recall a second time the Jews." (*Homily on Ep. to the Rom.*, Chapter 11)

St. Thomas examines a number of alternative interpretations of the phrase "resurrection of the dead" to settle on the following opinion: "What, I say, will such an admission effectuate, if not that it bring the Gentiles back to life? The Gentiles would be the believers whose faith has grown cold; or even that the totality, deceived by the Antichrist, fall and are restored to their pristine fervor by the admission of the Jews." (*Comm Ep. to the Rom. 11:15*)

J. Lémann resumes the argument: "One must expect that the figure of the Messiah, at a given moment of history, appear between two negations, the negation of the Jewish people, who do not want to recognize him, and the negation of the Gentiles as an assembly of nations, who will have abandoned him, after having known him." (*La Question du Messie*, p. 92)

We are indebted to Lémann for the definition of the biblical expression "apostasy of the Gentiles". It does not mean that all Gentile Christians will lose their faith, even to confine oneself to Europe. That there are still flourishing communities of Christians in Europe is in no way proof that the apostasy of the Gentiles has not taken place. The apostasy of the Gentiles is synonymous with the collapse of Christendom, not with the disappearance of Christianity. That Christendom, not Christianity, has indeed collapsed is affirmed both by Giuseppe de Rosa and Delumeau and in so many words.

Our question was: when, according to Scripture, is the accession of the Jews due to occur? Our answer is that it will take place simultaneously with the apostasy of the Gentiles.

Holy Scripture provides us with another significant circumstance. In Rm. 11:24, St. Paul teaches us that when the hour arrives, the admission of the Jews will be effectuated with relative ease: "If you (the Gentiles) were cut off from the natural wild olive and, contrary to nature, were grafted into the cultivated olive, so much the more will they who belong to it by nature be grafted into their own olive tree." As a matter of historical fact, the persecution of the Church by the Romans dragged on for three centuries. No comparable resistance need be expected from the Jews.

The Jewish sages dealt, in a parallel manner, with the same question, inquiring when complete redemption would come to the Jewish people. Their intuitions were, often enough, profound.

Rabbi Yohanan affirmed: "If you see that the generation is spiritually impoverished, wait for him," that is to say, you can expect the Messiah to come. Again, he said: "If you witness a generation laboring under a river of suffering, wait for him." To this deep insight, he added: "In the generation that will witness the arrival of the Son of David, Torah scholars will be few and far between, the rest will be consumed with anxiety; sorrow, troubles and persecution will increase in intensity, following one upon another without a breathing space."[15]

Rabbi Eliazar ben Avina predicted: "If you see empires struggling with one another, wait for the footsteps of the Messiah."

Other signs, more positive ones, of the approach of the Messiah would be: the ingathering of the exiles, the deliverance from political subjection to the Gentiles, success in war, and miraculous victories, which would make them forget their previous unhappiness. The final redemption would be the work of God himself. It would be preceded by dreadful wars between the powers of the world, when Israel would be homeless. The rabbis predict that at this moment Elijah would appear to announce their impending deliverance. Together the Messiah and Elijah would conduct Israel back to the Holy Land, which forthwith will become the spiritual center of mankind.

The reader may judge for himself how appropriate to the contemporary scene are the rabbinical forecasts. He will understand why influential rabbis in Israel have begun to air the view, eagerly but cautiously, that the hour of the complete redemption of the Jews is at hand. Indeed, a deep current of messianic spirituality courses through the Zionist enterprise from its onset.

Individual Admission or Admission En Masse

Father Benoit is of the opinion that "it is not sure, for example, that he (St. Paul) affirms a return en masse, under collective form". The alternative would be, it goes without saying, a slow absorption of individual Jewish converts, one by one, into the Gentile majority.

We reply: admission by slow absorption would never suffice to provoke the "resurrection of the dead". Does not the phrase suggest a sudden, highly dramatic event, a collective event?

The Jewish mentality is collective. It was shared by St. Paul, trained as he had been under Gamaliel. God has always treated the Jewish people collectively; the Exile was collective, the Holocaust was collective, the return to the Holy Land was collective; why should not its admission to the faith be collective?

Turning to the exegesis of history, the Ratisbonnes were convinced that the process of the collective admission of the Jews had already been initiated.

Let us address ourselves to their thesis.

XIII. THE IDENTITY OF POST-CHRISTIC JEWRY IN THE AGE OF APOSTASY

Theodor Ratisbonne, son of a rich Alsatian Jewish banker, entered the Catholic Church in 1827, after long conversations with the pious Madame Humann and the philosopher, Bautain. He was ordained in 1830. As usual, the family opposed his conversion. Alphonse, his younger brother, was particularly indignant. His resistance was overcome by the Blessed Virgin herself, who appeared to the young man while he was idling away his time waiting for a friend in the church of San Andrea delle Fratte in Rome. The apparition of Our Lady, one of the most outstanding religious events of the nineteenth century, took place on January 20, 1842. Soon Alphonse joined his brother in the priesthood.

"What touched me most," commented Theodor, "was the light thrown on the great question of the return of the Jews. The visible intervention of the Blessed Virgin in the event at Rome, seemed to me a presage of the imminent accomplishment of the promises concerning this people. The thought which dominated me from the very beginning of my vocation took possession also of my brother from the hour of the miracle."[1]

Under the illumination of a Marian grace of extraordinary intensity, Theodor developed a theory of the imminence of the accession of Jewry to the faith. It took the form of a Christian interpretation of modern Jewish history, stopping short of Zionism, since the Ratisbonnes died before Herzl launched his movement.

For Ratisbonne, as for Jewish historians in general, the modern period in Jewish life had been initiated by the French Revolution. The Act of Civil Emancipation brought to an end the static phase which had begun with the destruction of the second Temple and initiated a phase of transition, the end of which would be the entry *en masse* into the Church of post-Christic Jewry.

Ratisbonne has been criticized for describing the intervening history of Jewry as static. It is objected that it displays a great deal of change and creativity. There is the golden age of Hebrew literature in Spain, the mysticism of Luria, the Hassidic movement attached to the name of the Baal Shem Tov.

The objection fails to grasp the particular light under which Ratisbonne contemplated Jewish history. His point of view was theological. It focused on the status of post-Christic Jewry, fixed in the cadre of an insurmountable exile. Pseudo-Messiahs arose, only to collapse miserably. Gershom Scholem recounts the story of the last great pretender, Sabbatai Zevi (1562-1676), in a thousand pages of incomparable erudition. His conclusion is that Jewish pseudo-Messiahs were a uniformly disappointing lot.

Ratisbonne detailed the various consequences of Civil Emancipation, rapid acculturation to Gentile life, the decline of Orthodoxy, religious reform, the aggravation of anti-Semitism, and a wave of conversions to Christianity. Their number has been estimated at about two hundred thousand for the past century, not, of course, exclusively to the Catholic Church. Amongst them we find eminent spiritual personalities, to mention, for example, the venerable Father Libermann, founder of a congregation for missionary work in Africa; Herman Cohen, a famous pianist in his day who became a Carmelite friar and who is now being proposed for canonization; the Ratisbonne brothers themselves; and the Lémann brothers. The line continues into our century in names such as Raissa Maritain, Max Jacob, Gustave Mahler, René Schob, Karl Stern, David Goldstein, Rosa Levy, Eugene Zolli, Chief Rabbi of Rome. Henri Bergson stopped short of baptism so as not to appear to have deserted his people in face of the Nazi danger. Edith Stein, disciple and secretary of the philosopher Husserl, became a Carmelite nun, was tracked down by the Gestapo, ordered out of her convent and sent to Auschwitz, where she died in the company of her fellow-Jews. With her died her sister, Rose. The Discalced Carmelites promoted the cause of her canonization. On his visit to Auschwitz, Pope John Paul II recalled the memory of Edith Stein. He beatified her on May 1, 1987.

Struck by the coincidence of the two phenomena, the apostasy of the Gentiles, to which the French Revolution had given such violent expression, and the rapid advance of the Jew in European society, Theodor Ratisbonne announced that the prophecies, notably those of St. Paul, were in the process of being accomplished.

"The present time," he declared, "is evidently a transition between the state of immobility of the last eighteen centuries and a future regeneration which can only be the work of the Gospel. The civil and political emancipation of the Jews is but a prelude to a liberation of a higher order. Under the ruins of the Synagogue are being accumulated the materials for a new edifice, which has already begun to grow and though hardly issued from the earth, is already visible to all."[2]

Ratisbonne's merit lay in his determination of the transitional character of Jewish identity in the modern period. He underrated the difficulties that lay in store for the Jew and overrated the value of his institute; but there is no good reason for doubting the authenticity of his charism. It was manifestly inspired by the Blessed Virgin, it is in conformity with Church doctrine, and both brothers were entirely submissive to Church authority. The Ratisbonnes were, indeed, friends of the reigning popes. That Theodor's charism was the work of the Holy Spirit is brought out by its universality. The same kerygma reappears in the thought of the Lémann brothers. It is echoed in part by Newman and, from their side, by the most distinguished Jews of our time. Moses Hess, Theodor Herzl, Bialik, Jabotinsky, to mention a few, are all visionaries of a new future for the Jewish people. Bialik was convinced that our age was a period of transition from Orthodoxy through a phase of materialism to a spiritual renascence of the Jewish people which he could not define. One can talk safely of a renewal of the prophetic spirit in modern Jewry. Religious Zionists commonly view the return of Jews to the Holy Land as the initial stage of their complete redemption, the nature of which remains for them obscure. Israel Eldad saw in the capture of Jerusalem by the Israeli army in 1967 the precondition for the spiritual revival of the Jewish people.

The centrality of apostasy was the hilltop from which Christopher Dawson, in the name of the Gentiles, surveyed the state of the Christian religion in modern Europe. Barbara Ward extended his vision deep into the contemporary scene.

The kerygma of the Ratisbonnes implied a prophetical exegesis of biblical prophecies. "If," wrote Theodor, "one does not desire to interrogate the Gospel in order to understand this sad mystery, let him read the prophets of Israel. We cite only Moses and Daniel (cf. Lv. 26, Dn. 9:26)." He went on to conclude his argument with a passage vibrant with messianic excitement: "The time has come to have mercy on her, the hour has struck."

The fate of Theodor's message was a classical one. It ended up by being discredited by his own congregation. Actually, the latter has become disobedient to the Church, for Vatican Council II urged all religious institutes to return to the charism of their founders (*Perfectae Caritatis*, 2b).

Why was the doctrine of the Ratisbonnes so poorly received in ecclesiastical circles?

The charism of the Ratisbonnes required a response in faith to their kerygma, to which the intellectual climate in the Church was at that time unfavorable. For this the neo-scholastic movement was in part responsible, not that we mean to imply any criticism of St. Thomas himself. But it remains that seminarians were not taught the theology of history nor how to read the signs of the times. The sin was one of omission, not of commission. Compared with the atmosphere in the Jewish world, there was a distinct lack of the spirit of prophecy. The field was thus left clear by Catholic theologians only to be rapidly dominated by anti-Christian substitutes, especially those of Hegel and Marx. Their philosophies seemed to have met a genuinely felt need of the age, characterized as it was by a renewed interest in history. The very application of scientific methods to history led to a quest for meaning. It was to this need that Catholic theology failed to respond, with disastrous consequences for the Church in Europe.

Though the same causes of opposition to Ratisbonne's charism continue to exist, a new atmosphere has come into being in the post-conciliar Church, the creation of John XXIII and Vatican Council II. Its very presence measures the extent of the ground that had to be covered before the kerygma of Ratisbonne could find its natural setting in the ensemble of Christian thought. Today, the notions of charism, kerygma, prophecy are in the air. The official Church has imposed on Catholics the obligation of reading the signs of the times. The harvest may not yet be abundant, but the Spirit is at work.

The Doctrine of the Lémanns

The Lémanns, like the Ratisbonnes, were Catholic priests of Jewish origin. Both were deeply concerned with the Jewish problem as they perceived it in the light of their new faith. Their approach was systematic.

"We are dealing," began Joseph Lémann, "with a philosophy of history, which is inspired by the Bible and by events."

"It traces, in effect, and formulates the great lines of the simultaneous work of God and man…a sort of fifth Gospel!"

"All these who have devoted themselves to the philosophy of history, from St. Augustine to the Comte de Maistre, have spoken of cycles. As the cycles of truth and error extend, an increasing number of continents and of nations are englobed, each bringing its nuances and its passions, and so history became more and more universal."[3]

Lémann's words may be true of the progressive increase of the material of history, of historiography, but from the point of view of the meaning of history, the plan of salvation takes a linear course.

Joseph Lémann then turned his attention to the contemporary scene: "One must be deaf not to hear the cracking of the branches. Great God! What a noise! The cracking of France, the breaking off of Italy, the tearing out of Austria and the other nations. These are the branches of the Gentiles, which in turn are menaced by the shears."[4]

As for the Jewish scene, Joseph Lémann understood that the French Revolution had precipitated Jews into a society in a state of spiritual and moral decomposition. By imitating the Gentiles, they were rendering themselves inapt to fulfill the sublime designs of God. Nevertheless, emancipation had launched them on a slow if perilous voyage from incredulity to faith. Their entry into the Church would be the culminating point of their advance in other spheres, social, cultural, and financial.

"The conversion of the Jew," concluded Lémann, "has therefore begun, but their conversion, which resembles the first drops of rain falling scatteredly from a cloud, will it continue to exhibit this slow intermittent character, or, at a moment known only to God, will it turn into an immense benediction, which will astonish and rejoice the world?"[5] One theologian saw no more in Lémann's prophetic enthusiasm than an example of lyrical sentiment.

To sum up the thought of the Lémanns, the steady elevation of Jewish status, especially since the French Revolution, though interrupted and checked by antagonistic forces from within and without, was itself the process of the collective accession of the Jewish people to the Christian faith.

Predecessors

Joseph Lémann discovered the existence of an entire current of religious literature in France and Italy during the seventeenth and eighteenth centuries, dealing with the admission of Jewry to the Church.

The current had been set in motion by the disastrous blow inflicted on Christian unity by the Protestant reformers.

"The first to express fear," wrote Lémann, "at the state of apostasy, already well advanced at the time they lived and who allowed their lips or their pen to give voice to the painful previsions, whether God was not preparing to cut off certain corrupted nations, were Bossuet and Fénélon."

Bossuet cried out in alarm: "Listen, listen, O Christian, read your destiny in that of the Jews, read and listen to your heart... Should we not be terrified at the awful vengeance which overtook the Jews, since St. Paul warns us in the name of God, that our ingratitude would attract a similar punishment upon us."

Fénélon clamored in turn: "If God, terrible in his counsels towards the children of men, did not even spare the natural branches of the cultivated olive tree, how dare we hope that he will spare us, the wild branches, mere grafts, branches, dead and incapable of bearing fruit? What future has the faith amongst peoples corrupted down to the root? Cowardly and unworthy Christians, through you Christianity is rendered vile and unrecognizable: by you, the name of God is blasphemed amongst the Gentiles. Sin abounds, charity has grown cold, darkness deepens, the mystery of iniquity takes shape. ...The torch of the Gospel which should make the tour of the universe, touches the end of its course; the day of ruin approaches and the times hasten their pace."

"Both," continued Lémann, "in their sadness and anxiety, see a source of help for the Church of God: they aspire for the admission to the faith of Israel."

Bossuet went on to say, in speaking of the remnant of Israel: "The Lord will turn to them; he will wipe out their sins, and render to them the understanding of prophecies which they lost for so long a time…thus the Jews will return one day and they will return never to err again."

Lémann names the principal writers who contributed to revive interest in the ultimate destiny of Jewry: Duguet the Oratorian, Rondet, Deschamps, d'Houbigan and Belet.

"All these works," he says in *résumé,* "understand as a sign, as well as cause of the recall of the Jews, the blasphemy proffered against God and his Christ amongst the Nations. The Gentility of the Nations were called because of the blindness and ingratitude of the Jews. The Jews will be recalled because of the apostasy and the ingratitude, fomented amongst the Nations. And all these works proclaim: Indubitably, we have come to that pass."[6]

Lémann observed that chapters nine to eleven of the Epistle to the Romans became the object of fresh attention in the eighteenth century. The writers he mentioned were unanimous in their view that the wild, ingrafted branches of the Gentiles of Europe were being shaken by a terrible tempest, whereas the natural branches, the Israelites, were preparing to rise towards the olive tree and reoccupy their place. They dropped the polemical approach to Jews in favor of a kerygmatic one, announcing the forthcoming admission of the Jews to be a source of incalculable consolation for the Church and for the Gentiles themselves. As far back as 1643, one author appealed for a new attitude toward Jews, taking an example from the conduct of Joseph towards his brothers. Three centuries later, Pope John XXIII echoed these sentiments when he welcomed a group of representative Jews with the cordial words: "I am Joseph your brother."

The Constellation of Signs

Lémann was aware that the top two nuclear signs of the times, the apostasy of the Gentiles and the elevation of the Jewish status, were not taking place in a vacuum. They were set in a constellation of eschatological tendencies, of which Lémann singled out three for special mention.

"The first," he wrote, "is the rapid movement which carries all beings, peoples and things, towards a mysterious and irresistible end."

"The next important fact is the encounter of all peoples at the same time."

"The third important fact is the rising tide of persecution against Christians, lamentable, savage and perfidious."

Jean Guitton expressed a similar sentiment: "Increasing numbers have the impression that humanity is heading for a crisis, a final period, which will not only be the end of a period, but the end of all time."[7]

The force of Lémann's observations have grown, if anything, since he made them in 1912. The rate of historical change has become more vertiginous, the internationalization of communications more spectacular, the spread of militant atheism more triumphant. The modern world has seen a formidable series of anti-Christs, Marx, Lenin, Mao, Hitler, to confront whom the Church has produced a series of remarkable popes. The very configuration of world politics, the primary division into two blocks, crudely reflects the transcendental struggle between Michael and the Dragon. The destruction of Hiroshima and Nagasaki and the present fearful accumulation of nuclear bombs, poised to strike at any moment, underscore with lines of fire the Christian belief in a sudden, violent end to human history.

From the foregoing it should not be difficult to classify the signs of the present times into groups: positive, negative, ambiguous and neutral. Political Zionism will remain an ambiguous sign until the admission of the Jews has occurred.

Several popes have deplored the spread of atheism: Pius X in the first encyclical of his reign; Pius XI in *Miserentissimus Redemptor*; Benedict XV at the outbreak of the first World War.

Pope John Paul II has replied to the essential challenge of our time. In his first encyclical, *Redemptor Hominis*, he explains that the world has passed into a new phase of its history; one in which it is called upon to prepare itself for the Second Coming of the Lord. He furnishes the Christian with an eschatological framework of reference, which he asks to be henceforth applied to all human situations.

Redemptor Hominis is evidence to what extent the self-consciousness of the Church has matured since the first encyclical of Pius X. The eschatological perspective of John Paul II contrasts with the incarnational one which until now has prevailed in the Christian world.

From the central vision of John Paul II flows a renewed self-confidence, a mysterious serenity of which the pope himself has become the fountainhead. He has unveiled the secret of his far-reaching influence. He has situated the Church in the mighty flood of world history.

Our Lady, in her multiple apparitions during the last hundred or so years, brought each time a message of mingled hope and warning, always in relation to the events of the day, which is to say that she assumed the role of a prophet. Her apparition to Alphonse Ratisbonne takes on its full significance when placed against the background of the ensemble of her interventions.

The Theological Prophetism of Cardinal Newman

Newman had an intense theological vision of history. "It is not unprofitable," he warned in his book *Discussions and Arguments,* "to bear in mind that we are still under what may be called a miraculous system. I do not mean to maintain that literal miracles are taking place every day, but that our present state is a portion of a providential course, which began in miracle and at least, at the end of the world, will end in miracle."[8]

Newman practiced the reading of the signs of the times: "I make my anticipations according to the signs of the times."[9]

What is more, he was conscious of the value of an eschatological vision of history in the present circumstances: "I must think that the vision of anti-Christ as a supernatural power to come, is a great providential gain, as being a counterpoise to the evil tendencies of the age."[10]

Newman admitted the possibility of a prophetical exegesis of Dt. 28 and applied the chapter to the situation of post-Christic Jewry.

For what regards the Gentiles, he indicted the French Revolution in the following passage: "In the capital of that powerful and cultivated nation, there took place, as we well know, within the last fifty years, an open apostasy from Chrisitanity."

About the religious health of Europe, Newman declares energetically: "You may persist in calling Europe Catholic, though it is not."

He analyzes the state of the faith in Europe in a splendid but disturbing passage: "Is there no reason to fear that some Apostasy is gradually gathering, hastening on in this very day? For is there not at the very time, a special effort made almost all over the world, that is every here and there, more or less in sight or out of sight, in this or that place, but most visibly or formidably in its most civilized and powerful parts, an effort to be without Religion? Surely there is at this day a confederacy of evil, marshalling its hosts from all parts of the world, organizing itself, taking its measures, enclosing the Church as in a net, preparing the way for a general Apostasy from it."[11]

What is unique about the religious crisis is that Newman   ;

no remedy for it. His hero, Charles Redman, in *Loss and Gain,* utters the sentiment: "I cannot see how a nation like England, which has lost its faith, ever can recover it." Bossuet was anguished by a similar sentiment, which since Hegel and Nietzsche has been known as "the death of God". Indeed, God has died in the soul of the apostate Gentile. Apologetical arguments have become inefficacious, since a dead man does not listen. He has to be resurrected. Against this moment, God has held the Jews in reserve, to use the brilliant phrase of Duguet.

Though Newman did not treat of modem Jewry at any length, he remarked that "to rebuild the Temple, then, was to reestablish the Jews, as Jews, in their own land, an event, which, if prophecy is sure, never is to be".[12] The prevision is interesting in the light of the transitional character of the identity of the contemporary Jew. Herzl, in fact, was an atheist. He foresaw a state for Jews, not a Jewish state, in the theological sense of the term. It seems that the distinction escaped Augustin Lémann, who erred in believing that Zionism would never succeed in establishing a state.

The Abbé Arminjon

The Abbé Arminjon was familiar with the thought of the Lémanns. He is now known to have influenced St. Thérèse of Lisieux through his book, *End of the Present World.* What St. Thérèse read therein should explain her precipitate entry at the early age of fifteen into the silence of the Carmelite cloister, where she offered herself up as a holocaust of divine love. The following pages must have excited her thirst for immolation.

"A superficial study of the signs of the present time, the menacing symptoms of our political situation and of our revolutions, the continual growth of impiety corresponding to our progress in civilization and discoveries in the material order, lead one to foresee the proximity of the Man of Sin and the days of desolation which Jesus predicted for us."[13]

"If we do not succeed in opposing these excesses of evil...if the defection continues its course, one can predict that this war against God will inevitably lead to a total and consummate apostasy. "[14]

Monsignor Eugene Kevane, in his fine work *The Lord of History,* after expounding the teaching of John Henry Newman, describes Modernity "as a great revolt against God and very possibly as the Great Apostasy".[15]

XIV. THE MEANING OF HISTORY

One of the reasons why the doctrine of Ratisbonne did not obtain a fair hearing among theologians was because of its implicit theology of history and correlative theological prophetism, neglected in the manuals of the time.

"We are poor in the theology of history," comments P.L. Hug.[1] C.A. Rijk expressed the opinion "that we suffer from a total absence in the Church of a real theology of Israel, one which would be faithful to the biblical vision of things". He went on: "The manuals of theology deal with the Old Testament, but never with Judaism after the coming of Christ," and again, "When one considers the history of Christianity until the twentieth century and its attitude to Judaism one has the feeling that it was impossible for it to develop a true theology of Judaism, by which I mean a genuine religious reflection on the action of God by and through the Jewish People." As for the residual value of the Old Testament, Rijk confesses: "Specialists have not succeeded in making clear the significance of its message for Christians."

Jacques Maritain recognized the lack of a "wisdom of history" in his Thomist synthesis: "In our opinion, there is an entire field to be reconquered from Hegel and claimed by Christian wisdom. Will Thomist thought, one day, stimulated by the spirit of Augustine, enrich itself by his conjectures on the subject of the exegesis of history, so essential for reflection on culture? It would seem necessary to rewrite the *Discourse on Universal History* and a more modern development of the *City of God* would render service." *(Degrès du Savoir,* p. 609)

The Christian clergy is, by and large, reluctant to admit its ignorance in the field mapped out by Maritain. In face-to-face contact with the contemporary Jewish scene, the clergy's attitude is, at best, one of puzzled silence, or of embarrassed charity. Many escape from their embarrassment into platitudinous generalities,

145

or plunge into an imprudent and fanatical proselytism. In compensation for its feelings of frustration, the clergy often exhibits a great force of negation, hesitant to affirm but prompt to deny. A basic feeling of uncertainty carries it, often enough, far beyond the modest positions adopted by the specialists.

Where the Jews are concerned, the clergy is on the defensive, afraid to concede anything to the Jew, for fear of undermining Christian doctrine. Its perception of Jewish identity is, to speak of the majority, confused, if not downright false. How many clergymen are not content to define the Jew as a member of the Jewish race, though they should know perfectly well that there is no such thing as a Jewish race.

What then, we ask, is the theology of history? It is that branch of theology which treats of the plan of salvation (cf. Eph. I: 314). The ambiguities that vitiate the thought of Teilhard de Chardin stem from his failure correctly to define the formal object of the treatise.

The plan of salvation is at the heart of divine providence. It embraces human action in all times, whereas the art of history aims at giving a continuous account of past human actions and events only.

The plan of salvation takes the form of a redemptive cycle in three principal phases: an alliance, the breaking of the alliance together with its inevitable consequences and reestablishment of the alliance. As the cycle unrolls itself in time, it divides history into epochs, each introduced by an epoch-making event. Division and sub-division become the source of the progressive intelligibility of history .[2]

Theological prophetism extends intelligibility to concrete situations. It is none other than the reading of the signs of the times. Without theological prophetism, the Christian exposes himself to the sardonic criticism of Hegel, who complained that Christian theology was unable to come to grips with actualities. Naturally, Hegel esteemed his own philosophy to be more successful than Christian theology in this respect. The intellectual triumphalism of Marxism lies in its pretension to penetrate contemporary situations by the aid of an intellectual system, dialectical materialism, and there encounter an intelligible structure, the class conflict. The devil used an analogous vision with which to tempt Jesus, taking him up to a very high mountain and showing him all the kingdoms of the world and their splendor (cf. Mt. 4:8).

A sign of the times is, in turn, any historical phenomenon, person, or event in its relation to the plan of salvation. The task of theological prophetism is to determine the content of the relation.

We have already dealt, briefly enough, with the redemptive cycle as it is encountered in the Bible. It was later employed by the Fathers of the Church to develop a negative theology of post-Christic Jewry, polemically biased and semantically naive. Its fossilized residue remained in tranquil possession of the Christian mind until challenged by Vatican Council II.

As Maritain perceived, the present position in the Church where the theology of history is concerned is not its entire absence, but the need to revise and extend it. But it is not St. Augustine only who can provide the stimulus for the updating of the Christian theology of history; it is the study of Zionism.[2a] Cardinal Newman will undoubtedly play a decisive role in the prosecution of this immense task. His influence in shaping the mind of the official Church has been growing steadily ever since his death, to judge from the contents of papal encyclicals touching on the relation of the Church to the modern world.

Jesus, at the beginning of his public ministry, took the scroll of the Law in his hands one Saturday morning in the synagogue, read a passage from the prophet Isaiah, then sat down and declared: "Today this Scripture passage is fulfilled in your hearing" (Lk. 4:21). On other occasions he admonished the crowd for not reading the signs of the times (cf. Mt. 16:3; Lk. 12:56-57).

The Jewish tragedy may be ascribed to the inability of the contemporaries of Jesus to read the signs of the times. They possessed the science of Holy Scripture, but book knowledge was insufficient. The hour called for a wisdom which could be attained only by responding to the kerygma of Jesus. Without faith, the bewildered crowds could do no more than exclaim: "Is not this Joseph's son?" (Lk. 4:22).

It is the word "today" that characterizes the propositions of theological prophetism. The Council Fathers spoke its language when they declared that "now as before" the Jews are beloved by God on account of the Fathers.

Exegetes have no more than an indirect control over the propositions of theological prophetism insofar as these are the application, or actualization, of biblical prophecies. Directly, they can neither demonstrate them to be true nor false. They are free to say, "We do not believe," or dismiss them with the remark that the text admits of a variety of interpretations.

The sources of faith, such as Scripture, Tradition, the ordinary teaching authority of the Church, cannot furnish more than motives of credibility to propositions bearing on actualities, on the "today" and "now". The passage from fact to sign is discontinuous. A kerygma calls for a personal option, an option of faith, it being granted that in the last resort the option must submit to ecclesiastical control.

Such was precisely the dilemma confronting the contemporaries of Jesus. They had many and divergent views about the Messiah, his nature, and his origin. Was Jesus the Messiah? Even his miracles were insufficient to generate conviction, for they, too, could be interpreted in different ways.

Only by an act of faith could the Jew break through to the universal affirmation: "You are the Christ, the Son of the Living God".

The post-Conciliar crisis had been brewing for some time before the Council began. The Council, by calling on the priesthood to relate to actuality, precipitated the crisis. It exposed the incapacity of many priests to relate *theologically* to actuality. The same lacuna was revealed in the attitude of the clergy to the Council itself. No theological justification was proposed for the holding of the Council. Its reforms were received as so many empirical adaptations to immediate needs. Here lies the root of the schism of Lefèbvre. In other words, the Council itself was a sign of the times, one of the greatest. It became a victim of the general incapacity to read the signs of the times.

Flannery contrasted the exegesis of texts and the exegesis of events: "Unlike doctrinal theology," he wrote, "which is concerned with the internal order of revealed truths, historical theology follows these truths in the successive stages of their understanding, in their existential unfolding in history. Hence it must constantly rejudge former assumptions by present realities; it must pay close attention to historical developments and exegetical advances. Though it always remains intimately joined with doctrinal theology, its necessary counterpart, and pursues its study according to the light of reason under the light of faith, as does all theology, it must be more empirically orientated, both as to the subjects it treats and the manner in which it treats them. Israel is one of the subjects. Recent developments in Palestine will have a decisive influence on my interpretations."[3]

Another ecclesiastical writer, writing about twenty years before Flannery, gave expression to the older mentality: "What remedy can we suggest to restore peace in Palestine? None other than the departure of the Jews."[4]

Professor Skysgaard, a Protestant observer at Vatican Council II, called attention to the need for a concrete and historical theology.

Pope Paul VI welcomed the suggestion and took the initiative in setting up the Ecumenical Institute at Tantur, near Bethlehem, though to date its contribution to the development of a "concrete and historical theology" has not taken any clear-cut form. Indeed, David Jaeger of the Institute appeared to reject the very possibility of a Christian reading of the signs of the times, especially in his dialogue with Zionists.[5]

As we have said, the maturation of the mind of the official Church is reflected in the first encyclical of John Paul II; in it we read: "This eschatological scene has always to be applied to the history of man, always to be taken as a measure of human actions, as the essential framework of an examination of conscience for each and for everyone." It transpires then that the Council was not a purely pastoral Council. Far from it! It was an eschatological sign of the highest order. Obedient to the instruction of John Paul II, we intend applying the "eschatological scene" to Modern Zionism.

We recommend the reading of the encyclical to Professor de Epalza and those like him, for whom "the Palestinian problem is eminently a political problem".[6]

Theology of History in Jewish Literature

The redemptive cycle has dominated the self-evaluation by Jews of their unique if painful destiny.

The author of the book of the Apocalypse of Baruch, written shortly after the fall of Jerusalem, AD 70, held that God had scattered his people among the Gentiles, because of the sins of the remaining two tribes.

In the Fourth Book of Ezra, a composite work dating from about 120 AD, the writer describes in pathetic terms how he lay on his bed preoccupied by the mystery of the desolation of his country and the sufferings of his people. How could one, he asked himself, attribute them to the sins of the Jews when the pagans, who were even greater sinners, enjoyed wealth, prosperity, and power?

Josephus repeatedly affirms that the destruction of Jerusalem was a divine punishment for national sin.

The Talmud recounts the following tale about Rabbi Jose: "I heard a divine voice cooing like a dove and saying: *Woe to the children on account of whose sins I destroyed my house and burnt my temple and exiled them among the nations of the world.*"[7]

The same sentiment is found in the Targum to Lamentations, which dates from about 400 AD: "Jerusalem sinned a great sin, therefore has she become a wanderer." The author compares the Exile with the expulsion of Adam and Eve from the Garden of Eden.

The Targum to the Song of Songs, from about 200 AD, laments: "I, God, have already removed my Presence from your midst; how then can I return, seeing you have done evil things?"

We have mentioned the sublime Yehudah Halevi. In his celebrated *Kitab Al Khazari*, he probes the mystery of the Exile: it is the consequence of sin. All the same, the very state of Exile demonstrates that Jewry is the Elect People. Redemption will come when the people fulfills its vocation, the precondition of which has to be their return to the Holy Land. On the redemption of the Jews will depend, in turn, the redemption of mankind. Halevi timidly proposed to identify Jewry with the Suffering Servant of Yahve, only to correct himself by reflecting that perhaps after all it suffers for its own sins.

Nahman Krohmal (1785-1840) opposed the view of Hegel that a people can only shine once in history. He taught that Jewish history is governed, under providence, by recurring cycles of growth, development, and decline. Krohmal applied his cycles to Jewish history in an interesting way, ceasing with the expulsion of the Jews from Spain. He left it to be inferred that a phase of renewal could be expected for the future, a thought from which Zionism drew inspiration. The weakness of Krohmal as a theologian of Jewish history is that his cycles are not, strictly speaking, theological ones. They are conceived on the analogy of the cycle of nature, growth, maturation, decay.

Hruby was prepared to write that the Jewish People is punished by God in his own way. After the Holocaust, the question stands, in stark, monumental grandeur: what could have been the sin that brought on a punishment of such infinite proportions? The traditional answer of the rabbis, who attribute the punishment of the Exile to the sin of gratuitous enmity between Jews prior to the fall of Jerusalem, is no more adequate. On the Day of Remembrance for the victims of the Holocaust, it is never invoked. Rabbis must surely be conscious of the disproportion between their traditional explanation and the death of six million Jews two thousand years later. Having abandoned an unconvincing stance, they find themselves in the painful position of having no consolation, no light to offer a profoundly distressed nation.

XV. THE RETURN: MODERN ZIONISM

Flannery announced a fundamental biblical theme when he said that the history of Israel is a pattern of exiles and dispersions. Why should he not have added "and returns"?

The redemptive cycle closes with a return, spiritual and physical.

The Old Testament strikes the note of return as if on a giant gong. The motif is found in Amos (9:14-15), Isaiah (11:11-12), Ezekiel (28:25-26), Jeremiah (31:8-9), the Psalms (106:43-48), Chronicles (1 Chr. 16:35), Deuteronomy (30:2-3), Sirah (30:10), Maccabees (2 Mc. 1:27).

In Lk. 21:24, Jesus predicted, implicitly, the return to the Holy Land of the dispersed Jews and the reestablishment of their rule over Jerusalem. A. Heschel, famous Jewish theologian, surprisingly cited Lk. 21:24 in the same sense.

From Deuteronomy, it would seem that God awaits an act of national repentance before the material return of the people to their ancient homeland. In a Christian perspective, that would mean that the first Zionists should have been a group of repentant Israelite Christians making what we call the ideal return. We invoke the memory of Alphonse Ratisbonne as an example of Ideal Zionism. He founded a convent in Jerusalem thirty years before the first pioneers set up a Zionist colony. He died a saintly death and was buried in Ain-Karem, near Jerusalem.

It is a comment on the degree to which the historical identity of the Jewish converts has been shattered to have to admit that Ideal Zionism did not stand the least hope of materializing. Whatever the personal merits of the converts might have been, and at times they were great, most of them had no appreciation of their providential obligations. Notwithstanding, their faith may have furnished the act of repentance required by Deuteronomy.

God consequently moved the entire post-Christic Jewry to a spiritual and material return. But God's action is received according to the capacity of the receiver. The majority did not respond. Absorbed in careerism, atheism, socialism, communism, they drifted ever farther away from obedience to the divine intentions. The great prophetic voice of Moses Hess warned that they would die because they did not belong to the future; they went on their way, unheedingly.

Modern Zionism answered the call to return to the Holy Land, again, in diverse ways.

The Spiritual Zionism of Bialik approaches our conception of Ideal Zionism. In his programmatic speech, delivered at the opening of the Hebrew University on Mount Scopus in 1923, Bialik proclaimed: "We have come here to seek neither riches nor power." He continued: "Following the decree of Cyrus, a few tens of thousands of Babylonian exiles rejoined this broad but poor land, to form a small, insignificant community. Some hundreds of years had not passed, when in it arose an Israelite, son of a Jewish carpenter, who brought the message of redemption to the pagan world and prepared the way for the messianic age.

"Two thousand years have passed since then, and we are witnesses that not all the idols have disappeared from the earth. In the place of the old idols new ones have arisen, no better than their predecessors. Now comes the Balfour Declaration! Israel gathers in its land for the third time. Why should not the wonder take place this time also?

"Who knows whether from behind the walls of its Seminaries in the last days a teaching may not be proclaimed, conscious of its responsibilities for the destiny of mankind as a whole and ready to spread to all nations. Indeed, it is not for nothing that the hand of God has held this people suspended over Sheol, in the anguish of the fear of destruction, for thousands of years, only to restore it to its home for the third time.

"The Book of Chronicles is the last book of the Old Testament, but not the last book of Israel's history. To its two parts a third will be added, perhaps longer and more important than its predecessors. That book begins with Adam, Seth and Noah, and ends with the Declaration of Cyrus, which prepared, five hundred years later, the gospel of redemption for the idolators of antiquity. Without a doubt, the third part will begin with the Balfour Declaration and end in a new gospel, the gospel of redemption for mankind."

Simon Halkine describes the search for a new faith among the Hebrew writers of our time: "(Hebrew) Literature meditates humbly on the final consequences of the Jewish renaissance and on the sublimity of the human destiny implied, even though obscurely, in this renaissance. But it remains uncertain when it comes to formulating the new relation between the Jew and the last ends, between the destiny of man in the world, of man's role in the cosmos, and God." Heschel esteemed that it would be presumptuous even to try.

Halkine went on: "One is struck by the comfort that Hebrew poets always draw from an infinite faith in the following idea: 'Israel is bruised, Israel bleeds, so that the world may learn no more to wound, learn to put a stop to bloodshed and the infliction of pain.'

"The idea of mission which Reform Judaism preached in a manner somewhat hollow and self conscious secretly nourishes a good part of Hebrew poetry, the most inspired and the richest in promise, reflecting on the sorrow of Jews and trying to discover an explanation. Naturally it does not offer an explicit doctrine.

"The courageous abstraction, the vigorous exposition of a dogmatic doctrine frightens the Hebrew imagination, precisely because the intensity of the new life borders on a religiosity which escapes formulation.

"A day will come when one will recognize in a considerable part of Hebrew literature a new, multiple and modem enunciation on the theme of redemption.

"Only when all these conditions are united will the Jewish community be able, in time, to assume the function for which it appears to be well suited, to be the guide of other peoples."[1]

One asks, with due respect, whether Halkine was not making himself preposterous by proposing for the Jewish people the vocation of the Catholic Church. Jews are today one-half percent of the world population, a percentage which shrinks as the world population expands and Jewish families restrict their natality. Jewish society is eroded by skepticism, materialism, eroticism. Its moral standing has been undermined by the prolonged Jewish-

Arab conflict. According to Halkine it possesses no new doctrine, no new spiritual energy.

Yet we do not deny that the nostalgic belief in a universal mission is justified. The whole question is: how can it be implemented?

The Prophetic Zionism of Moses Hess (1812-1875) astounds by the precision of its forecasts. In his classic of Modem Zionism, *Rome and Jerusalem,* published as far back as 1862, Hess situated the future return of the Jews to the Holy Land in an eschatological framework which vividly recalls *Redemptor Hominis.*

"We are at the eve of the Sabbath of History," announced Hess. "It (the messianic era) is the era in which the Jewish nation and all historic peoples will rise again to new life, the time of the 'resurrection of the dead', of the 'return to the Lord', of 'the new Jerusalem'.

"The hard covering that surrounds the hearts of our cultured Jews will be shattered only by a blow from without, one that world events are preparing and which will probably fall in the near future."

Hess made it clear that the destruction of European Jewry would be the work of German anti-Semites.

Furthermore, Hess predicted the return of the Jews to the Holy Land following the tragedy, and the erection of a state. "After the last catastrophe, the approach of which is attested by unmistakable signs of the times, the Jewish people will receive its full rights as a nation and find its legitimate place in world history.

"It is to be well understood that we speak of a Jewish settlement in the Orient. We do not mean to imply a total emigration of Occidental Jews to Palestine. Even after the establishment of a Jewish State, the majority of the Jews, who live at present in the civilized Occidental countries, will undoubtedly remain where they are."

Then these preliminary conditions have been established; "the rigid forms of Orthodoxy, the existence of which was justified before the century of rebirth, will naturally, through the productive power of the national idea and the historical cult, relax and become fertile. It is only with the national rebirth that the religious genius of the Jews will again be reinspired with the prophetic spirit.

"Reformers, rabbinists and Chassidim will disappear from

Jewish history after the crisis has passed."

What will replace Orthodox Judaism?

Moses Hess answered with outstanding frankness: "The cult which we will one day introduce in the new Jerusalem can and must, for the present, remain an open question."

The fate of Moses Hess was again that of the prophets. His flaming intuitions were ignored and when the catastrophe occurred, it came as a ghastly surprise to the majority of Jews. What is astonishing is that Hess was famous as one of the founders of Modern Zionism!

Religious Judaism reacted in various ways to Zionism: favorable, ambivalent, rejectionist. The Mizrachi current has always collaborated with Political Zionism; Agudat Yisrael has been ambivalent; the Neturei Karta rejectionist, to the point of refusing to acknowledge the authority of the State of Israel.

Evidently, if Moses Hess was right, Religious Zionism has no future. Gershon Scholem was of the same opinion.[2] "I think," he esteemed, "that Judaism is in for changes of form. Certain historical forms are not destined to survive forever, and I strongly doubt whether the traditional Jewish structures are going to survive in their present form, although it is certainly desirable that something should, and reasonable to assume that something will remain.

"If you ask me today, whether in the light of all that has happened in the last fifty years, I believe that the Jewish future lies in the traditional Orthodox framework, my answer is no."

On the other hand, Scholem was equally sure that Secular Zionism is not destined to inherit the future: "I do not think that Zionism's Secular vision is the ultimate vision, the last word."

What is Scholem's final word on the Israeli experiment?

As he came to understand it, after fifty years of personal experience, the actual situation of Jewish society in the State of Israel is one of a dialectic transition, the opposing poles of the dialectic being Orthodox Judaism and Secular Zionism. The future belongs to neither; rather, it belongs to an original synthesis of both, to be engendered by a messianic crisis.

"Can this entry into history take place," he asks anxiously, "without leading to the abyss of a messianic crisis? Even if, at present, this crisis appears to have been virtually forestalled, it remains the question which the Jew of today poses to himself for the present and the future, after a past so grandiose and intimidating."[3]

What is peculiar to Scholem is that he appears to reject the need for a new institutionalized community, in which case he would be in disagreement with Bialik and Buber.

The Political Zionism of Theodor Herzl (1860-1904) is one among many forms of Zionism. The Dreyfus Affair aroused in Herzl a presentiment of disaster looming ahead for European Jewry. He desired their immediate evacuation to a safe refuge. His state was conceived as a permanent shelter for distressed Jews, one which would break the vicious circle of their wandering. Originally, then, Herzl was not a Zionist, but a Territorialist, ready to consider any place suitable for his purposes. He settled for Palestine, after making contact with Jewish sentiment, especially that of Russian Jewry. The possibility of an Arab reaction to his project entirely escaped his notice.

The achievements of the young State of Israel in the last thirty years have been brilliant, but they have not been successes for Zionist ideology. J. Talmon, in his book *The Age of Violence,* expresses his considered opinion that Political Zionism can no more be looked upon as the solution of the Jewish problem. If anything, it was a reaction to the problem in terms of Jewish nationalism.

In effect, Herzlian Zionism desired ardently to provide a secure refuge for the Jews of Europe, threatened by anti-Semitism. Instead, the threat materialized, the six million died horribly, while the Zionist movement stood by, helpless to save the victims. After the storm had passed, a refuge was set up, but no one will pretend that it is secure.

Ben-Gurion's Zionism put the accent on the "ingathering of the exiles". In the thirty years or so of its existence, the State of Israel has only succeeded in assembling a representative number of Jews. American Zionists have publicly declared that they do not consider themselves under any moral obligation to emigrate to Israel, a declaration which dealt a mortal blow to the dream of Ben-Gurion. It is true that a number of desperate cases found a home in Israel in the years following the establishment of the State, but against the fact must be weighed the destruction of flourishing communities of Jews in Arab countries in the wake of the foundation of the new State.

Most Jews in distress have preferred to seek shelter elsewhere than in Israel. North African Jews streamed to France where the Jewish community has swelled to nearly seven hundred thousand. Most South African Jews who felt inclined to leave South Africa have preferred emigrating to an English-speaking country. Russian Jews continue to head for America. More disheartening for Zionism is the emigration of Jews from Israel. Between ten to twenty thousand of them "descend" each year from the national home to repopulate the Diaspora.

Leon Pinsker (1821-1891), one of the founders of Modern Zionism, expounded a psychological theory of anti-Semitism in his classic, *Auto-Emancipation,* according to which the existence of a Jewish State would bring about the normalization of relations between Jews and Gentiles. The author of these pages has spent thirty years in Israel, during which period Israelis have not ceased to lament that their State is not a normal one. Relations with Arabs have even grown progressively worse, though the peace treaty with Egypt may herald a brighter future. Professor Amnon Rubenstein sums up the history of the vain search for normalization in his book *From Herzl to Gush Emunim and Back.*[4]

Ahad Ha'am promised to halt assimilation in the Diaspora by his Cultural Centre. Statistics indicate that the rate of assimilation, to judge by the percentage of mixed marriages, has soared.

Religious Zionism aspired to found a "Torah State", that is, to place the State under rabbinical law. It has not succeeded. Professor G. Weiler wrote a book, *Jewish Theocracy,* to demonstrate that it could never succeed, that Judaism and Jewish political sovereignty are incompatible both in theory and in practice.

Coming to the universal spiritual mission of the State of Israel as a model society for others to imitate, W. Laqueur dryly observes that one speaks less and less about it as time goes on.

Maritain correctly evaluates Modern Zionism for Christians. He insists on the necessity for distinguishing between the bare fact of the return of Jews to the Holy Land after an interval of close to two thousand years and the particular forms that the return has taken. God has willed a representative body of Jews to return to their ancient homeland for purposes of his own. To these ends he has made use of many instruments, including Modern Zionism, however imperfect it might have been; are we not, all of us, imperfect instruments in the hand of God? Political Zionism did succeed in bringing back a limited number of Jews to the Holy Land; it did not solve the Jewish problem, in whatever way one may choose to formulate it.

"No more," explains Maritain, "than individualistic liberalism, or than the pluralist régime we have been discussing, can the Zionist State do away with the law of the desert and of the Galut... essential to the mystical body and the vocation of Israel in the state of separation."[5]

Flannery assessed Modem Zionism in the same way: "I have quoted," he wrote, "Fathers Faccio, Congar, Iglesias and Monsignor Journet, who have in one way or another, suggested that the State of Israel may be a strategem of divine providence to drive Israel into a blind alley of grace.

"With Congar, we may think that God wished to bring a representative cross-section of the Jewish people to the Holy Land in order to bring it face to face with the great question of the Messiah. Israel's restoration to the land of the promise, even though under secular auspices, may thus be a distant preparation for her final encounter with grace."[6]

Similar views have been expressed by many other Christians, to mention only, amongst the Catholics, Hruby, André Richard, Paul Claudel, Jean Toulat, Marcel Dubois, René Laurentin.

The Commission of French Bishops for Relations with Jews issued a remarkable document in which it invites Christians to ponder the possible significance of Zionism: "Both Christians and Jews find themselves called upon to answer the essential question, whether the assembling of dispersed Jews, though taking place under the compulsion of persecution and subject to the play of political forces, may not turn out finally, in spite of the many dramas, to be a means of God's justice for the Jewish people and, at the same time, for all peoples of the earth."[7]

In the perspective drawn by these words, the identity of the Israeli Jews could be defined as pre-Christian.

Was the very idea of a Jewish State in Palestine a moral one? It is notorious that Arabs do not think so. Whatever be the rights and wrongs on either side, the Christian should hold firmly to a transcendental point of view about the Judeo-Arab conflict. The return of the Jews to the Holy Land after two thousand years of exile is a sign of the times and a fulfilment of prophecy, the capture of Jerusalem in 1967 no less so, though no Christian interpretation of these events will ignore the legitimate rights of the Palestinians.

Zionist ideology may have collapsed, leaving the State of Israel without a goal but not without a function, for it assures the security of Israeli Jews, a providential absolute.

A. N. Whitehead, in his day, foresaw nothing but catastrophe for the Zionist experiment. As one who has lost his faith, he had deprived himself of the higher wisdom which the eschatological perspective offers to the Christian.

XVI. ALLEY OF GRACE

Why, it is objected, if it is true that Jewish society in Israel is being prepared for admission to the faith, should there be no palpable indications pointing in that direction? The objection overlooks the many-sided nature of the preparation for an act of faith, remote, immediate, intellectual, moral, positive and negative. It overlooks also its collective dimension.

The primary step is well under way, the rapid de-judaization of the Israeli Jew who no more accepts the Talmud as the inclusive norm for his life.

At this point, let us recall the severe setbacks suffered by Orthodoxy since the French Revolution. The emancipated Jew, by his very entry into Gentile society, was obliged to abandon Jewish customs. For instance, the ghetto Jew had been exempt from military service; the emancipated Jew was liable to be conscripted into Gentile armies, where he could not observe the dietary prescriptions proper to his religion. The emancipated Jew preferred to marry and divorce civilly, rather than appear before a rabbinical tribunal. The upshot of these and other changes in the lifestyle of the emancipated Jew was to restrict progressively the intervention of the rabbi to the four walls of the synagogue.

The First World War amputated the enormous reservoirs of Russian Jewry as a recruiting field for the rabbinate. The Second World War annihilated similar reservoirs in Poland.

The movement for the reform of the Jewish religion reduced Orthodox Judaism to a minority in the United States where, at present, dwell the greatest concentration of Jews, since the destruction of European Jewry. But even in Israel, Orthodoxy is a minority of thirty percent in confrontation with a hostile majority.

The consciousness of their diminished status had thrown Orthodox Jews on the defensive. They are more unyielding than ever in their interpretation of rabbinical law, helping in this way to render unbridgeable the gap between themselves and the secularists.

Admission to the faith would imply a decisive change in identity. Zionism deliberately set out to provoke such a change. The erstwhile ghetto-dweller has turned into a successful farmer and an equally successful soldier. The new model of the Jew is illustrated in the stream of autobiographies and biographies, to which we have already made passing allusion. From this abundant source we signal out for special praise the admirable autobiography by Yigal Allon, *My Father's House,* a monument of enduring literary value in which the author pays tribute to the Zionist pioneers who sought to rebuild not only a country and a state, but themselves.

Approaching the faith, a person is bound to make acquaintance with the Bible and with the history of the Jewish people. In this connection we encounter an extraordinary fact: Zionism has created a modern culture, based on the Bible. In the last analysis, it is in the Bible that the Zionist seeks for justification. So is explained the paradox of a Socialist government, secularist in mentality, imposing on school children an intensive biblical education. Young boys and girls enter for Bible competitions on a national and international level. There is a special competition for the Army. The international Bible competition arouses widespread popular interest. The prizes are distributed in the presence of the highest dignitaries of the State. Biblical themes spill over into Israeli music, ballet, theatre, literature, the plastic arts, the press, and, of course, politics. The Hebrew-speaking Israeli has the great advantage of being able to read the Old Testament in the original language itself, a phenomenal cultural event in our century. Zionism cultivates the love of the land. The desire for knowledge about its geography, history, fauna, flora, and so on are insatiable, to judge from the institutes that have been created to supply the information, and the books and studies that pour out on the subject in an endless stream. Archaeology, which in Israel is notably a biblical archeology, is the national hobby. The Israeli Jew digs into the past to discover his future. He uses archaeology in the search for his own identity.

The encounter with the New Testament begins in the classroom, where the Israeli child, having reached a suitable age, has a booklet on Christian origins placed before him.[1]

Jesus on the Israel Horizon

Professor Zweig has published the results of a sociological inquiry into the subject of Jesus in the State of Israel in a book, *Israel: The Sword and the Hap: the Mystique of Violence and the Mystique of Redemption.* (See Bibliography.) The subtitle expresses Zweig's view that two incompatible aspirations struggle for the domination of the soul of the Israel Jew: Political Zionism and Spiritual Zionism.

In the introduction of Zweig's book we read: "The strange transformation which the Jewish people are undergoing in their new land is inexplicable to Israelis themselves, in spite of their constant search for meaning. They feel that they are caught up in a whirlwind of mighty currents of history, stretching from ancient times to more recent upheavals in Europe, enacting a drama far transcending their own existence. In fact, they are caught between two mystiques, the mystique of violence and the mystique of redemption. Both of them have always flourished in the Holy Land, the land of innumerable holy and unholy wars. Both mystiques now wrestle tenaciously for the soul of Israel. Which mystique is going to win in the end? Does the answer depend on the peace settlement, or does the peace settlement depend on the answer?

"The contest between the mystique of violence and the mystique of redemption is the most fateful and crucial conflict on which the future of Israeli society depends. It is the conflict between the two conceptions of society, two visions, in fact two Israels. In a way, it expresses also the discord between Israel and the Diaspora.

"The new Israeli, who styles himself a robust and sturdy native, buoyant and self-confident, is, in spite of all his transformations, still a Jew, who did not escape the fate of his ancestry. The anti-Jewish hatred from which he wanted to escape is still about him, among the Arabs in his midst and the Arabs who surround him... The supreme ethico-religious vocation of his ancestry is still his inheritance and his responsibility, of which he cannot divest himself. True, he is a warrior now, not a warrior with a field marshal's baton in his knapsack, but rather one with the staff of a prophet in his hand."

Coming to Jesus, Zweig comments: "The figure of Jesus, the

Jew from Nazareth, looms large on the Israeli horizon, although not much is said about him openly and most Jews cautiously refrain from mentioning his name in public. Still he is very much in the mind of the Israeli Jews, more now than ever, and the awareness of his shadow in Israel is constantly growing."

"In Galilee, the most beautiful and inspiring part of Israel, he is the dominating figure. Every site of antiquity and every beauty spot in Galilee bears his footprints. He is still walking by the sea of Galilee (cf. Mt. 4:18), on the Sabbath day he enters the synagogue in Capernaum (cf. Mt. 4:12-17), in Tabgha, close to Capernaum, he performs the miracle of the loaves and the fishes (cf. Lk. 9:16-17). On the Mount of Beatitudes, which overlooks the waters of the lake, he utters his immortal Sermon on the Mount. Of course, Nazareth is the centre of his life and Jerusalem, the scene of his last ministry. Much of the charm and magnetism of the Holy Land is due, not only to echoes of the Old Testament, but also to echoes of Jesus' life. Being confronted with Jesus in this way is a new experience for the Jew. In the Diaspora, Jesus looked alien to the Jew, an outsider, an interloper. But in Israel, he is seen as the Jew from Nazareth, a native of this country, a Sabra,[2] with claims to the land as strong as any. He cannot be brushed aside as a foreign influence."

Amusingly, Zweig remarks that Jesus is a first-class tourist attraction. On a higher level, the Israeli Jew has to surrender to the evidence that, if his land and his Bible have a world-wide resonance, the responsible agents were not Orthodox Jews, but Jesus and his band of Sabra disciples.

Nor does it escape them that Jesus was also instrumental in facilitating their return to the Holy Land. Zionism counted Christian sympathizers away back from the nineteenth century onwards. In the establishment of the State, did they not receive support from Churchill, Roosevelt, Truman, not to mention the Christian states who voted in favor of partition and the subsequent admission of Israel to the United Nations?

When the Jews returned to Israel, they had to redefine their historical identity. To do so they had to link the Third Commonwealth with the Second Commonwealth of the Jews, which was the time of Jesus' ministry. The fateful question arises: were their forefathers right in rejecting Jesus? True, at that time they had not alternative, for to accept Jesus would have meant to sign their death warrant as a people.

But now, how does the challenge of Jesus appear? Do Jews who have returned to their land need the props of the ritual Law to retain their identity now that they have their own land, state, language, and culture?

The discovery of the Dead Sea Scrolls has injected a surprising element into the argument. It came at the very moment of the emergence of the State, a remarkable coincidence, almost providential. The Scrolls demonstrate that the ethics and ideas of Jesus were a product of an organic growth spread over the last centuries of Mosaic Judaism. What Zweig affirms here, we say in passing, has been supported by Professor Flusser, Orthodox Jew and eminent exegete of the New Testament.

Zweig continues: "They show Jesus as a genuine product of the land, a native growth of the Second Commonwealth. If Israel is heir to the Second Commonwealth, is she not heir also to the most significant spiritual message of that Commonwealth? Rabbinical Judaism was the Judaism of the Diaspora. What is the Judaism of the Third Commonwealth to be? Should it not incorporate the most important message of the preceding Commonwealth?

"The mystery of this simple Jew from Nazareth, who managed to conquer almost the whole world and whose spiritual power was stronger than that of the whole of Jewry, is puzzling to the Israeli Jew. Who was he? Where lies the secret and mystery of his power? How did this Jew manage to attract the immense love and admiration of the whole world, while the Jews attracted only hatred and contempt? How did he manage to fulfill the task set in the Bible for the Jews, to serve as a light unto the nations, while the Jews failed miserably? Why was it that only he managed to shape and mold the world while the Jews played a losing game, rolling in the dust? Why has the genius of Jesus never been repeated within Jewish gates? And will it be repeated?"

Zweig notes the recurring expression of hope by Jews that Israel may produce good tidings for humanity, similar to that of Jesus. He quotes the very passage from Bialik's speech on Mount Scopus, which we brought to the attention of the reader. But how to realize these hopes, asks Zweig pertinently, so long as the most significant message of the Second Commonwealth is ignored?

"The old religion practised by the Orthodox," observes Zweig, "is ritualistic, petrified, ossified and deprived of vivifying, life-enhancing and tender forces, while the rest of society, the majority, is atheistic, agnostic, or religiously indifferent, disinterested and unconcerned."

The growing disappointment with the atmosphere of armed violence and the erosion of secularist, humanitarian ideals have combined to create an ideological vacuum in Israel. Yet, Jews remain a people with profound aspirations and spiritual needs. The new society must rebuild its spiritual foundations or crumble.

The catastrophes and triumphs of our generation are intensely felt. Nevertheless, the culminating point in the development of Jewish identity has not been reached, a culminating creed has not been created, the ideal synthesis of Jewish existence has not emerged. There is no purified reflection on the unique historical moment, to use Durkheim's phrase, no all-embracing, dynamic ideal to act as a catalyst of emotion, as a focus of national communal interest, as a spur for a dynamic drive towards the fulfilment of the age-long aspirations of Jewry.

What is interesting is that Zweig is not a Christian. He asks only whether the incorporation of the message and personality of Jesus as a major prophet for Israel is not the answer to the spiritual and moral predicament of Jewish society in the State of Israel. He believes that the acceptance of Jesus will make "all the difference in the fight for survival by the Israeli Jews, in their development as a nation and as a spiritual force in the world, as well as the peaceful settlement of their conflict with the Arab nations."

Really, what more can one ask for?

From Zweig we understand that, as the Israeli Jew passes from Bethlehem to Jerusalem, from Jerusalem to Nazareth, from Nazareth to Capernaum, he undergoes a quiet but efficacious catechism; the very stones cry out!

Practicalities

There are four methods of apostolate towards Jews: active individual proselytizing, passive proselytizing, pseudo-ecumenism, and the eschatological apostolate.

Active individual proselytizing is the classical form of missionary work. It is present when a Christian takes the initiative in persuading a Jew to accept Christianity.

Missionary activity of the sort described, directed towards Jews, has a long history, beginning with the abortive attempts of St. Peter and St. Paul. This history is marred by missionary methods which must be characterized as unjust or uncharitable: unjust, such as in the case of forced baptisms; uncharitable, in the forced attendance of Jews at Christian sermons. Once converted, powerful pressures were brought upon the convert to assimilate. In Spain and Portugal, literally thousands of converts were wrenched away from contact with their people and their historical identity systematically destroyed. A pseudo-theology of post-Christic Jewry justified these excesses before the Christian conscience. The policy of active proselytizing draws strength from Mt. 28:19, where Jesus commands the Church to go out and baptize all nations. True! But he does not command how to go about it in each case. Where the Jews are concerned, God, in fact, had drawn a veil over their eyes, until the time should arrive for them to accede, collectively, to the faith. During that period, only a remnant would believe. Never has the Christian mission to the Jews succeeded in overcoming what was a divine decree. The Christian missionary willfully blinded himself to the fact that he was menacing the survival of the Jewish people and exciting the enmity of an intelligent, vocal, and outraged world community. The relentless obstinacy of the Christian missionary in pursuing his policy of proselytizing Jews is a glaring example of religious fanaticism.

Passive proselytizing occurs when the Jew takes the initiative in pressing for admission into the Church. The priest is then called upon to treat the case on its merits. He may be alive to the dangers for the historical identity of the Jew should he convert, but his duty is to the conscience of the individual. The rest he must confide to

God, responsible in the first case for the *démarche*.

Far from us to suggest that the Christian should not bear witness to his faith by manifesting a discreet but persistent good will towards Jews. That in itself is a program. Is it not the duty of a Christian to show charity to all?

In principle, Jews should have no valid objection to offer against passive proselytizing. Let it be recalled that the Synagogue confronts a similar problem and that the rabbi handles it in a similar way. Each year, thousands of Gentiles are received into Judaism, both in Israel and in the Diaspora. We testify that rabbis in Israel are under constant pressure from politicians to facilitate conversion procedures.

Proselytizing produced a small category of converts who found themselves stranded between two worlds. The Jews saw them as traitors who had lost their sense of responsibility towards the ongoing destiny of the Jewish people, as a group which had burnt its bridges with fellow-Jews to pass over to the protection of the more powerful majority. Between themselves, the converts had a common past, but no common present, no common future. Confused about their identity, they repelled each other, before repelling Jews. As we have remarked, their capacity for collective action to date has been *nil*.

A letter was published by Christian authorities in the State of Israel which formulated their view of the convert in these words: "A Jew who has become a Christian, remains a member of his people, as he has been since his birth."[3]

Unfortunately, the letter has had no practical effect, if it was ever intended to have one. The clergy continues to act as if the opposite were true.

Father U. A. Floridi severely criticized Soviet policy towards Jews because it does not allow them to develop their proper culture as do other nationalities. When has the Christian Church ever encouraged Jewish converts to develop their proper culture?[4]

Pseudo-ecumenism, to turn to the third method of apostolate, is an attempt to apply the principle of ecumenism to relations between the Christian and the Jewish worlds. We say *"pseudo-ecumenism"* because ecumenism was first intended to facilitate the union of the

Christian churches, not as a form of apostolate to the Jews.

We agree that dialogue between Jews and Christians can serve a useful purpose and that the study of Judaism is an excellent program for encouraging better relations between the two bodies. However, pseudo-ecumenism serves too often to mask the real problems at issue. In practice, the pseudo-ecumenical apostolate turns out to be a substitute for a reading of the signs of the times, a program of evasion. The pseudo-ecumenist has difficulty in confronting certain specific issues, the most painful of which is the Jewish-Arab conflict. The reason is not far to seek. As an ecumenist, he is obliged to be even-handed in his approach. What, then, will be his attitude in the event of a war between Jew and Arab? Let not the reader imagine that we are inventing situations. Jewish authorities in Israel on the outbreak of war have had occasion to reproach ecumenists for not even telephoning to express their regret.

Another peculiarity of the pseudo-ecumenist policy is to make the existence of the convert a source of embarrassment to the ecumenist. Here again, the reason is simple. The pseudo-ecumenist protests to the Jew that he has no intention of converting him. The presence of a convert would undermine his posture; the presence of several converts would threaten to ruin his *démarche* altogether. The convert, consequently, must neither be seen nor heard.

The eschatological approach takes its point of departure in a reading of the signs of the times. It is oriented to the collectivity, not to individuals. It focuses attention on the status of the Jewish convert, who is envisaged as that part of Jewry which has accepted the Law of Christ. It accepts the transitional nature of Jewish identity in modern times. It is conscious of the overpowering influence of divine providence in the process of the admission of Jewry to the faith. It limits the human role to collaborating with the intentions of providence. It is aware that the action of the divine in history is the source of an inexhaustible, messianic spirituality, ready to wait patiently on the sidelines, or to act with promptitude, as the occasion may require. It is, finally, sensitive to Jewish objections against the Christian mission, but also to the extent to which the Jew is responding to the pressure of a loving providence.

The spirituality which clothes the doctrinal skeleton of the eschatological apostolate with flesh and blood is messianic. Messianic spirituality may be defined as the discovery of the divine in history. More particularly, it discovers the divine plan of salvation in history. A splendid example of messianic spirituality is found in St. Paul. Having meditated profoundly on the mystery of the salvation of Israel, he ends the eleventh chapter of the Epistle to the Romans with a hymn to God's mercy and wisdom: "How deep are the riches and the wisdom and the knowledge of God! How inscrutable his judgments, how unsearchable his ways!" (Rm. 11:33) In addition to the two divine attributes of wisdom and knowledge, one sees reflected in Israel's history the power of God, extending from one end of time to the other, the severity and mercy of God, to which St. Paul makes allusion in another passage of the Epistle to the Romans, the gratuitous goodness of God's salvific will, his patience with disobedient man, how God is able to draw good from the greatest of evils. Messianic spirituality contemplates the centrality of Jesus Christ for history in general, and for the history of Jewry in particular. Its gaze then focuses on the Mystical Body of Christ, His Church, with which the Jew is called upon finally to associate himself, and not, let it be said, directly with the Church of the Gentiles. His mind and heart unite in contemplation of the Blessed Virgin, sole link between Israel and its redemption through Jesus Christ. Messianic spirituality complacently considers the role of the saints in the apostolate, of St. John the Baptist, the precursor of Jesus, and of St. Joseph, who together stand as a bridge between the Old and New Dispensations, of Saints Peter and Paul, who were forced to abandon the apostolate, discouraged.

Above all, messianic spirituality draws on inexhaustible sources of spiritual motivation and inspiration from its discovery of the presence of the God of Israel, active in contemporary history.

The practical program of the eschatological apostolate is, in the first place, kerygmatic. Its kerygma of the signs of the times is directed to the Church as a whole before being addressed to others.

Beyond the kerygma, there is room for study, for the development of the theology of history, for the analysis of Jewish-Christian relations throughout the ages, for a serious evaluation of Judaism and Zionism.

New wine should be poured into new wineskins or it goes to waste. The Jewish convert should be encouraged to correct the deficiencies of his situation by common action with other converts. Together, they would endeavor to establish a policy for their own collective future and another for relations with Jewry. The ultimate object of their associating would be to petition the official Church to set up a Hebrew community, juridically approved by the Holy See. Individual petitions have been received in Rome from priests, religious, and faithful around the world. To them should be added the unanimous recommendation of the Synod of the Southern African Catholic Bishops' Conference sitting in Plenary Session.[5]

It has to be recognized that the time is not ripe for a Hebrew community in the Church, here and now. A great deal of preparatory work is necessary. As they stand, few converts have any desire to enter into association with one another. They do not grasp the obligation which the possession of the "election factor" imposes on them. Their sense of responsibility towards the destiny of their own people is feeble. Their historical identity has been disintegrated. The few that are inclined to assert their identity are discouraged and shrink back. Nothing less than the encouragement of the official Church could change the situation.

We call the work of preparation of the converts the internal apostolate; it is an integral part of the eschatological program.

Speaking by and large, the idea of a community for converts arouses suspicions. We have it in writing that there are some who see the proposal as an insidious attempt to set up a church within a church. Whatever its eventual shape and form, the community will have to be juridically approved by Rome.

It is further objected that the proposal to set up a community for converts would appear to Jews as a subtle standing invitation to conversion.

We reply that Jews have been the most strident in criticizing the convert for alienating himself and his descendants from participation in Israel's destiny. Why should they complain, if the convert accepts the criticism and takes steps to correct his situation?

If the existence of a Hebrew-Catholic community demonstrates to the Jews that the official Church does not intend to bring about the destruction of Jewry by assimilation, that would be a great gain for the Church. If the existence of a Hebrew-Catholic community should facilitate the admission of Jewry, the gain should be laid to the account of divine providence.

Another objection points to the number of converts, too small, it is said, to form an association. Our Lord founded his Church on twelve! The real problem is not one of numbers. In the last hundred and fifty years there have been plenty of converts. But so long as the régime of assimilation condemns them to absorption, the number of available converts at any given moment will always be small. A beginning must be made by changing the régime of assimilation with its cruel effects on the identity of the convert. Every Jewish convert needs to be registered as an Israelite at the moment of baptism and his descendants likewise. During his catechism he should be taught the doctrine of the Church concerning the identity of the Jewish people. After all, the existence of the "election factor" places an obligation on the Church to act in consequence by encouraging converts to associate in order to build their new identity in continuity with their past. Associations of converts, regional and international, should formulate their collective position towards their people of origin, towards Zionism and the State of Israel, their views on the Jewish-Arab conflict, on the possibilities of collaboration with Jewish bodies. The building of a Hebrew-Christian identity would involve them in a full Hebrew cultural program, with the accent on the Hebrew education of their children. In other words, the community will not be built on converts as they are, but on converts who have been instructed in their unique vocation and its concomitant responsibilities.

The spectre of Judaeo-Christianity is another source of suspicion. We reply that Jewish converts are not Judaeo-Christians. What characterized Judaeo-Christianity was its conviction that the Law of Moses was still necessary for salvation. Whatever be the ultimate form of the community, its statutes will be drawn up by the Church. As for liturgical problems, they should be the last consideration. In the absence of a community, the elaboration of a Hebrew-Christian liturgy is a purely theoretical exercise.

The charge of racialism hurled against the proposal for a

Hebrew community in the Church dishonors those who make it. The objection arises from the fear that an Israelite community in the church would inevitably exclude the Gentiles. But every authentic Israelite community in history has aggregated Gentiles to itself, under certain conditions. An approved Hebrew-Catholic community would enjoy similar authority.

The community, when it comes into being one day, will be seen for what it is: an eschatological sign of the times, raised up before a Church in crisis and for the encouragement of a jaded world.

In a discourse to a delegation of the Orthodox Coptic Church, John Paul II declared: "Unity, whether on the universal level or the local level, does not mean uniformity or absorption of one group by another. It is rather at the service of all groups to help each live better the proper gifts it has received from God's spirit."[6]

To the thought so appropriately expressed by the Holy Father, we respond with a fervent Amen!

REFERENCES

(For the full data in each instance consult the Bibliography)

CHAPTER I (A Case of Conscience)

1. *Encyclopaedia Judaica* 3 (1971) 209-210; 10 (1971) 53-65, esp. 63; 12 (1971) 72, 147; *Verdicts* 16 (1962) 2428-2455, esp. 2428, 2449; Litvin & Hoenig: *Jewish Identity*, pp. 2-3; Stiassny, M. J.: *Proche-Orient Chrétien* 23 (1963) 42-49.

2. Zuckerman & Basoq (eds.): *The Book of the Ghetto Wars*, pp. 480-486.

3. A tourist visa was valid only for three months.

4. *Register of Laws* 6-7-50, No. 51, p. 159.

5. *Register of Laws* 8-4-52, No. 95, p. 146 para. 2; Sha'ava M.: *Personal Law in Israel*, p. 103.

6. *Register of Laws* 1-9-54, no. 163, p. 174, Amendment para. 2.

7. The term "excluding clause" will henceforth designate the phrase "providing that there had been no change of *dat*".

8. Litvin & Hoenig: *Jewish Identity*, p. 154.

9. *Verdicts* 16 (1962) 2428-2455.

10. Katz, J.: *Tradition and Crisis*, p. 254.

11. *Verdicts* 16 (1962) 2428-2445.

12. *Verdicts* 16 (1962) 2432-2437; Kurman, A.: *Who and What is a Jew*, pp. 356-402; *Proche-Orient Chrétien* 20 (1970) 57.

13. Litvin & Hoenig: *Jewish Identity*, p. 143.

14. *Proche-Orient Chrétien* 8 (1958) 179-180; 269-273; 372-374; 9 (1959) 366-368; 10 (1960) 79-81.

15. *Proche-Orient Chrétien* 7 (1957) 333-343; 9 (1959) 77-78.

16. Litvin & Hoenig: *Jewish Identity*, p. 143.

17. *Proche-Orient Chrétien* 5 (1955) 74; Ben-Chorin, Sh.: "Judenchristen in Israel", *Israel Nachrichten*, 15-7-77, p. 7.

18. *Proche-Orient Chrétien* 3 (1953) 171.

19. Chouraqui, A.: *Lettre á un ami Chrétien*, p. 54.

20. *Proche-Orient Chrétien* 5 (1955) 70.

21. *Proche-Orient Chrétien* 15 (1965) 268-269; 16 (1966) 249-250; 16 (1966) 384-384.

22. Stiassny, M. J.: *Proche-Orient Chrétien* 20 (1970) 52-60; Kurman, A.: *Who and What is a Jew*, p. 167 ff.

23. Litvin & Hoenig: *Jewish Identity*, p. 121.

24. *Proche-Orient Chrétien* 16 (1966) 249.

25. *Proche-Orient Chrétien* 20 (1970) 52-60.

26. Minkowitz, M.: *The Issue of Who is a Jew*. The author stresses the necessity of a law regulating marriage if Jewish identity is to be conserved.

27. *Perception*, Vo. 2, No. Feb. 1979, p. 1.

28. *Register of Laws* 19-3-70, No. 586, p. 34; Sha'va, M.: *Personal Law in Israel*, p. 104 (21); 361 (108); *Proche-Orient Chrétien* 20 (1970) 57 ff.

29. Kurzweil, B.: *Our New Literature*, Jer. 1959. See H. Herzberg, The Struggle of Baruch Kurzweil, "Ha'aretz", 22-10-1976, p. 18.

30. Leibowitz, Y.: *Judaism, The Jewish People*, p. 188.

31. Steinletz, A: Reported in "Ha'aretz", 12-5-78, Supplement, p. 24.

32. *Verdicts* 16 (1962) 2432, para. 2.

33. *Verdicts* 16 (1962) 2438.

34. *Verdicts* 16 (1962) 2440.

35. *Verdicts* 16 (1962) 2440.

36. Ratosh, Y. (ed): *From Victory to Defeat; Encyclopaedia Judaica* 10 (1971) 53-62, esp. 62; 13 (1971) 1573-1574; *Proche-Orient Chrétien* 5 (1955) 170.

37. Culi, Y.: *Me'am Le'oz*, p. 39.

38. *Proche-Orient Chrétien* 5 (1955) 75; 18 (1968) 273; 10 (1971) 53: 761-785, esp. 776; *New Catholic Encyclopaedia* 12 (1967) 1009: 8 (1966) 130-132, esp. 131 f.

39. *New Catholic Encyclopaedia* 12 (1967) 1009-1010, esp. 1009; Macdonald, J.: *The Theology of the Samaritans*, pp. 14, 277, 335, 338.

40. Macdonald, J.: *The Theology of the Samaritans*, p. 29.

41. *Proche-Orient Chrétien* 5 (1955) 75.

42. *Encyclopaedia Judaica* 14 (1971) 725-758, esp. 746-747.

43. *Proche-Orient Chrétien* 3 (1953) 77.

44. Baker, D.: *Christian News from Israel*, 21 (1970) 32-35; 21 (1970) 20-23; *Proche-Orient Chrétien* 20 (1970) 332.

45. *Proche-Orient Chrétien* 18 (1968) 265.

46. *Proche-Orient Chrétien* 18 (1968) 265.

47. *Proche-Orient Chrétien* 20 (1970) 196.

48. 15th April 1957.

49. Drayton, R. H.: *The Laws of Palestine*, 3 (1934) 2132.

50. Drayton, R. H.: *The Laws of Palestine*, 2 (1934) 1294-1295.

51. *Verdicts* 16 (1962) 2454, para. 5.

52. Proche-Orient Chrétien 20 (1970) 333.

53. Litvin & Hoenig: *Jewish Identity*, pp. 334-345.

54. Proche-Orient Chrétien 9 (1959) 171, 367.

55. Proche-Orient Chrétien 3 (1953) 358-359.

56. Silberg, M.: *Personal Status in Israel*, pp. 350 ff.

57. Hruby, K.: *Le Concept et L'Experience*. pp. 55-94. esp. p. 77.

58. Kurman, A. quotes the Council of Trent to the effect that a person cannot be a Jew and a Christian at one and the same time, p. 382.

59. Derczansky, A.: *Sidic* 4 (1971-34).

CHAPTER II (History of the Jewish Identity Problem)

1. Margolis and Marx: *A History of the Jewish People*, p. 630 ff.

2. Maritain, J.: *The Social and Political Philosophy of Jacques Maritain*, p. 209.

3. *Encyclopaedia Judaica* 8 (1971) 407-121.

4. Hruby, K.: *Le Concept et L'Experience Historique*, pp. 69 ff.

5. Rosenbloom, N. H.: *Luzzato's Ethico-Psychological Intetpretation*, p. 117.

6. Leibowitz, Y: *Judaism, The Jewish People*, p. 121; Weiler, G.: *Jewish Theocracy*, pp. 163-179.

7. *Encyclopaedia Judaica* 14 (1971) 23 ff.

8. Klausner, J.: The Writings of. ..Jer. 1955-1957.

9. *Encyclopaedia Judaica* 3 (1971) 207.

10. *Encyclopaedia Judaica* 3 (1971) 770-783.

11. Aron, R.: *De Gaulle, Israel and the Jew*, p. 41.

12. Sartre, J. P.: *Antisemite and Jew*, p. 68.

13. *Verdicts* 16 (1962) 2445.

14. Scholem, G.: *On Jews and Judaism* , p. 34.

CHAPTER III (Ahad Ha'amism, or New Lamps for Old)

1. Laqueur, W.: *A History of Zionism*, p. 33.

2. Simon, L.: *Ahad Ha'am*, p. 281.

3. Simon, L.: *Ahad Ha'am*, p. 106.

4. Kurzweil, B.: *Our New Literature*, p. 192.

5. Gordon, A. D.: *Writings*, Vol. I, p. 239; Vol. 3, p. 35.

6. Ben-Gurion, D.: *The Eternity of Israel*, p. 223.

7. Ben-Gurion, D.: *The Eternity of Israel*, p. 448.

8. Scholem, G.: *On Jews and Judaism* , p. 34.

9. Scholem, G.: *On Jews and Judaism* , p. 34.

10. Buber, M.: *On Judaism*, pp. 9, 16-17.

11. *Encyclopaedia Talmudica* (Eng.) Vol. I, cols. 7-8; Litvin & Hoenig: *Jewish Identity*, pp. 318-319.

12. *Encyclopaedia Judaica* 10 (1971) 58.

13. Leibowitz, Y.: *Judaism, The Jewish People*, p. 19.

14. Kurzweil, B.: *Our New Literature*, p. 191.

15. Simon, L.: *Ahad Ha'am*, p. 290.

16. Simon, L.: *Ahad Ha'am*, p. 100.

17. Heschel, A.: *The Insecurity of Freedom*, p. 210.

18. Laqueur, W.: *A History of Zionism*, p. 599.

19. Eldad, I.: *And So, On to Jerusalem*, p. 35.

20. Weiler, G.: *Jewish Theocracy*, p. 178.

21. Weiler, G.: *Jewish Theocracy*, pp. 171-173.

22. Leibowitz, Y.: *Judaism, The Jewish People*, p. 75.

23. Leibowitz, Y.: *Judaism, The Jewish People*, p. 153.

24. *Encyclopaedia Judaica* 10 (1971) 53-65, esp. 62.

CHAPTER IV (Ahad Ha'am Interrogated)

1. Ratosh, Y.: *From Victory to Defeat*, p. 120.

2. Kurman, A.: *Who and What Is a Jew*, p. 193.

3. *Encyclopaedia Judaica* 10 (1971-54-65, esp. 63).

4. Herman, S. See Kurman, p. 290.

5. *Proche-Orient Chrétien* 3 (1953) 145-149.

6. Leibowitz, Y.: *Judaism, The Jewish People*, pp. 50, 73, 188-9.

7. Bar-on, M.: Reported in *Jerusalem Post*, Supplement, 21-5-1972, p. 18.

8. Rakman, E.: Reported in *Ha'aretz*, Supplement, 12-5-78, p. 8.

9. *Proche-Orient Chrétien* 7 (1957) 356 f; 15 (1965) 272.

10. Hruby, K.: *Le Concept et L'Expénence*, p. 66.

11. *Proche-Orient Chrétien* 5 (1955) 168.

12. Rubinstein, A.: *Sources of Contemporary Jewish Thought*, p. 29.

13. *Proche-Orient Chrétien* 7 (1957) 261-267; 328-333; (1958) 168-170; 272-274 etc.

CHAPTER V (Words! Words! Words!)

1. *Encyclopaedia Universalis* 9 (1971) 521.

2. Noth, M. *Storia d'Israele*, p. 17.

CHAPTER VI (Jesus and Jewish Identity: From Mosaic Judaism to the Church)

1. Hruby, K.: *Le Concept et L'Expénence*, p. 84.

2. Fisher, E.: *Faith Without Prejudice*, p. 68.

3. Larcher, C.: *L'Actualite Chrétienne*, p. 246.

4. Darlap, A.: *Mysterium Salutis*, Vol. I, p. 201.

5. Newman, J. H.: "The Principle of Continuity," pp. 199-217, in *Sermons Bearing on Subjects of the Day* (1885), Sermon 15.

6. Newman, J. H.: "The Christian Church, A Continuation of the Jewish;" Sermon XIV, in *Sermons on Subjects of the Day* (1885), p. 197.

7. Flusser, D.: *Judaism and Christian Sources* (Heb.), p. 455.

8. Rordorf, W.: *Sabbat et Dimanche*, p. 178.

9. Newman, J. H.: "The Principle of Continuity," pp. 206-208.

10. Newman, J. H.: "The Principle of Continuity," p. 200.

11. Newman, J. H..: "The Christian Church, A Continuation of the Jewish Church, in *Sermons Bearing on Subjects of the Day* (1885) 190.

12. Newman, J. H.: "The Christian Church, A Continuation of the Jewish Church," in *Sermons Bearing on Subjects of the Day* (1885) p. 192.

13. Newman, J. H.: "The Christian Church, A Continuation of the Jewish Church," in *Sermons Bearing on Subjects of the Day* (1885) p. 195.

14. Dodd, C. H.: *Le Parabole del Regno*, p. 113.

CHAPTER VII (From Mosaic Judaism to Rabbinism)

1. Naftal, A. M.: *The Talmud and its Makers* (Heb.) Vol. I, p. 13.

2. *Loeb Classical Library,* Vol 7, p. 173.

3. *Encyclopaedia Judaica* Vol. 14, 725-758; Samaritans; Vol. 10, 761-785: Karaites; Vol. 14, 23-28: Reform Judaism; Vol. 5, 901-906: Conservative Judaism; Vol. 10, 58-59: Doenmeh; Vol. II, 1018-1025: Marranos; Vol. 4, 1068-1069: the Black Jews; Vol. 6, 1143-II54: Falashas; Vol. 4, 493-498: Benei Israel.

4. Maritain, J.: *The Social and Political Philosophy of Jacques Maritain*, p. 202.

5. Danielou and Chouraqui: *The Jews, Views and Counterviews*, p. 47.

6. Baum, G.: "The Doctrinal Basis for a Jewish–Christian Dialogue," in *The Ecumenist,* Vol. 6, No.4, pp. 145-152.

7. Maritain, J.: *op. cit.,* p. 202.

CHAPTER VIII (The Theological Identity of the Post-Christic Jewish People)

1. Hruby, K.: *Le Concept et L'Expérience Historique*, p. 64.

2. Urbach, E. E.: *The Sages*, p. 192.

3. Journet, C. H.: "The Mysterious Destinies of Israel," in *The Bridge* 2 (1956-57) 35-90, esp. 36.

4. Cited by Schoeps, H. J.: *The Jewish-Christian Argument*, p. 149.

5. Rijk, C. A.: "The Catholics and Jews after 1967: A New Situation," in *New Blackfriars*, Oct. 1968, p. 20.

CHAPTER IX (Has the Election Been Revoked?)

1. Benoit, P.: *L'Eglise et Israël*, p. 38.

2. Frizzel, L.: *SIDIC* 2 (1969) 27.

3. George, A.: *Rev. Bib.* 65 (1968) 481-525, esp. 524, footnote 92.

4. *La Civilta Cattolica:* 87 (4) (1936) 37-46; 88 (2) (1937) 418-431; 88 (2) (1937) 497-510, esp. 500.

5. Figueras, P.: "A Midrashic Interpretation," *Liber Annuus,* XXX (1980) 159-166.

6. *Nouvelles Chrétiennes d'Israel* 22 (1973) 255-258, esp. p. 256.

7. *Christian News from Israel* (Eng.) 23 (4) (12) (1973) 252-255, esp. 253.

8. Hruby, K.: *The Jerusalem Colloquium*, p. 92.

CHAPTER X (Objections and Refutations)

1. *L'Osservatore Romano* (Fr. Ed.) (I Fév. 1977) pp. 5-7.

2. *Encyclopaedia Universalis* 9 (1971) 552.

3. Versfeld, M.: *A Guide to the City of God*, p. 68.

4. Newman, J. H.: "The Tree Beside the Waters," Sermon 13, pp. 248-249, in *Sermons Preached on Various Occasions.*

CHAPTER XI (The Moral Dimension of Post-Christic Jewish Identity)

1. *Service International de Documentation Judeo-Chrétienne* 3 (1970) 22-23, esp. 32.

2. Flick and Alszeghy: *Il Peccato Originale*, p. 315.

3. Maritain, J.: *The Social and Political Philosophy of Jacques Maritain*, p. 201.

4. Isaac, J.: *Jésus et Israël*, pp. 405-406.

5. *Summa Theologica*: 3a pars, art. 4, 5, 6.

6. Scholem, G.: "Kabbalah," p. 72: *Encyclopaedia Britannica*, 15 (1974) 107-108.

CHAPTER XII (The Historical Consequences of the Sin of Unbelief)

1. Newman, J. H.: *Grammar of Assent*, p. 435.

2. *Jerusalem Bible,* New Testament, Luke, p. 129, footnote "e".

3. *La Civiltà Cattolica:* 119 (1968) 122-135, esp. p. 134.

3b. Testa, P. E.: *Genesi*, vol. I, p. 50.

4. Delumeau, J.: Le Christianisme, va-t-il mourir? see Chapter I.

5. Von Rad, Gerhard: "so far, no direct correspondence, Babylonian or extra-biblical (to the story of Original Sin), has been found." *Genesi*, tr. from German by Giovanni Moretto, Brescia 1978, p. 122.

6. *The Zohar*, Soncino Press, Vol. I, p. 47.

7. Newman, J. H.: *Grammar of Assent*, p. 435.

8. Newman, J. H.: *Sermons Bearing on Subjects of the Day*, pp. 205-206.

9. Maritain, J.: *The Social and Political Philosophy of Jacques Maritain*, p. 195.

10. Flannery, E.: *The Bridge* 3 (1958) 301-324, esp. 324.

11. Wiedekehr, D.: *Mysterium Salutis* (Fr. tr.): *Dogmatique de L'Histoire du Salut*, II (1975) 147.

12. Newman, J. H.: *Grammar of Assent*, p. 435.

13. Maritain, J.: *The Social and Political Philosophy of Jacques Maritain*, p. 203.

14. L'*Osservatore Romano*, Nov. 16/17, 1970.

15. Meisels, M.: *Judaism*, p. 569.

CHAPTER XIII (The Identity of Post-Christic Jewry in the Age of Apostasy)

1. Anonymous: *Les Frères Ratisbonne*, pp. 80-81.

2. Ratisbonne, Th.: *Rayons de Vérité.*, pp. 215-243, esp. 229.

3. Lémann, J.: *L'Entrée des Israélites*, p. 274.

4. Lémann, J.: *Les Nations Frémissantes*, p. vi.

5. Lémann, J.: *Les Nations Frémissantes*, p. 200.

6. Lémann, J.: *L'Entrée des Israélites*, pp. 263-284.

7. Guitton, J.: *Esprit et Vie* (Ami du Clergé) 73 (1963) 262 ff.

8. Newman, J. H.: *Discussions and Arguments*, p. 75.

9. Newman, J. H.: *Idea of a University*, p. 386.

10. Newman, J. H.: *Discussions and Arguments*, p. 75.

11. Newman, J. H.: *Discussions and Arguments*, p. 59.

12. Newman, J. H.: *Essays on Miracles*, p. 342.

13. Arminjon, Abbé: *Fin du Monde Présent*, p. 61.

14. Arminjon, Abbé: *Fin du Monde Présent*, p. 63, footnote.

15. Kevane, Eugene: *The Lord of History: Christocentrism and the Philosophy of History.* St. Paul Editions, Boston, Mass., 1980, p. 94.

CHAPTER XIV (The Meaning of History)

1. *New Catholic Encyclopaedia* 7 (1967) 30.

2. Collingwood, G.: *The Idea of History*, pp. 49-52, esp. 50.

2a. Billot, L.: *La Parousie*, pp. 327-350.

3. Flannery, E. H.: *The Bridge*, 3 (1958) 3°1-324.

4. Anonymous, *La Civiltà Cattolica*, 89 (1938) 76-82, esp. 81.

5. Jaeger, D.: *Tantur Papers*, p. 66: He appears to reject the possibility of a Christian reading of the signs of the times, especially in his dialogue with Zionism.

6. *Acta Apostolicae Sedis*: 55 (1963) 734-735.

7. *La Civiltà Cattolica*, 123 (1972) 504.

CHAPTER XV (The Return: Modern Zionism)

1. Halkine. S.: *La Littérature Hébraique Moderne*, pp. 164-165.

2. Scholem. G.: *On Jews and Judaism in Crisis*, p. 22.

3. Scholem. G.: *Le Messianisme Juif*, p. 66.

4. Rubenstein. Amnon: *From Herzl to Gush Emunim and Back*.

5. Maritain, J.: *The Social and Political Philosophy of Jacques Maritain*, p. 210.

6. Flannery. E.: *The Bridge* 3 (1958) 324.

7. *Nouvelles Chrétiennes d'Israël* 23 (1973) 255-258. esp. pp. 257-258; see Appendix 3. p. 7.

CHAPTER XVI (Alley of Grace)

1. *Proche-Orient Chrétien* 23 (1973) 369.

2. Native-born Israeli Jew.

3. *Proche-Orient Chrétien* 13 (1963) 321.

4. *La Civiltà Cattolica 115* (1964) 127-138, esp. 138.

5. Personal communication from the Primate of South Africa, Cardinal Owen McCann, dated 12 February 1982.

6. *L'Osservatore Romano* (It.) 119 (1972) 2.

LIST OF ABBREVIATIONS

AAS   *Acta Apostolicae Sedis*, Rome

BJ(E)   *The Jerusalem Bible* (Eng.), New York, 1966

BT   *The Babylonian Talmud*, Soncino Press, London

CC   *La Civiltà Cattolica* (periodical of the Jesuit Order, Rome)

EJ   *Encyclopaedia Judaica*, Jerusalem, 1971

ET (Eng.) *Encyclopaedia Talmudica*

EU   *Encyclopaedia Universalis*, Paris, 1968

MS   *Mysterium Salutis* (Fr. tr.) 15 Vols., Einsiedeln, 1965

NCE   *New Catholic Encyclopaedia*, New York, 1967

Oss.Rom. *L 'Osservatore Romano*, Vatican City

POC   *Proche-Orient Chrétien* (White Fathers), Jerusalem

SDB   *Supplement du Dictionnaire de la Bible* (Pirot et Robert), Paris 1966

SIDIC   *Service International de Documentation Judaeo-Chrétienne*, Rome

BIBLIOGRAPHY

Alon, Gedaliah. *The Jews in Their Land in the Talmudic Age* (70-640). Magnes Press, Hebrew University, Jerusalem. 1980 (English translation).

Ahad Ha'am. *Collected Works.* (Hebrew) Jerusalem, 1960.

Anonymous. *Les Frères Ratisbonne et Notre Dame de Sion.* Beauchesne, Paris, 1931.

Arminjon, Abbé. *Fin du Monde Présent et Mystères de la Vie Future.* L'Oeuvre S. Paul, Paris, 1863; re-edited by the Carmel of Lisieux, 1964.

Auclair, Raoul. *Le Jour de Yahve.* Editions P. Tequi, Paris, 1975.

Aron, Raymond. *De Gaulle, Israel and the Jews.* Deutsch, London, 1969.

Baeck, Leon. *The Essence of Judaism.* Schoken, New York, 1948.

Begin, Menachem. *The Revolt: The Story of the Irgun.* Steimatzsky, Jerusalem, 1977.

Ben-Gurion, David. *The Eternity of Israel.* Ayanot, Tel Aviv, 1964 (Hebrew).

Benoit, Pierre, O. P. *L'Eglise et Israël.* Apostolat des Editions, Paris, 1968.

Bialik, Hayyim Nachman. *Collected Works.* Devir, Tel Aviv, 1938 (Hebrew).

Billot, Louis (Cardinal). *La Parousie.* Beau Chesne, Paris, 1920.

Breuer, Isaac. *Concepts of Judaism.* Israel Universities Press. Jerusalem, 1974.

Buber, Martin. *On Judaism.* Schoken, New York, 1967.

Chouraqui, André. *Lettre à un Ami Chrétien.* Fayard, Bordeaux, 1971.

Collingwood, Robin George. *The Idea of History.* Oxford University Press, New York, 1957.

Culi, Ya'aqov (1689-1732). *Me 'am Lo 'ez.* Moznaim, New York, 1977 (Series: The Torah Anthology, English translation).

Daniélou, J. and Chouraqui, A. *The Jews: Views and Counterviews.* Newman Press, New York, 1967.

Dawson, Ch. *Religion and the Rise of Western Culture.* Image Books, New York, 1958.

Dawson, Ch. *Medieval Essays.* Image Books, New York, 1959.

Dawson, Ch. *Understanding Europe.* Image Books, New York, 1960.

Dayan, Moshe. *The Story of My Life.* Weidenfeld and Nicolson, London, 1966 (translated from the Hebrew).

Delumeau, Jean. *Le Christianisme, va-t-il mourir?* Hachette, Paris, 1978.

Dodd, Charles Harold. *Le Parabole del Regno*. Paideia Editrice, Brescia, 1976 (Original title, *The Parables of the Kingdom*).

Drayton, Robert Harry. *The Laws of Palestine*. Waterloo and Sons, London, 1934; Vols. I-III.

Dubois, Marcel Jacques. *Vigiles à Jerusalem*. Morel, Paris, 1976.

Dubois, Marcel Jacques. *Paradoxes et Mystéres d'Israël*. Maison Saint Isaïe, Jerusalem, 1977.

Dubois, Marcel Jacques. *Israël, Poète de Dieu*. Editions d l'Olivier, Jerusalem, 1977.

Elon, Amos. *The Israelis: Founders and Sons*. Sphere Books, London, 1971.

Eldad, Israel. *And so, on to Jerusalem: Collected Reflections in Commemoration of Liberated Jerusalem*. Yahdav, Jerusalem, 1968 (Hebrew).

Figueras, Pau. A *Midrashic Interpretation of the Cross as Symbol*. Studium Biblicum Franciscanum, Jerusalem, 1980.

Fisher, Eugene. *Faith Without Prejudice: Rebuilding Christian Attitudes Towards Judaism*. Paulist Press, New York, 1977.

Flannery, Edward H., S. J. *The Anguish of the Jews, Twenty-three Centuries of Anti-Semitism*. Macmillan, New York, 1965.

Flusser, David. *Jésus*. Seuil, Paris, 1970 (translated from the German).

Flusser, David. *Jewish Sources in Early Christianity*. Hashomer Hatsa'ir, Tel Aviv, 1979 (Hebrew).

Friedman, John. *The Redemption of Israel*. Sheed and Ward, London, 1947.

Goldman, Nahum. *Community of Fate: Jews in the Modern World*. Israel Universities Press, Jerusalem, 1977.

Gordon, A. D. *Collected Writings*. Hapoel Hatsa'ir, Tel Aviv, 1957 (Vols. I-III).

Halkine, Simon. La *Littérature Hebraïque Moderne: Ses Tendances, Ses Valeurs*. Presses Universitaires, Paris, 1958 (translated from the English).

Halevi, Judah (1080-1144). *Kitab Al Khazari*. Cailingold, London, 1931.

Harkabi, Yehoshua. *Palestine et Israël*. Ed. L'Avenir, Geneve, 1972.

Herman, Simon N. *Israelis and Jews: The Continuity of an Identity*. The Jewish Publication Society of America, Philadelphia, 1971.

Herzl, Theodore. *L 'Etat Juif*, Gesher, Jerusalem, 1954.

Heschel, Abraham Joshua. *The Insecurity of Freedom*. Schoken, New York, 1966.

Heschel, Abraham Joshua. *Israel, an Echo of Eternity*. Farraz, New York, 1973.

Hess, Moses. *Moses and Jerusalem*. Bloch, New York, 1918.

Hruby, Kurt. *"Le Concept et l'Expérience historique de la Nation"*, in *The Jerusalem Colloquim on Religion, Peoplehood, Nation and Land*. Truman Research Institute, Jerusalem, 1970.

Isaac, Jules, *Jesus et Israel.* Fasquelle, Paris, 1959.

Isaac, Jules. *L'Enseignement du Mepris.* Fasquelle, Paris, 1967.

Jaeger, David (ed). *Tantur Papers on Christianity in the Holy Land.* Ecumenical Institute for Theological Research, Tantur, Israel, no date.

Katz, Jacob. *Tradition and Crisis: Jewish Studies at the End of the Middle Ages.* Schoken, New York, 1961.

Kevane, Eugene. *The Lord of History: Christocentrism and the Philosophy of History.* St. Paul Editions, Boston, 1980.

Klausner, Joseph. *Collected Writings.* Mada, Jerusalem, 1955-1957 (Hebrew; 15 vols.).

Krochmal, Nachman. *The Writings of Rabbi Krochmal* (1785-1840). Ayanot, Berlin, 1924. (Hebrew)

Kurman, Abraham. *Who and What is a Jew?* Kfar Habad, Tel Aviv, 1974 (Hebrew; private edition).

Kurzweil, Baruch. *Our New Literature: Continuity or Revolution?* Schoken, Jerusalem, 1959 (Hebrew).

Laqueur, Walter. *A History of Zionism.* Weidenfeld and Nicolson, London, 1972.

Larcher, C., O. P. *L'Actualité Chrétienne de l'Ancien Testament d'aprés le Nouveau Testament.* Cerf, Paris, 1962.

Leibowitz, Yeshayahu. *Judaism, the Jewish People and the State of Israel.* Schoken, Tel Aviv, 1975 (Hebrew).

Lémann, Joseph. *L'Entrée des Israelites dans la Sociéte Prancaise et les Etats Chrétiens.* Lecoffre, Paris, 1886.

Lémann, Joseph. *Les Nations Frémissantes contre Jésus et son Eglise.* Poussielgue, Paris, 1879.

Litvin, Baruch (compiler) and Hoenig, Sidney B. (Ed.). *Jewish Identity: Modern Response and Opinions on the Registration of Children of Mixed Marriages: David Ben-Gurion's Query to Leaders of World Jewry — A Documentary Compilation.* Feldheim, Jerusalem and New York, 1970.

Mann, Peggy. *Golda: The Life of Israel's Prime Minister.* Washington Square Press, New York, 1972.

Maritain, Jacques. *Distinguer pour Unir: Les Degrés du Savior.* Desclée de Brouwer, Paris, 1963.

Maritain, Jacques. *The Social and Political Philosophy of Jacques Maritain: Selected Readings.* Doubleday, New York, 1955.

Maritain, Jacques. *De l'Eglise du Christ: La personne de l'Eglise et son personnel.* Desclée de Brouwer, Paris, 1970.

Margolis, Max and Mark, Alexander. *A History of the Jewish People.* The Jewish Publication Society of America, Philadelphia, 1927.

Meiseles, Meir. *Judaism: Thought and Legend: Anthology on Ethics and Philosophy Throughout the Ages.* Lipa Friedman, Benei Brak, Tel Aviv, no date.

Minkovitch, Meyer. *The Issue of who is a Jew in a historico-legal perspective.* Sepher-Hermon Press, New York, 1975 (Hebrew).

Mussner, Franz. *Il Popolo della Promessa: Per il dialogo cristiana-ebraico.* Citta Nuova Editrice, Roma, 1982 (translated from the German).

Newman, John Henry. *Sermons Preached on Various Occasions.* Burnes and Oates, London, 1887.

Newman, John Henry. *The Idea of a University Defined and Illustrated.* Longmans, London, 1889.

Newman, John Henry. *Sermons Bearing on Subjects of the Day.* Rivingtons, London, 1885; esp. Sermon XV, "The Principle of Continuity Between the Jewish and Christian Churches".

Newman, John Henry. *An Essay in Aid of a Grammar of Assent.* Longmans, London, 1889.

Newman, John Henry. *Essays on Biblical and Ecclesiastical Miracles.* Longmans, London, 1885.

Newman, John Henry. *Loss and Gain.* Burnes and Oates, London, 1886.

Newman, John Henry. *Discussions and Arguments on Various Subjects.* Longmans, London, 1888.

Noth, Martin. *Storia d'Israele.* Paideia Editrice, Brescia, 1975.

Naftal, A. M. *The Talmud and its Makers.* Yavneh Publishing House, Tel Aviv, 1972 (Vol. I-II; Hebrew).

Osterreicher, J. M. *The Walls are Crumbling: Seven Philosophers Discern Christ.* Hollis and Carter, London, 1953.

Peres, Shimon. *David's Sling: the Arming of Israel.* Willner, Birkenhead, 1970.

Pinsker, Leo. *Auto-Emancipation: A Call to His People by a Russian Jew.* Rital Searl, London, 1947.

Philo. *Works: Loeb Classical Library.* Heinemann, London, 1968.

Rad, Gerhard von. *Genesi: Traduzione et Commento.* Paideia Editrice, Brescia, 1978.

Ratisbonne, Théodore. *Rayons de Vérité.* Palme, Paris, 1874.

Ratosh, Yonathan (ed), *From Victory to Defeat.* Hadar, Tel Aviv, 1976 (Hebrew).

Rosenbloom, Noah H. *Luzzato's Ethico-Psychological Interpretation of Judaism.* Yeshiva University, New York, 1965. (Studies in Torah Judaism, no. 7).

Rubenstein, Amnon. *From Herzl to Gush Emunim and Back.* Shocken, Jerusalem-Tel Aviv, 1980 (Hebrew).

Rubenstein, Aryeh. *Sources of Contemporary Jewish Thought.* Hardon, Jerusalem, 1972.

Sartre, Jean-Paul. *Anti-Semite and Jew.* Schoken, New York, 1973.

Scholem, Gershom. *On Jews and Judaism in Crisis: Selected Essays.* Schocken, New York, 1976.

Scholem, Gershom. *Sabbatai Sevi.* Princeton Press, Princeton, 1973 (translated from the Hebrew by J. Z. Werblowsky).

Scholem, Gershom. *Kabbalah.* Keter, Jerusalem, 1974 (Library of Jewish Knowledge).

Scholem Gershom. *The Messianic Idea in Judaism and Other Essays in Jewish Spirituality.* Schocken, New York, 1971.

Shawa, Manashe. *Personal Law in Israel.* Massada, Tel Aviv; 1976 (Hebrew).

Silberg, Moshe. *Personal Status in Israel.* Akdom, Jerusalem, 1965 (Hebrew).

Talmon, Jacob. *The Age of Violence.* Am Oved, Tel Aviv, 1974 (Hebrew).

Testa, P. E., ofm: *Genesi,* in series *La Sacra Bibbia,* 2 vols. Marietti, Torino, 1969.

Urbach, Ephraim E. *The Sages, Their Concepts and Beliefs.* Magnes Press, Hebrew University, Jerusalem, 1971 (Hebrew).

Weiler, Gershon. *Jewish Theocracy.* Am Oved, Tel Aviv, 1976 (Hebrew).

Weizman, Ezer. *On Eagle's Wings.* Weidenfeld and Nicolson, London, 1976.

The Zohar. Soncino Press, London, 1973 (Five volumes).

Zuckerman, Y. and Basory, Y. (eds). *The Book of the Ghetto Wars* (Heb.) Hakibbutz Hame'uhad, Tel Aviv, 1956 (Hebrew).

Zweig, Ferdynand. *Israel, the Sword and the Hap: The Mystique of Violence and the Mystique of Redemption.* Heinemann, London, 1969.

PERIODICALS

Christian News from Israel; Ministry of Religious Affairs, Jerusalem.

Nouvelles Chrétiennes d'Israël; Ministry of Religious Affairs, Jerusalem.

Esprit et Vie (1' Ami du Clergé), Langres, France.

New Blackfriars (review of the English Dominicans), Cambridge, UK

Perception. Evangelicals United for Zion. New Jersey, USA (since defunct).

Liber Annuus, annual of the Studium Biblicum Franciscanum, Franciscan Press, Jerusalem.

Register of Laws. (Sefer ha-huqim), Government of Israel, Jerusalem.

The Bridge: a Yearbook of Judeo-Christian Studies. The Institute of Judeo-Christian Studies, Seton Hall University, Pantheon Books, New York.

Verdicts of the Supreme Court of Israel (Heb.) (Abbreb. Verdicts)., Government Printers, Jerusalem.

The Ecumenist. A Journal for Promoting Christian Unity. Paulist Fathers, Inc. 304 West 58th St., New York, NY 10019.

Lectio Divina. Cerf, Paris Series.

APPENDIX I

DECLARATION OF THE SECOND VATICAN COUNCIL ON THE ATTITUDE OF THE CHURCH TOWARD THE JEWS: *NOSTRA AETATE* No. 4 (October 28, 1965)

"Sounding the depths of the mystery which is the Church, this sacred Council remembers the spiritual ties which link the people of the New Covenant to the stock of Abraham.

"The Church of Christ acknowledges that in God's plan of salvation the beginning of her faith and election is to be found in the patriarchs, Moses and the prophets. She professes that all Christ's faithful, who as men of faith are sons of Abraham (cf. Gal. 3:7), are included in the same patriarch's call and that the salvation of the Church is mystically prefigured in the exodus of God's chosen people from the land of bondage. On this account the Church cannot forget that she received the revelation of the Old Testament by way of that people with whom God in his inexpressible mercy established the ancient covenant. Nor can she forget that she draws nourishment from that good olive tree onto which the wild olive branches of the Gentiles have been grafted (cf. Rom. II:17-24). The Church believes that Christ who is our peace has through his cross reconciled Jews and Gentiles and made them one in himself (cf. Eph. 2:14-16).

"Likewise, the Church keeps ever before her mind the words of the apostle Paul about his kinsmen: 'They are Israelites, and to them belong the sonship, the glory, the covenants, the giving of the law, the worship, and the promises; to them belong the patriarchs, and of their race according to the flesh, is the Christ' (Rom. 9:4-5), the son of the virgin Mary. She is mindful, however, that the apostles, the pillars on which the Church stands, are of Jewish descent, as are many of those early disciples who proclaimed the Gospel of Christ to the world.

"As holy Scripture testifies, Jerusalem did not recognize God's

moment when it came (cf. Lk. 19:42). Jews for the most part did
not accept the Gospel; on the contrary, many opposed the spreading
of it (cf. Rom. 11:28). Even so, the apostle Paul maintains that the
Jews remain very dear to God, for the sake of the patriarchs, since
God does not take back the gifts he bestowed or the choice he
made. Together with the prophets and the same apostle, the Church
awaits the day, known to God alone, when all peoples will call on
God with one voice and 'serve him shoulder to shoulder' (Soph.
3:9; cf. Is. 66:23; Ps. 65:4; Rom. 11:11-32).

"Since Christians and Jews have such a common spiritual
heritage, this sacred Council wishes to encourage and further
mutual understanding and appreciation. This can be obtained,
especially, by way of biblical and theological enquiry and through
friendly discussions.

"Even though the Jewish authorities and those who followed
their lead pressed for the death of Christ (cf. John 19:6), neither
all Jews indiscriminately at that time, nor Jews today, can be
charged with the crimes committed during his passion. It is true
that the Church is the new people of God, yet the Jews should not
be spoken of as rejected or accursed as if this followed from holy
Scripture. Consequently, all must take care, lest in catechizing or
in preaching the Word of God, they teach anything which is not in
accord with the truth of the Gospel message or the spirit of Christ.

"Indeed, the Church reproves every form of persecution
against whomsoever it may be directed. Remembering, then, her
common heritage with the Jews and moved not by any political
consideration, but solely by the religious motivation of Christian
charity, she deplores all hatreds, persecutions, and displays of anti-
Semitism leveled at any time or from any source against the Jews.

"The Church always held and continues to hold that Christ out
of infinite love freely underwent suffering and death because of
the sins of all men, so that all might attain salvation. It is the duty
of the Church, therefore, in her preaching to proclaim the cross
of Christ as the sign of God's universal love and the source of all
grace." — from Austin Flannery, O. P. (ed.) *Vatican Council II:
The Conciliar and Post Conciliar Documents* (New York: Costello,
1975), pp. 740-742.

APPENDIX II

VATICAN COMMISSION FOR RELIGIOUS RELATIONS WITH JUDAISM: GUIDELINES AND SUGGESTIONS FOR IMPLEMENTING THE CONCILIAR DECLARATION *NOSTRA AETATE* (1 December 1974)

The Declaration *Nostra Aetate,* issued by the Second Vatican Council on 28 October 1965, "on the relationship of the Church to non-Christian religions" (n. 4), marks an important milestone in the history of Jewish-Christian relations.

Moreover, the step taken by the Council finds its historical setting in circumstances deeply affected by the memory of the persecution and massacre of Jews which took place in Europe just before and during the Second World War.

Although Christianity sprang from Judaism, taking from it certain essential elements of its faith and divine cult, the gap dividing them was deepened more and more, to such an extent that Christian and Jew hardly knew each other.

After two thousand years, too often marked by mutual ignorance and frequent confrontation, the Declaration *Nostra Aetate* provides an opportunity to open or to continue a dialogue with a view to better mutual understanding. Over the past nine years, many steps in this direction have been taken in various countries. As a result, it is easier to distinguish the conditions under which a new relationship between Jews and Christians may be worked out and developed. This seems the right moment to propose, following the guidelines of the Council, some concrete suggestions born of experience, hoping that they will help to bring into actual existence in the life of the Church the intentions expressed in the conciliar document.

While referring the reader back to this document, we may simply restate here that the spiritual bonds and historical links binding the Church to Judaism condemns (as opposed to the very spirit of Christianity) all forms of anti-Semitism and discrimination, which in any case the dignity of the human person alone would suffice to condemn. Further still, these links and relationships render obligatory a better mutual understanding and renewed esteem.

On the practical level in particular, Christians must therefore strive to acquire a better knowledge of the basic components of the religious tradition of Judaism, and they must strive to learn by what essential traits the Jews define themselves in the light of their own religious experience.

With due respect for such matters of principle, we simply propose some first practical applications in different essential areas of the Church's life, with a view to launching or developing sound relations between Catholics and their Jewish brothers.

I. Dialogue

To tell the truth, such relations as there have been between Jew and Christian have scarcely ever risen above the level of monologue. From now on, real dialogue must be established.

Dialogue presupposes that each side wishes to know the other, and wishes to increase and deepen its knowledge of the other. It constitutes a particularly suitable means of favoring a better mutual knowledge and, especially in the case of dialogue between Jews and Christians, of probing the riches of one's own tradition. Dialogue demands respect for the other as he is, above all, and respect for his faith and his religious convictions.

In virtue of her divine mission, and her very nature, the Church must preach Jesus Christ to the World (*Ad Gentes*, 2). Lest the witness of Catholics to Jesus Christ should give offense to Jews, they must take care to live and spread their Christian faith while maintaining the strictest respect for religious liberty in line with the teaching of the Second Vatican Council (Declaration *Dignitatis Humanae*).

They will likewise strive to understand the difficulties which arise for the Jewish soul—rightly imbued with an extremely high, pure notion of the Divine transcendence—when faced with the mystery of the Incarnate Word.

While it is true that a widespread air of suspicion, inspired by an unfortunate past, is still dominant in this particular area, Christians, for their part, will be able to see to what extent the responsibility is theirs and deduce practical conclusions for the future.

In addition to friendly talks, competent people will be encouraged to meet and to study together the many problems deriving from the fundamental convictions of Judaism and of Christianity. In order not to hurt (even involuntarily) those taking part, it will be vital to guarantee, not only tact but a great openness of spirit and diffidence with respect to one's own prejudices.

In whatever circumstances as shall prove possible and mutually acceptable, one might encourage a common meeting in the presence of God, in prayer and silent meditation, a highly efficacious way of finding that humility, that openness of heart and mind, necessary prerequisites for a deep knowledge of oneself and of others. In particular, that will be done in connection with great causes such as the struggle for peace and justice.

II. Liturgy

The existing links between the Christian liturgy and the Jewish liturgy will be borne in mind. The idea of a living community in the service of God, and in the service of men for the love of God, such as it is realized in the liturgy, is just as characteristic of the Jewish liturgy as it is of the Christian one. To improve Jewish-Christian relations, it is important to take cognizance of those common elements of the liturgical life (formulas, feasts, rites, etc.) in which the Bible holds an essential place.

An effort will be made to acquire a better understanding of whatever in the Old Testament retains its own perpetual value (cf. Dei Verbum 14-15), since that has not been cancelled by the later interpretation of the New Testament. Rather, the New Testament brings out the full meaning of the Old, while both Old and New illumine and explain each other (cf. ibid. 16). This is all more important since liturgical reform is now bringing the text of the Old Testament ever more frequently to the attention of Christians.

When commenting on biblical texts, emphasis will be laid on the continuity of our faith with that of the earlier Covenant, in the perspective of the promises, without minimizing those elements of Christianity which are original. We believe that those promises were fulfilled with the first coming of Christ. But it is none the less true that we still await their perfect fulfilment in his glorious return at the end of time.

With respect to liturgical readings, care will be taken to see that homilies based on them will not distort their meaning, especially when it is a question of passages which seem to show the Jewish people as such in an unfavorable light. Efforts will be made so to instruct the Christian people that they will understand the true interpretation of all the texts and their meaning for the contemporary believer.

Commissions entrusted with the task of liturgical translation will pay particular attention to the way in which they express those phrases and passages which Christians, if not well informed, might misunderstand because of prejudice. Obviously, one cannot alter the text of the Bible. The point is that with a version destined for liturgical use there should be an overriding preoccupation to bring out explicitly the meaning of a text, while taking scriptural studies into account.

The preceding remarks also apply to introductions to biblical readings, to the Prayer of the Faithful, and to commentaries printed in missals used by the laity.

III. Teaching and Education

Although there is still a great deal of work to be done, a better understanding of Judaism itself and its relationship to Christianity has been achieved in recent years thanks to the teaching of the Church, the study and research of scholars, as also the beginning of dialogue. In this respect, the following facts deserve to be recalled.

It is the same God, "inspirer and author of the books of both Testaments" *(Dei Verbum,* 16), who speaks both in the old and new Covenants.

Judaism in the time of Christ and the Apostles was a complex reality, embracing many different trends, many spiritual, religious, social and cultural values.

The Old Testament and the Jewish tradition founded upon it must not be set against the New Testament in such a way that the former seems to constitute a religion of only justice, fear and legalism, with no appeal to the love of God and neighbor (Deut. 6:5; Lev. 18:18; Matt. 22:34-40).

Jesus was born of the Jewish people, as were his Apostles and a large number of his first disciples. When he revealed himself as the Messiah and Son of God (cf. Matt. 16:16), the bearer of the new Gospel message, he did so as the fulfilment and perfection of the earlier Revelation. And, although his teaching had a profoundly new character, Christ, nevertheless, in many instances took his stand on the teaching of the Old Testament. The New Testament is profoundly marked by its relation to the Old. As the Second Vatican Council declared: "God, the inspirer and author of the books of both Testaments, wisely arranged that the New Testament be hidden in the Old and the Old be made manifest in the New" *(Dei Verbum,* 16). Jesus also used teaching methods similar to those employed by the rabbis of his time.

With regard to the trial and death of Jesus, the Council recalled that "what happened in his passion cannot be blamed upon all the Jews then living, with distinction, nor upon the Jews of today" *(Nostra Aetate,* 4).

The history of Judaism did not end with the destruction of Jerusalem, but rather went on to develop a religious tradition. And, although we believe that the importance and meaning of that tradition were deeply affected by the coming of Christ, it remains nonetheless rich in religious values.

With the prophets and the apostle Paul, "the Church awaits the day, known to God alone, on which all peoples will address the Lord in a single voice and 'serve him with one accord' (Soph. 3:9)" *(Nostra Aetate,* 4).

Information concerning these questions is important at all levels of Christian instruction and education. Among sources of information, special attention should be paid to the following: catechisms and religious textbooks; history books; the mass-media (press, radio, cinema, television).

The effective use of these means presupposes the thorough

formation of instructors and educators in training schools, seminaries and universities.

Research into the problems bearing on Judaism and Jewish-Christian relations will be encouraged among specialists, particularly in the fields of exegesis, theology, history and sociology. Higher institutions of Catholic research, in association, if possible, with other similar Christian institutions and experts, are invited to contribute to the solution of such problems. Wherever possible, chairs of Jewish studies will be created, and collaboration with Jewish scholars encouraged.

IV. Joint Social Action

Jewish and Christian tradition, founded on the Word of God, is aware of the value of the human person, the image of God. Love of the same God must show itself in effective action for the good of mankind. In the spirit of the prophets, Jews and Christians will work willingly together, seeking social justice and peace at every level—local, national and international.

Conclusion

The Second Vatican Council has pointed out the path to follow in promoting deep fellowship between Jews and Christians. But there is still a long road ahead.

The problem of Jewish-Christian relations concerns the Church as such, since it is when "pondering her own mystery" that she encounters the mystery of Israel. Therefore, even in areas where no Jewish communities exist, this remains an important problem. There is also an ecumenical aspect to the question: the very return of Christians to the sources and origins of their faith, grafted on to the earlier Covenant, helps the search for unity in Christ, the cornerstone.

In this field, the bishops will know what best to do on the pastoral level, within the general disciplinary framework of the Church and in line with the common teaching of her magisterium. For example, they will create some suitable commissions or secretariats on a national or regional level, or appoint some competent person to promote the implementation of the conciliar directives and the suggestions made above.

On 22 October 1974, the Holy Father instituted for the universal Church this Commission for Religious Relations with the Jews, joined to the Secretariat for Promoting Christian Unity. This special Commission, created to encourage and foster religious relations between Jews and Catholics—and to do so eventually in collaboration with the other Christians—will be, within the limits of its competence, at the service of all interested organizations, providing information for them, and helping them to pursue their task in conformity with the instructions of the Holy See.

The Commission wishes to develop this collaboration in order to implement, correctly and effectively, the express intentions of the Council. (Reprinted from: *Christian News from Israel* 25(1974)91-94).

APPENDIX III

A DECLARATION OF THE FRENCH EPISCOPAL COMMISSION FOR RELATIONS WITH JUDAISM (16 APRIL 1973)

I. The Existence of the Jewish People Challenges the Christian Conscience

The present-day existence of the Jewish people, its often precarious state throughout its history, the tragic ordeals that it has undergone in the past and above all in recent times, and its partial regathering in the Land of the Bible signify more and more, for Christians, a reality which may bring them nearer to a better understanding of their own faith and illuminate their own lives.

The permanence of this people all down the ages, its survival over many other civilizations, its presence as a stern and exigent partner confronting Christianity are facts of the highest importance which we dare not treat with either indifference or contempt.

The Church, which attaches itself to the name of Jesus Christ and which through him, finds itself, from its first origin, forever linked with the Jewish people, perceives in the age-long, unbroken, being of Jewry a sign which it would fain comprehend with absolute truth.

II. How Slowly the Christian Conscience Travels!

On 28 October 1965, the Second Vatican Council solemnly promulgated the declaration *Nostrae Aetate,* in which is a chapter on the Jewish people. We reaffirm the importance of this text, wherein it is recalled that the Church "is nourished from the root of the veritable olive tree onto which have been grafted the branches of the wild olive-tree—the Gentiles." It is our duty, as the Episcopal Commission for Relations with Judaism, to show forth the present import of this declaration and to point out its applications.

The attitude taken up by the Council should be looked upon

as a beginning rather than an end. It marks a turning point in the Christian outlook on Judaism. It opens up a way and permits us to make an exact appraisal of our task.

The declaration is built upon a return to the scriptural sources. It breaks with the standpoint of an entire past. It calls for a new attitude towards the Jewish people on the part of Christians from now on, not only in the domain of human relations but also in that of faith. Obviously, it is not possible in a single day to reexamine all the pronouncements recorded in the Church over the centuries, or every historical posture portrayed. The Christian conscience has, nonetheless, started this process, which reminds the Church of its Jewish roots. The main thing is that it be begun, that it reach every stratum of the Christian people and that it be everywhere pursued with honesty and vigor.

III. The Eternal Mission of the Jewish People

It is not possible to regard the Jewish "religion" simply as one among the religions that presently exist on this earth. It is through the people of Israel that belief in the One God has been engraved in the history of mankind. It is through the people of Israel that, albeit with certain differences, monotheism became the shared legacy of the three great families which stem from the heritage of Abraham: Judaism, Christianity, Islam.

According to Bible revelation, it was God Himself Who made the Jewish people, schooled it, and taught it His designs, sealing an eternal Covenant with it (Genesis 17:7) and endowing it with a vocation that Saint Paul terms irrevocable (Romans 11:29). To it we owe the Pentateuch, the Prophets and the other sacred Books which complete its message. Assembled by tradition, written and oral, these teachings were received by the Christians, without the Jew being in any wise thereby dispossessed of them.

Even if, for Christianity, the Covenant is renewed in Jesus Christ, Judaism must be regarded by Christians as a reality that is not merely social and historical but primarily religious, not as the relic of a venerable, antiquated past, but as a living reality for all time. The chief signs of this vitality of the Jewish people are the testimony of its collective loyalty to the One God; its fervor in studying the Scriptures to discover, in the light of Revelation, the meaning of human life; its search for identity in the midst of other peoples, and its constant effort to be gathered together again in a reunified community. For us Christians these signs put a question which goes to the very heart of our faith: What is the precise mission of the Jewish people in the Divine plan? What expectancy inspires it, and how does that expectancy differ from or resemble our own?

IV. Teach Nought Unconformable with the Spirit of Christ (Nostra Aetate, 4, paragraph 2)

a) It is urgent that Christians should once and for all stop picturing the Jew to themselves in terms of cliches that have been forged by a centuries-old aggressiveness; let us utterly expunge, and in all circumstances battle bravely against, caricatures unworthy of any decent person, and even more so of any decent Christian— for example, the travesty of the Jew who, with an innuendo of scorn or aversion, is said to be "not like the others", or of the "usurious, ambitious, conspiratorial" Jew, or, more alarming yet in its consequences, of the Jew as a "deicide". These scandalous descriptions which, alas, are still current in our days, whether in explicit fashion or obliquely, we denounce and condemn insistently. Anti-Semitism is a legacy from the pagan world, but it has been further reinforced in a Christian ambiance by pseudo-theological arguments. The Jew is deserving of our attention and our esteem, and often, our admiration, sometimes, surely, of friendly and fraternal criticism, but always of our love. Love is perhaps what he has lacked most, and it is in that respect that the Christian conscience has been most guilty.

b) It is a theological, historical, and juridical error indiscriminately to hold the Jewish people responsible for the passion and death of Jesus Christ. The Catechism of the Council of Trent long ago rebuked that error (Part I, cap. 5, II). If it is historically true that responsibility for the death of Jesus was shared in varying degree by certain Jewish and Roman authorities, the Church holds that "it is on account of the sin of all men that Christ, in his immense love, bowed himself to his passion and his death so that all might gain salvation" *(Nostra Aetate,* 6).

Notwithstanding the contention in an ancient but questionable exegesis, one cannot infer from the New Testament that the Jewish people is shorn of its elect status. On the contrary, Scripture as a whole prompts us rather to discern in the solicitous allegiance of the Jewish people to its Law and its Covenant the sign of God's allegiance to His people.

c) It is a fallacy to set Judaism as a religion of fear against Christianity as a religion of love. The fundamental article of the Jewish faith, the Shema, begins with the words: "Thou shalt love the Lord thy God", and goes on to enjoin love of one's fellow man (Leviticus 19:19). This is the starting point of the preaching of Jesus and is thus a doctrine common to Judaism and Christianity.

The sense of God's transcendence and allegiance, of His justice and mercy, of repentance and forgiveness of sins, are basic elements of Jewish tradition. Christians who lay claim to the same values would err in believing that they have nothing more to learn, even today, from Jewish spirituality.

d) Contrary to widely held opinions, it must be asserted that the doctrine of the Pharisees is not the reverse of Christianity. The Pharisees sought to make the Law become life for every Jew by so interpreting its precepts as to adapt them to the different circumstances of existence. Contemporary researches have yielded clear evidence that the Pharisees, as also the Sages of the Talmud, were by no means strangers to the inner meaning of the Law. It is not these manifestations that Jesus decries when he denounces the attitude of certain Pharisees or the formalism of their teaching. It appears, moreover, that it was because the Pharisees and the early Christians were close to one another in many ways that they fought so bitterly at times over the traditions handed down from the era of the Patriarchs and the interpretation of the Mosaic Law.

V. Reaching a Just Understanding of Judaism

Christians, if only for their own sakes, should acquire a true and living knowledge of Jewish tradition.

a) A genuinely Christian catechesis must affirm the ongoing value of the Bible in its entirety. The First Covenant indeed has not been made obsolescent by the new, but is its root and source, its foundations and its promise. If it is true that, for us, the Old Testament does not disclose its ultimate meaning save in the light of the New Testament, this in itself presumes that it shall be welcomed and recognized, first, in its own right (cf. 2 Tim. 3:16). One must not forget that, by his obedience to the Torah and by his prayer, Jesus, a Jew by virtue of his mother, the Virgin Mary, accomplished his ministry in the midst of the people of the Covenant.

b) The effort must be exerted to present the special vocation of this people as being "the Sanctification of the Name". Here is one of the essential dimensions of synagogal prayer, whereby the Jewish people, invested with a priestly mission (Exodus 19:6), offers the totality of man's acts to God and glorifies Him. This vocation makes of the life and prayer of the Jewish people a benison for all the nations on earth.

c) To regard the precepts of Judaism as no more than practices of constraint is to underestimate them. Its rituals are acts to break the day-to-day pattern of existence and remind those who observe them of the lordship of God. Pious Jews greet as God's gifts the Sabbath day and rites whereof the purpose is to sanctify the works of men. Above and beyond their literal significance, they are light and joy for the Jew along the path of life (Psalms 119). They are a form of "building Time itself" and of giving thanks for all of creation. And, indeed, all existence must be related to God, as Paul reminded his brothers (I Cor. 10:30-31).

d) The dispersion of the Jewish people is to be understood in the light of its recorded history.

If Jewish tradition regards the trials and exile of the people as a punishment for its disloyalties (Jeremiah 13:17, 20, 21-23), it is nevertheless still the case that, since the time of Jeremiah's letter to the exiles of Babylon (ibid., 29:1-23), the life of the Jewish people in the Diaspora has also had a positive import: through its trials, the Jewish people is called upon to "sanctify the Divine Name" among the nations.

Christians must ceaselessly combat the anti-Jewish, Manich an temptation to look upon the Jewish people as accursed on the pretext that it has been a victim of unending persecution. Rather, according to Scripture's own testimony (Isaiah 53:2-4), to undergo suffering is often the effect and reminder of the prophetic state.

e) It is more difficult than ever today to pass a calm theological judgment on the movement of return of the Jewish people to "its" Land. That being so, first and foremost we cannot, as Christians, overlook the gift vouchsafed long ago by God to the people of Israel of a Land wherein it was summoned to dwell again (cf. Genesis 12:7; 26:3-4; 28:13; Isaiah 43:5-7; Jeremiah 16:15; Zephaniah 3:20).

Ever in history, Jewish existence has been constantly divided between life in dispersion among the nations and aspiration to nationhood in its own Land. It is a striving that creates many problems for the Jewish conscience itself. To understand the striving and the controversy which it provokes in all it dimensions, Christians must not allow themselves to be led away by interpretations that misconceive the communal and religious ways of life of Judaism, or by well-meant but hurriedly adopted political standpoints. They should take account of the interpretation which the Jews themselves set upon their regathering about Jerusalem—in the name of their faith, they consider it as a blessing.

This return, and its repercussions, put justice to the test. On the political level, there is a confrontation between different requirements of justice. Beyond the legitimate diversity of political options, the universal conscience cannot deny the Jewish people, which has undergone so many vicissitudes in the course of its history, the right, and the means, to its own political being among the nations. That right, and these possibilities of existence, can no longer be withheld by the nations from those who, by reason of local conflicts resulting from their return, are presently the victims of serious situations of injustice. So let us turn attentive eyes to this Land visited by God, and cherish the eager hope that it become a place where all its inhabitants, Jews and non-Jews, may live in peace. It is a cardinal question that faces Christian and Jew alike, to know whether the regathering of the scattered congregations of the Jewish people, end-product of the interplay of persecution and political forces, will, in the end, prove, or fail to prove, to be one of the paths of Divine justice for the Jewish people, and, at the same time, for all the peoples on earth. How can Christians remain uninterested in what is being decided in that Land today?

VI. Promote Mutual Understanding and Respect (Nostra Aetate 4, paragraph 2)

In most cases, encounters between Jews and Christians are still marked today by mutual ignorance and, at times, a certain mistrust. This ignorance and this mistrust have been in the past and can still in the future be the source of grave misunderstanding and terrible ills. We consider it essential and urgent that priests, faithful Christians, and all who are responsible for education, on whatever level they stand, should strive to inculcate in Christians a better understanding of Judaism, of its traditions, its customs and its history.

The first condition is for all Christians to respect the Jew at all times, whatever his way of being a Jew. They should seek to understand him as he understands himself, instead of judging him according to their own modes of thought. Let them respect his convictions, his aspirations, his rites and the attachment which he vows to them. Let them also understand that there can be different ways of being a Jew and of recognizing oneself as Jewish, without detriment to the fundamental unity of Jewish existence.

The second condition is that in meetings between Christians and Jews each should recognize the other's right fully to proclaim his faith without suspicion of wishing thereby to suborn a person disloyally away from his own community and join his own. Such intent must be eschewed, not only because of respect for the other party which every dialogue with any person, whoever he may be, demands but even more for a special reason which Christian laymen and above all clergy will do well to bear in mind. It is that the Jewish people, as a nation, was the object of an "Eternal Covenant" without which the "New Covenant" itself would have no being. Therefore, far from envisaging the disappearance of the Jewish community, the Church realizes itself as in quest of a living link with it. A great opening of the spirit, distrust of their own prejudices and an acute sense of the psychological conditioning of the individual are, when such problems have to be faced, indispensable assets in the pastors of the Church. Even if, in the present-day context of "a frontierless civilization", there are personal actions that fall outside the governance of either community, the respect which the two communities have for each other in reciprocity should not on that account be affected.

VII. The Church and the Jewish People

a) The Jewish people, by virtue of its special vocation, is conscious of having been given a universal mission to the nations. The Church, for its part, deems that its own mission cannot but be inscribed in that same universal plan of salvation.

b) Israel and the Church are not complementary institutions. Permanence, in a confrontation of Israel and the Church, is the sign of the incompletion of God's design. The Jewish people and the Christian people are thus in a situation of reciprocal questioning or, as Paul says, of "jealousy" on the issue of unity (Romans 11:14, cf. Deut. 32:21).

c) The words of Jesus himself and the teaching of Paul testify to the role of the Jewish people in the accomplishment of the final unity of mankind, as a union of Israel and the nations. Thus the quest for its unity which Judaism pursues today cannot be alien to God's plan of salvation. Nor can it be without kinship to the efforts of Christians in search of their own unity.

But if the Jews and Christians do accomplish their vocation by following distinct courses, history shows that their ways intersect again and again. Is not their common concern one for messianic times? It is, therefore, to be desired that they will at long last enter upon the path of mutual recognition and understanding, and that, casting aside their ancient enmity, they will turn to their Father in one and the same movement of hope, which will bespeak a promise for the entire globe. — (*Christian News from Israel*, 23(1973)252-255).

APPENDIX IV

CONSTITUTION OF THE SECOND VATICAN COUNCIL: *LUMEN GENTIUM* PAR. 16

"Finally, those who have not yet received the gospel are related to the People of God in various ways. There is, first, that people to which the covenants and promises were made, and from which Christ was born according to the flesh (cf. Rom. 9:4-5): in view of the divine choice, they are a people most dear for the sake of the fathers, for the gifts of God are without repentance (cf. Rom. 11:25-29)." — from Flannery, *op. cit.,* p. 367.

APPENDIX V

THE DEVELOPMENT OF HEBREW CHRISTIANITY: CREDAL AND ECCLESIOLOGICAL QUESTIONS: THE PROBLEM OF CONTEXTUALIZATION
By Pastor O. C. M. Kvarme

(Norwegian Church of Elijah, Haifa, Israel, published in TANTUR Papers on Christianity in the Holy Land, Jerusalem, 1979, pp. 315-342, as a comment on the private edition of *Jewish Identity*, by Elias Friedman.)

"The most thorough attempt to work out a proper understanding of Hebrew Christianity, leading to a proposal for the solution of the dilemma, has been undertaken by Father Elias Friedman of the Carmelite Order, particularly in his book *Jewish Identity*. Since the Jewish people receives its primary identity from the Election, which is now fulfilled in Christ, the only solution for the modern crisis of Jewish identity is a Hebrew-Christian one. On the basis of a 'theological prophetism' Friedman accepts the validity of the application of Old and New Testament prophecy to the Jewish People today, with respect both to their return to the Land and their future general conversion. From a biblical and humanistic point of view, however, he asserts that it is important for Hebrew Christians to keep their distinct national identity and proposes that a Hebrew-Catholic Community be canonically erected within the Roman Catholic Church on the same basis as, for example, the Maronite and Melkite Communities.[1*] In addition, the Hebrew character of this community should be expressed through the incorporation of elements from the Synagogue, elements compatible with the principles of Christianity, following the example of the Church of nearly two thousand years ago."

"Although Father Elias Friedman's proposals have been

---

* N.B. The comparison is purely analogical in the mind of the present author.

discussed in various circles, they have not been acted upon as yet. It is, therefore, only within the *Opus Sancti Jacobi* and through a Hebraized ritual that Hebrew Catholics are able to express their identity, their other means of doing so being commitment to and identification with the State of Israel. As this state of affairs leaves unresolved the problem of the national distinction of Hebrew Catholics and the question of their role within the Church, the contribution made by Father Elias Friedman is still a challenge that ought not to be allowed to die away."

APPENDIX VI

P.O. Box 19199
Jerusalem
25 June 1979

The Reverend Elias Friedman, O.C.D.
P.O. Box 9047
31090 Haifa, Israel

Dear Father Elias,

On my return from annual vacation on 17 June, I found your letter of 28 May last concerning certain assertions by Professor D. Flusser, and by a writer in *Civiltà Cattolica* (1937), page 500:

"You are well aware that when Orthodox Christians return to the obedience of Rome, they are asked only to express acceptance of the Holy Father and His teachings, while conserving all their rites, customs, language and traditions which are not opposed to Catholic truth. I personally see no reason why this should not apply to persons of Jewish descent." The *Civiltà* writer confuses "nazionalità giudaica" with the "special character and special claims" mentioned by Prof. Flusser.

"Whether we were Jews or pagans, we are the ones He has called" (Rom. 9:24); "I, an Israelite, descended from Abraham through the tribe of Benjamin, could never agree that God has rejected His people" (ib. 11:1); the Jews "as the chosen people... are still loved by God" (ib. 11:28); "How rich are the depths of God...to Him be glory for ever!" (ib. 11:33-36).

It is well known that the two great fears of the Jewish people are liquidation and assimilation, and I personally believe we should enable them to accept Christ and His Church without assimilation, just as Syrian, Armenian and other Orthodox do when returning to Catholicism. Be assured of my best wishes for your efforts in this respect and my desire to be of assistance in securing their acceptance.

In union of prayers I remain, dear Father,

Yours devotedly in Christ,

/s/ + William Aquin Carew
Apostolic Delegate of Jerusalem

APPENDIX VII

ARCHDIOCESE OF PRETORIA
Archbishop's House, Main Street,
Pretoria, South Africa

26th January, 1973.

Rev. Father Elias Friedman,
"Stella Maris" — Mount Carmel,
HAIFA, Israel.

Dear Father Elias,

As I mentioned in my brief note to you last month, the two copies of your script *Jewish Identity* were safely delivered to me by Mr. Ford Niehaus, President of the National Council of Catholic Men; one of these I sent to Cardinal McCann in Capetown, but His Eminence is still in Rome—very ill, I am sorry to say—and I have no doubt that your manuscript will be kept in Capetown until he returns. I am sending a copy of this letter to Mr. Niehaus, to keep him informed.

I have read your manuscript very carefully, and with the keenest interest, nodding my head in agreement as I passed from chapter to chapter! As you know, my views and those of other members of the South African hierarchy are in full accord with yours.

Your manuscript deserves close and critical study by truly competent persons: it is not enough for Cardinal McCann and myself (and other local bishops) to read it and give an approbation in generalised terms—in any case South Africa is very far away from the centre of things, and what S. A. does is not likely to have any repercussions, favourable or otherwise. If you agree, I would like to hand your manuscript to the staff of St. John Vianney Seminary, with a request that they study it, and give us a proper critique. You may, however, have other ideas as to how it is to be brought to the attention of those who really count—in America and Europe.

For myself, I cordially accept your thesis. The definition of Israel as the Chosen People (page 17) expressive of their Election, is wholly acceptable, and the Election "is one, unique and beyond time...by the very nature of things absent in non-Israelites or non-Jews". But there must be a new synthesis between Election and Law "to restore equilibrium to the national identity, which Secular Zionism has disturbed" (page 26).

On page 38 you state in a single paragraph the purpose of your paper and its whole conclusion that "assuming the conversion of the Jewish people to Christianity, their national identity can only be conserved, on condition of their entering a Hebrew-Catholic Community, canonically erected." When you stated this conviction in your previous papers, there were some dissenters; for myself, once again, I accept it sincerely—for reasons that I cannot go into here, but which accord very closely with your own. There will still be those, however, who will not accept it—or at least with the proviso that it must be left to the individual Jewish convert to decide whether to become (formally, canonically) a member of the Hebrew-Catholic Community.

To me, *your whole vision is an inspiring one,* but far from being merely visionary: it is highly practical. In fact, I see no hope of the Jewish people of the world moving in to occupy their rightful place in the Church of Christ other than as a Hebrew-Catholic community. It cannot wait longer; the time is now, before it is rendered more difficult by the terrible inroads that are being made upon the Jewish people (in common with the other peoples of the world) by humanism run riot. With kindest regards,

Sincerely in Christ,

/s/ + John C. Garner, Archbishop

APPENDIX VIII

Commission for Religious Relations with the Jews

NOTES
on the correct way to present the Jews and Judaism in
preaching and catechesis in the Roman Catholic Church

Preliminary considerations

On March 6th, 1982, Pope John Paul II told delegates of
episcopal conferences and other experts, meeting in Rome to study
relations between the Church and Judaism:
"...you yourselves were concerned, during your sessions, with
Catholic teaching and catechesis regarding Jews and Judaism
...We should aim, in this field, that Catholic teaching at its
different levels, in catechesis to children and young people,
presents Jews and Judaism, not only in an honest and objective
manner, free from prejudices and without any offence, but
also with full awareness of the heritage common" to Jews and
Christians.

In this passage, so charged with meaning, the Holy Father plainly
drew inspiration from the Council Declaration *Nostra Aetate* § 4,
which says:
"All should take pains, then, lest in catechetical instruction
and in the preaching of God's Word they teach anything out of
harmony with the truth of the Gospel and the spirit of Christ"; as
also from these words: "Since the spiritual patrimony common
to Christians and Jews is thus so great, this sacred Synod wishes
to foster and recommend mutual understanding and respect..."

In the same way, the *Guidelines and Suggestions for
implementing the conciliar declaration Nostra Aetate* (§ 4) ends
its chapter III, entitled "Teaching and Education", which lists a
number of practical things to be done, with this recommendation:

"Information concerning these questions is important at all levels of Christian instruction and education. Among sources of information, special attention should be paid to the following:
-catechisms and religious textbooks;
-history books;
-the mass media (press, radio, cinema, television).
The effective use of these means presupposes the thorough formation of instructors and educators in training schools, seminaries and universities" (AAS 77, 1975, p. 73).
The paragraphs which follow are intended to serve this purpose.

I. Religious Teaching and Judaism

1. In *Nostra Aetate* § 4, the Council speaks of the "spiritual bonds linking" Jews and Christians and of the "great spiritual patrimony" common to both, and it further asserts that "the Church of Christ acknowledges that, according to the mystery of God's saving design, the beginning of her faith and her election are already found among the patriarchs, Moses and the prophets".

2. Because of the unique relations that exist between Christianity and Judaism — "linked together at the very level of their identity" (John Paul II, 6th March, 1982) — relations "founded on the design of the God of the Covenant" *(ibid),* the Jews and Judaism should not occupy an occasional and marginal place in catechesis: their presence there is essential and should be organically integrated.

3. This concern for Judaism in Catholic teaching has not merely a historical or archeological foundation. As the Holy Father said in the speech already quoted, after he had again mentioned the "common patrimony" of the Church and Judaism as "considerable": "To assess it carefully in itself and with due awareness of the faith and religious life of the Jewish people *as they are professed and practised still today,* can greatly help us to understand better certain aspects of the life of the Church" (emphasis added). It is a question then of *pastoral* concern for a still living reality closely related to the Church. The Holy Father has stated this permanent reality of the Jewish people in a remarkable theological formula, in his

allocution to the Jewish community of West Germany at Mainz, on November 17th, 1980: "...the people of God of the Old Covenant, which has never been revoked..."

4. Here we should recall the passage in which the *Guidelines and Suggestions* (I) tried to define the fundamental condition of dialogue: "respect for the other as he is", knowledge of the "basic components of the religious traditions of Judaism," and again learning "by what essential trait the Jews define themselves in the light of their own religious experience" (Introd.).

5. The singular character and the difficulty of Christian teaching about Jews and Judaism lies in this: that it needs to balance a number of pairs of ideas which express the relation between the two economies of the Old and New Testament:

Promise and Fulfilment
Continuity and Newness
Singularity and Universality
Uniqueness and Exemplary Nature

This means that the theologian and the catechist who deal with the subject need to show in their practice of teaching that:

-promise and fulfilment throw light on each other;
-newness lies in a metamorphosis of what was there before;
-the singularity of the people of the Old Testament is not exclusive and is open, in the divine vision, to a universal extension;
-the uniqueness of the Jewish people is meant to have the force of an example.

6. Finally, "work that is of poor quality and lacking in precision would be extremely detrimental" to Judaeo-Christian dialogue (John Paul II, speech of March 6th, 1982). But it would be above all detrimental — since we are talking of teaching and education — to Christian identity (*ibid.*).

7. "In virtue of her divine mission, the Church" which is to be "the all-embracing means of salvation" in which alone "the fullness of the means of salvation can be obtained" (Unit. Red. 3); "must of her nature proclaim Jesus Christ to the world" (cf. *Guidelines and Suggestions,* I). Indeed we believe that it is through him that ʍ e go to the Father (cf. Jn. 14:6) "and this is eternal life, that they

know thee the only true God and Jesus Christ whom thou has sent" (Jn. 17:3).

Jesus affirms *(ibid.* 10:16) that "there shall be one flock and one shepherd". The Church and Judaism cannot then be seen as two parallel ways of salvation and the Church must witness to Christ as the Redeemer for all, "while maintaining the strictest respect for religious liberty in line with the teaching of the Second Vatican Council (Declaration *Dignitatis Humanae)" (Guidelines and Suggestions,* I).

8. The urgency and importance of precise, objective and rigorously accurate teaching on Judaism for our faithful follows too from the danger of anti-Semitism, which is always ready to reappear under different guises. The question is not merely to uproot from among the faithful the remains of anti-Semitism still to be found here and there, but much rather to arouse in them, through educational work, an exact knowledge of the wholly unique "bond" *(Nostra Aetate,* 4) which joins us as a Church to the Jews and to Judaism. In this way, they would learn to appreciate and love the latter, who have been chosen by God to prepare the coming of Christ and have preserved everything that was progressively revealed and given in the course of that preparation, notwithstanding their difficulty in recognising in Him their Messiah.

II. Relations between the Old¹ and the New Testament

1. Our aim should be to show the unity of biblical Revelation (O. T. and N.T.) and of the divine plan, before speaking of each historical event, so as to stress that particular events have meaning when seen in history as a whole—from creation to fulfilment. This history concerns the whole human race and especially believers. Thus the definitive meaning of the election of Israel does not become clear except in the light of the complete fulfilment (Rom. 9-11) and election in Jesus Christ is still better understood with reference to the announcement and the promise (cf. Heb. 4:1-11).

2. We are dealing with singular happenings which concern a singular nation but are destined, in the sight of God who reveals his purpose, to take on universal and exemplary significance.

The aim is moreover to present the events of the Old Testament not as concerning only the Jews but also as touching us personally. Abraham is truly the father of our faith (cf. Rom. 4:11-12; Roman Canon: *patriarchae nostri Abrahae*). And it is said (I Cor. 10:1): "Our fathers were all under the cloud, and all passed through the sea". The patriarchs, prophets and other personalities of the Old Testament have been venerated and always will be venerated as saints in the liturgical tradition of the Oriental Church as also of the Latin Church.

3. From the unity of the divine plan derives the problem of the relation between the Old and New Testaments. The Church already from apostolic times (cf. 1 Cor. 10:11; Heb. 10:1), and then constantly in tradition, resolved this problem by means of typology, which emphasizes the primordial value that the Old Testament must have in the Christian view. Typology, however, makes many people uneasy and is perhaps the sign of a problem unresolved.

4. Hence, in using typology, the teaching and practice of which we have received from the Liturgy and from the Fathers of Church, we should be careful to avoid any transition from the Old to the New Testament which might seem merely a rupture. The Church, in the spontaneity of the Spirit which animates her, has vigorously condemned the attitude of Marcion[2] and always opposed his dualism.

5. It should also be emphasized that a typological interpretation consists in reading the Old Testament as preparation and, in certain aspects, outline and foreshadowing of the New (cf. e.g., Heb. 5:5-10, etc.). Christ is henceforth the key and point of reference to the Scriptures: "the rock *was* Christ" (I Cor. 10:4).

6. It is true then, and should be stressed, that the Church and Christians read the Old Testament in the light of the event of the dead and risen Christ, and that on these grounds there is a Christian reading of the Old Testament which does not necessarily coincide with the Jewish reading. Thus, Christian identity and Jewish identity should be carefully distinguished in their respective reading of the Bible. But this detracts nothing from the value of the Old Testament in the Church and does nothing to hinder Christians from profiting discerningly from the traditions of Jewish reading.

7. Typological reading only manifests the unfathomable riches of the Old Testament, its inexhaustible content and the mystery of which it is full, and should not lead us to forget that it retains its own value as Revelation that the New Testament often does no more than resume (cf. Mk. 12:29-31). Moreover, the New Testament itself demands to be read in the light of the Old. Primitive Christian catechesis constantly had recourse to this (cf. e.g., 1 Cor. 5:6-8; 10:1-11).

8. Typology further signifies reaching towards the accomplishment of the divine plan, when "God will be all in all" (I Cor. 15:28). This holds true also for the Church which, realised already in Christ, yet awaits its definitive perfecting as the Body of Christ. The fact that the Body of Christ is still tending towards its full stature (cf. Eph. 4:12-19) takes nothing from the value of being a Christian. So also the calling of the patriarchs and the Exodus from Egypt do not lose their importance and value in God's design from being at the same time intermediate stages (cf. e.g., *Nostra Aetate*, 4).

9. The Exodus, for example, represents an experience of salvation and liberation that is not complete in itself, but has in it, over and above its own meaning, the capacity to be developed further. Salvation and liberation are already accomplished in Christ and gradually realised by the sacraments in the Church. This makes way for the fulfilment of God's design, which awaits its final consummation with the return of Jesus as Messiah, for which we pray each day. The Kingdom, for the coming of which we also pray each day, will be finally established. With salvation and liberation the elect and the whole of creation will be transformed in Christ (Rom. 8:19-23).

10. Furthermore, in underlining the eschatological dimension of Christianity we shall reach a greater awareness that the people of God of the Old and the New Testament are tending towards a like end in the future: the coming or return of the Messiah—even if they start from two different points of view. It is more clearly understood that the person of the Messiah is not only a point of division for the people of God but also a point of convergence (cf. *Sussidi per l'ecumenismo* of the diocese of Rome, n. 140). Thus

it can be said that Jews and Christians meet in a comparable hope, founded on the same promise made to Abraham (cf. Gen. 12:1-3; Heb. 6:13-18).

11. Attentive to the same God who has spoken, hanging on the same word, we have to witness to one same memory and one common hope in Him who is the master of history. We must also accept our responsibility to prepare the world for the coming of the Messiah by working together for social justice, respect for the rights of persons and nations and for social and international reconciliation. To this we are driven, Jews and Christians, by the command to love our neighbour, by a common hope for the kingdom of God and by the great heritage of the Prophets. Transmitted soon enough by catechesis, such a conception would teach young Christians in a practical way to cooperate with Jews, going beyond simple dialogue (cf. *Guidelines*, IV).

III. Jewish Roots of Christianity

1. Jesus was and always remained a Jew, and his ministry was deliberately limited "to the lost sheep of the house of Israel" (Mt. 15:24). Jesus is fully a man of his time and of his environment — the Jewish Palestinian one of the first century, the anxieties and hopes of which he shared. This cannot but underline both the reality of the Incarnation and the very meaning of the history of salvation, as it has been revealed in the Bible (cf. Rom. 1:3-4; Gal. 4:4-5).

2. Jesus' relations with biblical law and its more or less traditional interpretations are undoubtedly complex and he showed great liberty towards it (cf. the "antithesis" of the Sermon on the Mount: Mt. 5:21-48, bearing in mind the exegetical difficulties; his attitude to rigorous observance of the Sabbath: Mk. 3:1-6, etc.).

But there is not doubt that he wished to submit himself to the law (cf. Gal. 4:4), that he was circumcised and presented in the Temple like any Jew of his time (cf. Lk. 2:21.24), that he was trained in the law's observance. He extolled respect for it (cf. Mt. 5:17-20) and invited obedience to it (cf. Mt. 8:4). The rhythm of his life was marked by observance of pilgrimages on great feasts, even from his infancy (cf. Lk. 2:41-50; Jn. 2:13; 7-10 etc.). The importance of the cycle of the Jewish feasts has been frequently underlined in the Gospel of John (cf. 2:13; 5:1, 7:2.10.37; 10:22, 12:1; 18:28; 19:42; etc.).

3. It should be noted also that Jesus often taught in the Synagogues (cf. Mt. 4:23; 9:34 Lk. 3:14-18; Jn. 18:20 etc.) and in the Temple (cf. Jn. 18:20 etc.), which he frequented as did the disciples even after the Resurrection (cf. e.g., Acts 2:46; 3:1:21:26 etc.). He wished to put in the context of synagogue worship the proclamation of his Messiahship (cf. Lk. 4:16-21). But above all he wished to achieve the supreme act of the gift of himself in the setting of the domestic liturgy of the Passover, or at least of the paschal festivity (cf. Mk. 14:1,12 and parallels; Jn. 18:28). This also allows of a better understanding of the "memorial" character of the Eucharist.

4. Thus the Son of God is incarnate in a people and in a human family (cf. Gal. 4:4; Rom. 9:5). This takes away nothing—quite the contrary—from the fact that he was born for all men (Jewish shepherds and pagan wise men are found at his crib: Lk. 2:80-20; Mt. 2:1-12) and died for all men (at the foot of the cross there are Jews, among them Mary and John: Jn. 19:25-27, and pagans like the centurion: Mk. 15:39, and parallels). Thus, he made two peoples one in his flesh (cf. Eph. 2:14-17). This explains why with the *Ecclesia ex gentibus* we have, in Palestine and elsewhere, an *Ecclesia ex circumcisione,* of which Eusebius for example speaks (H.E. IV, 5).

5. His relations with the Pharisees were not always or wholly polemical. Of this there are many proofs:

-It is Pharisees who warn Jesus of the risks he is running (Lk. 13:31);

-Some Pharisees are praised — e.g., "the scribe" of Mk. 12:34;

-Jesus eats with Pharisees (Lk. 7:36; 14:1).

6. Jesus shares, with the majority of Palestinian Jews of that time, some pharisaic doctrines: the resurrection of the body; forms of piety, like almsgiving, prayer, fasting (cf. Mt. 6:1-18) and the liturgical practice of addressing God as Father; the priority of the commandment to love God and our neighbor (cf. Mk. 12:28-34). This is so also with Paul (cf. Acts 23:8), who always considered

his membership of the Pharisees as a title of honour (cf. ibid. 23:6; 26:5; Phil. 3:5).

7. Paul also, like Jesus himself, used methods of reading and interpreting Scripture and of teaching his disciples which were common to the Pharisees of their time. This applies to the use of parables of Jesus' ministry, as also to the method of Jesus and Paul of supporting a conclusion with a quotation from Scripture.

8. It is noteworthy too that the Pharisees are not mentioned in accounts of the Passion. Gamaliel (Acts 5:34-39) defends the apostles in a meeting of the Sanhedrin. An exclusively negative picture of the Pharisees is likely to be inaccurate and unjust (cf. *Guidelines,* Note 1; cf. AAS, loco cit. p.76). If in the Gospels and elsewhere in the New Testament there are all sort of unfavourable references to the Pharisees, they should be seen against the background of a complex and diversified movement. Criticisms of various types of Pharisees are moreover not lacking in rabbinical sources (cf. the *Babylon Talmud,* the *Sotah* treatise 22b, etc.). "Phariseeism" in the pejorative sense can be rife in any religion. It may also be stressed that, if Jesus shows himself severe towards the Pharisees, it is because he is closer to them than to other contemporary Jewish groups (cf. supra n. 17).

9. All this should help us to understand better what St. Paul says (Rom 11:16 ff) about the "root" and the "branches". The Church and Christianity, for all their novelty, find their origin in the Jewish milieu of the first century of our era, and more deeply still in the "design of God" *(Nostra Aetate,* 4), realised in the Patriarchs, Moses and the Prophets *(ibid.),* down to its consummation in Christ Jesus.

IV. The Jews in the New Testament

1. The *Guidelines* already say (note I) that "the formula 'the Jews' sometimes, according to the context, means 'the leadership of the Jews' or 'the adversaries of Jesus', terms which express better the thought of the evangelist and avoid appearing to arraign the Jewish people as such".

An objective presentation of the role of the Jewish people in the New Testament should take account of these various facts:

a) The Gospels are the outcome of long and complicated editorial work. The dogmatic constitution *Dei Verbum,* following the Pontifical Biblical Commission's Instruction *Sancta Mater Ecclesia,* distinguishes three stages: "The sacred authors wrote the four Gospels, selecting some things from the many which had been handed on by word of mouth or in writing, reducing some of them to a synthesis, explicating some things in view of the situation of their Churches, and preserving the form of proclamation, but always in such fashion that they told us the honest truth about Jesus" (n. 19).

Hence it cannot be ruled out that some references hostile or less than favourable to the Jews have their historical context in conflicts between the nascent Church and the Jewish community. Certain controversies reflect Christian-Jewish relations long after the time of Jesus.

To establish this is of capital importance if we wish to bring out the meaning of certain Gospel texts for the Christians of today.

All this should be taken into account when preparing catechesis and homilies for the last weeks of Lent and Holy Week (cf. already *Guidelines* II, and now also *Susside per l'ecumenismo nella diocesi di Roma,* 1982, 144 b).

b) It is clear on the other hand that there were conflicts between Jesus and certain categories of Jews of his time, among them Pharisees, from the beginning of his ministry (cf. Mk. 2:1-11.24; 3:6 etc.).

c) There is moreover the sad fact that the majority of the Jewish people and its authorities did not believe in Jesus — a fact not merely of history but of theological bearing, of which St. Paul tries hard to plumb the meaning (Rom. chap. 9-11).

d) This fact, accentuated as the Christian mission developed, especially among the pagans, led inevitably to a rupture between Judaism and the young Church, now irreducibly separated and divergent in faith, and this stage of affairs is reflected in the texts of the New Testament and particularly in the Gospel. There is no question of playing down or glossing over this rupture; that could only prejudice the identity of either side. Nevertheless it certainly does not cancel the spiritual "bond" of which the Council speaks *(Nostra Aetate,* 4) and which we propose to dwell on here.

e) Reflecting on this in the light of Scripture, notably of the chapters cited from the epistle to the Romans, Christians should never forget that the faith is a free gift of God (cf. Rom. 9:12) and that we should never judge the consciences of others. St. Paul's exhortation "do not boast" in your attitude to "the root" (Rom. 11:18) has its full point here.

f) There is no putting the Jews who knew Jesus and did not believe in him, or those who opposed the preaching of the apostles, on the same plane with Jews who came after or those of today. If the responsibility of the former remains a mystery hidden with God (cf. Rom. 11:25), the latter are in an entirely different situation. Vatican II in the declaration on *Religious Liberty* teaches that "all men are to be immune from coercion...in such wise that in matters religious no one is to be forced to act in a manner contrary to his own beliefs. Nor...restrained from acting in accordance with his own beliefs" (n. 2). This is one of the bases —proclaimed by the Council — on which Judaeo-Christian dialogue rests.

2. The delicate question of responsibility for the death of Christ must be looked at from the standpoint of the conciliar declaration *Nostra Aetate,* 4 and of *Guidelines and Suggestions* (§ III): "What happened in (Christ's) passion cannot be blamed upon all the Jews then living without distinction nor upon the Jews of today", especially since "authorities of the Jews and those who followed their lead pressed for the death of Christ". Again, further on: "Christ in his boundless love freely underwent his passion and death because of the sins of all men, so that all might attain salvation" *(Nostra Aetate,* 4). The *Catechism* of the Council of Trent teaches that Christian sinners are more to blame for the death of Christ than those few Jews who brought it about — they indeed "knew not what they did" (cf. Lk. 23:24) and we know it only too well (Pars I, caput V, Quaest, XI). In the same way and for the same reason, "the Jews should not be presented as repudiated or cursed by God, as if such views followed from the holy Scriptures" *(Nostra Aetate,* 4), even though it is true that "the Church is the new people of God" (*ibid.*).

V. The Liturgy

1. Jews and Christians find in the Bible the very substance of their liturgy: for the proclamation of God's word, response to it, prayer of praise and intercession for the living and the dead, recourse to the divine mercy. The Liturgy of the word in its own structure originates in Judaism. The prayer of Hours and other liturgical texts and formularies have their parallels in Judaism as do the very formulas of our most venerable prayers, among them the Our Father. The eucharistic prayers also draw inspiration from models in the Jewish tradition. As John Paul II said (Allocution of March 6th, 1982): "...the faith and religious life of the Jewish people as they are professed and practised still today, can greatly help us to understand better certain aspects of the life of the Church. Such is the case of liturgy..."

2. This is particularly evident in the great feasts of the liturgical year, like the Passover. Christians and Jews celebrate the Passover: the Jews, the historic Passover looking towards the future; the Christians, the Passover accomplished in the death and resurrection of Christ, although still in expectation of the final consummation (cf. supra n. 9). It is still the "memorial" which comes to us from the Jewish tradition with a specific content different in each case. On either side, however, there is a like dynamism: for Christians it gives meaning to the eucharistic celebration (cf. the antiphon "O sacrum convivum"), a paschal celebration and as such a making present of the past, but experienced in the expectation of what is to come.

VI. Judaism and Christianity in History

1. The history of Israel did not end in 70 A.D. (cf. *Guidelines,* II). It continued, especially in a numerous Diaspora which allowed Israel to carry to the whole world a witness — often heroic — of its fidelity to the one God and to "exalt him in the presence of all the living" (Tobit 13:4), while preserving the memory of the land of their forefathers at the hearts of their hope (Passover Seder).

Christians are invited to understand this religious attachment which finds its roots in Biblical tradition, without however making their own any particular religious interpretation of this relationship (cf. *Declaration* of the US Conference of Catholic Bishops, November 20, 1975).

The existence of the State of Israel and its political options should be envisaged not in a perspective which is in itself religious, but in their reference to the common principles of international law.

The permanence of Israel (while so many ancient peoples have disappeared without a trace) is a historic fact and a sign to be interpreted within God's design. We must in any case rid ourselves of the traditional idea of a people *punished,* preserved as a *living argument* for Christian apologetic. It remains a chosen people, "the pure olive on which were grafted the branches of the wild olive which are the gentiles" (John Paul II, 6th March, 1982, alluding to Rom. 11:17-24). We must remember how much the balance of relations between Jews and Christians over two thousand years has been negative. We must remind ourselves how the permanence of Israel is accompanied by a continuous spiritual fecundity, in the rabbinical period, in the Middle Ages, and in modern times, taking its start from a patrimony which we long shared, so much so that "the faith and religious life of the Jewish people as they are professed and practised still today, can greatly help us to understand better certain aspects of the life of the Church" (John Paul II, March 6th, 1982). Catechesis should on the other hand help in understanding the meaning for the Jews of the extermination during the years 1939-1945, and its consequences.

2. Education and catechesis should concern themselves with the problem of racism, still active in different forms of anti-Semitism. The Council presented it thus: "Moreover, (the Church) mindful of her common patrimony with the Jews and motivated by the Gospel's spiritual love and by no political considerations, deplores the hatred, persecutions and displays of anti-Semitism directed against the Jews at any time and from any source" *(Nostra Aetate* 4). The *Guidelines* comment: "the spiritual bonds and historical links binding the Church to Judaism condemn (as opposed to the very spirit of Christianity) all forms of anti-Semitism and discrimination, which in any case the dignity of the human person alone would suffice to condemn" *(Guidelines,* Preamble).

Conclusion

Religious teaching, catechesis and preaching should be a preparation not only for objectivity, justice, and tolerance, but also for understanding and dialogue. Our two traditions are so related that they cannot ignore each other. Mutual knowledge must be encouraged at every level. There is evident in particular a painful ignorance of the history and traditions of Judaism, of which only negative aspects and often caricature seem to form part of the stock ideas of many Christians.

That is what these notes aim to remedy. This would mean that the Council text and "Guidelines and Suggestions" would be more easily and faithfully put into practice.

+ Johannes Cardinal Willebrands   (President)
Pierre Duprey   (Vice President)
Jorge Mejia   (Secretary)

REFERENCES

1. We continue to use the expression *Old Testament* because it is traditional (cf. already 2 Cor. 3:14) but also because "Old" does not mean "out of date" or "outworn". In any case, it is the *permanent* value of the O.T. as a source of Christian Revelation that is emphasised here (cf. *Dei Verbum*, 3).

2. A man of gnostic tendency who in the second century rejected the Old Testament and part of the New as the work of an evil god, a demiurge. The Church reacted strongly against this heresy (cf. Irenaeus).

N. B. The "Notes" offer three principles which bear directly on our argument:

I) it calls for the underlining of the eschatological dimension of Christianity (II, 18)

2) it gives a more central position to Jews and Judaism than was the case in the past (I, 2)

3) it offers the equivalent of a definition of a "sign" of the times: a "sign" is an historical fact to be interpreted in the light of God's plan of salvation (VI, 33).

The "Notes" mention one example of such a "sign", the permanence of Israel; but we are entitled to ask whether there are any other "signs" present in our time and what they might signify.

What is required is a systematic reading of *all* the signs of our times, based on the prophecies of both Testaments.

— Author

INDEX

The Association of Hebrew Catholics aims at combating the alienation of Catholics of Jewish origin from their historical identity as Israelites, by petitioning the Holy See to approve the establishment of an Israelite Community in the Church, such a community to serve as an eschatological sign of the times.

The Miriam Press, a non-profit lay apostolate, faithful to the Magisterium, will publish and distribute literature by and about Hebrew Catholics, on Hebrew Catholic spirituality and on matters relating to Zion and the Church.

For information regarding
The Association of Hebrew Catholics or
The Miriam Press, write to:

The Miriam Press
4120 W. Pine Blvd.
St. Louis, MO 63108

CPSIA information can be obtained
at www.ICGtesting.com
Printed in the USA
FFOW04n1950230316
22531FF